Programming Language Essentials

INTERNATIONAL COMPUTER SCIENCE SERIES

Consulting Editor A D McGettrick University of Strathclyde

SELECTED TITLES IN THE SERIES

Programming Language Essentials

Henri E. Bal
Dick Grune

Vrije Universiteit, Amsterdam

ADDISON-WESLEY
PUBLISHING
COMPANY

Wokingham, England • Reading, Massachusetts • Menlo Park, California
New York • Don Mills, Ontario • Amsterdam • Bonn • Sydney • Singapore
Tokyo • Madrid • San Juan • Milan • Paris • Mexico City • Seoul • Taipei

Cover designed by Chris Eley
and printed by The Riverside Printing Co. (Reading) Ltd.

Printed and bound in Great Britain by T.J.Press (Padstow) Ltd, Cornwall.

First printed 1994. Reprinted 1994.

ISBN 0-201-63179-2

British Library Cataloguing-in-Publication Data
A catalogue record for this book is available from the British Library.

Library of Congress Cataloguing-in-Publication Data is available

Preface

Aims and objectives

The aim of this book is to provide a concise introduction to the essentials of programming languages. Although many good books on programming languages exist, most are several hundred pages long. We believe that, in an age in which the pressure on the curriculum, lecturers and students increases with every new development, shorter books are becoming more attractive. In addition, we felt from the start that it should be possible to cover the area of programming languages in about 250 pages by focusing on principles rather than specifics. The book is not intended as an introduction to any existing language in particular.

Today's students can expect to be called upon, in the course of their professional careers, to work with several different programming paradigms, some of which have not yet been invented. To prepare the student for this, the book contains chapters on language principles for each of the four paradigms most in evidence today: imperative, object-oriented, functional and logic. It contains an additional chapter on parallel and distributed programming, since they will become more and more important, and a chapter covering half a dozen less prominent paradigms, in order to widen the student's horizon.

Readers who have finished this book can expect to be able to understand, interpret and evaluate any material, books, articles or manuals on programming languages, and to follow new developments.

Audience

Our audience is students who need a clear view of the field of programming languages but do not need to be experts on any of its aspects. We expect students to have some experience in programming in one or two imperative languages. Experience of programming in non-imperative languages or of parallel programming is not a prerequisite, and we do not require students to have a mathematical background. We do expect them to be willing to study rather than just read.

The book will also be of interest to professional programmers who have substantial experience in programming, say, C, FORTRAN or Ada. They can use this book for a quick overview of aspects of programming languages they were not aware of, and of different programming paradigms which may become important to them soon (such as object-oriented programming or parallel programming).

We have written this book with a rather heterogeneous audience in mind. In our own course, the audience consists of computer science students in various stages of their education, plus the occasional interested student from a related department. This book is not intended to fit seamlessly into any existing curriculum, but rather to be applicable anywhere an audience of interested, non-novice computer science students can be found.

Use of the book in a course

The size of the book allows it to be used in several ways. With its 270 pages, it can fill most or all of a one-semester course. We have used the book as the main material in a course of 13 weekly lectures of two hours' duration. Experience with this course suggests that the book contains enough material to fill a full 13-week course.

Alternatively, lecturers may prefer to allow some time to discuss additional material on specific languages of their choice, since the book does not cover any language in depth. In our course, for example, we spent the first few lectures on a short introduction to Ada (using a separate book), to acquaint the students with a large real-world language.

Finally, the book can also be used for half-semester courses. These condensed courses are being used at several universities in order to free time for other areas in which students have chosen to become experts. The size of this book makes it more suitable than many others for half-semester courses, although there still might not be enough time to discuss all the chapters in full detail.

Features

To achieve our goal of packing sufficient up-to-date material into a sufficiently short course, this book uses a combination of features: conciseness, extensive coverage of all major paradigms, a simple structure, extensive

treatment of parallel and distributed languages, an overview of other paradigms and chapter summaries.

Conciseness

A key feature of the book is its conciseness, which was achieved not by
omitting important issues but by avoiding verbosity and repetitiveness. Difficult concepts are explained in detail and illustrated with examples, but
simpler concepts are described briefly. Each feature is explained once
rather than in several settings. Also, as said before, we focus on principles
rather than specifics. We discuss language-specific features only if we feel
they help to explain general principles.

Apart from two or three paragraphs on BNF, the book contains no
mathematics and no formalisms. This is a conscious choice. It is clear that
a full understanding of the syntax, context conditions and semantics of programming languages can be achieved only through the appropriate formalisms, but such formalisms come at a price. It is our experience that
computer science students have to spend considerable amounts of time on a
formalism to reach the point at which the knowledge begins to pay off, and
we do not expect that kind of time to be available in a course that strives to
bring the student up to date in several programming paradigms.

We do not discuss language features that used to intrigue people
decades ago but are now outdated, such as computed gotos and call-by-
name parameter passing. Short examples are used to illustrate concepts and
features, but elaborate case studies have been avoided.

Extensive coverage of all major paradigms

The imperative paradigm is discussed in more detail than the other major
paradigms (object-oriented, functional and logic), but the other paradigms
are also covered extensively. For each paradigm we discuss the main principles and language concepts, using well-known languages to illustrate
them. For each paradigm we also briefly describe other relevant languages.

Simple structure

The book is organized essentially as one chapter per paradigm, which leads
to a very simple structure. A more traditional approach would have been to
devote several chapters to different language concepts, followed by one
chapter for each paradigm, showing how the concepts are applied in the
paradigm. Our book does not employ this approach; it describes each concept in the appropriate chapters, where they best make sense. Polymorphism, for example, is discussed in the chapters on object-oriented and
functional paradigms, rather than in a chapter of its own.

Extensive treatment of parallel and distributed languages

We think that parallel and distributed systems will play an important role in the near future, so we treat programming languages for such systems in depth, in a separate chapter. We describe recent ideas as well as traditional facilities.

Overview of other paradigms

Many languages outside the major paradigms exist, which students may at first sight just classify as 'funny' languages. Chapter 7 shows how these languages fit in with the rest of the programming world. It shows that the programming language landscape is open-ended, and discusses how to approach less conventional languages such as PIC, APL, SETL and SQL.

Summaries, exercises and bibliographies

Each chapter contains a summary and exercises, with which students can evaluate and test their understanding of the material discussed in the chapter. The answers to most exercises are collected in an appendix. Each chapter also contains a bibliographical section, with references to relevant books and journals. In selecting bibliographical references, we have often preferred more accessible and up-to-date material over original publications. We do not want to put our students off library usage by directing them to references that in the end they find they cannot get hold of. Also, it is easier to obtain references to original papers starting from modern material than the other way round.

Outline of structure

The book contains an introductory chapter, followed by four chapters on each of the major paradigms. Chapter 6 is on parallel and distributed languages and Chapter 7 on other paradigms. Appendix A contains literature references to all languages mentioned in the book, and answers to most exercises can be found in Appendix B. The outline of the seven chapters is given below. Each of Chapters 2 to 6 ends with a section that briefly describes example languages.

Chapter 1 describes *aspects of programming languages* which are relevant for the chapters that follow. It explains how programming languages evolved over the past decades, what exactly a paradigm is and which paradigms are used. It also discusses syntactic and semantic issues. One of the most important tasks of programming languages is to reduce the complexity of programming. Techniques to achieve this (such as decomposition and abstraction) are therefore summarized briefly here. Finally, the chapter describes how programs are processed (by a compiler or an interpreter), and takes a brief look at programming environments.

Chapter 2 is concerned with the *imperative languages*. It describes the following concepts: data (types and declarations), state (assignment, expressions and input/output), flow of control and program composition. ANSI C and Ada 9X are used to illustrate these concepts.

Chapter 3 addresses *object-oriented languages*. It first discusses the principles of object-oriented design and programming. Many different concepts are used in object-oriented languages, and they interact in subtle ways. Classes and inheritance are introduced, followed by discussions on class hierarchies, types and polymorphism, which all relate to classes. Next, dynamic binding and reference semantics are discussed. These concepts are illustrated by examples written in C++. Some attention is paid to ways of applying the new techniques.

Chapter 4 is on *functional languages*. It first discusses the advantages and disadvantages of functional languages. Next, the concepts of lists, types, polymorphism, higher-order functions, currying, lazy evaluation and equations and pattern matching are discussed and illustrated by Miranda code. Several example applications in Miranda are given.

Chapter 5 describes *logic programming languages*, of which Prolog is by far the most important representative. The main concept in these languages is the Horn clause, which is discussed first. Subsequently, logical variables, relations and data structures are described. Example programs in Prolog are given.

Chapter 6 deals with *parallel and distributed languages*. These languages need ways of expressing parallelism, communication and synchronization. Most of this chapter is devoted to communication and synchronization through shared variables or message passing. The examples are given mainly in a pseudo notation and in Ada 9X.

Chapter 7 shows that many *other paradigms* exist besides those discussed thus far. It describes additional general-purpose paradigms (constraint programming, access-oriented programming and single-datastructure languages) and additional special-purpose paradigms (dataflow programming, little languages, database languages and real-time languages).

Acknowledgements

We owe many thanks to the following people, who were willing to spend the time and effort to read drafts of our book and to supply us with many thoughtful and useful comments: Erik Baalbergen, John Barnes, Raoul Bhoedjang, Leendert van Doorn, Anton Eliëns, Rutger Hofman, Ceriel Jacobs, Frans Kaashoek, Koen Langendoen, Andrew McGettrick, Lourens van der Meij, John Romein, Tim Rühl, Chengzheng Sun, Andy Tanenbaum and the anonymous reviewers.

We also would like to thank the students of the Spring 1993 Programming Languages class, Michiel Koens, Paul-Erik Raué and Frans Simon van Leeuwen, for their sometimes very detailed comments.

We are grateful to Addison-Wesley's Simon Plumtree, Alan Grove and Annette Abel for all their help and comments during the writing of this book. We gladly acknowledge the help Ralph Griswold and Wiebren de Jonge provided on detailed questions. Bertrand Meyer helped us with the description of Eiffel and provided the Eiffel code for the example program in Chapter 3.

In the compilation of the bibliography we have benefited greatly from the electronic library system Melvyl, kindly made available to the public by the University of California.

We thank the Faculteit Wiskunde en Informatica of the Vrije Universiteit for the use of the equipment.

Henri E. Bal   email: bal@cs.vu.nl, URL: http://www.cs.vu.nl/~bal
Dick Grune   email: dick@cs.vu.nl, URL: http://www.cs.vu.nl/~dick

Hoofddorp/Amstelveen
December 1993

Contents

1

Aspects of Programming Languages

One of the jokes circulating among computer scientists is the following: 'What happens if you have a problem and ask a computer scientist to write a program to solve it? The answer: the scientist will come back a year later, presenting you with a brand new programming language ideally suited for solving your problem.'

While intended as a joke, it shows both the frustration over existing programming languages and the strong involvement that researchers feel in programming language design. The number of programming languages in use in the world is estimated to be between 2000 and 4000. Over a decade ago, the US Department of Defense decided to standardize on a single (new!) programming language. At that time, people were writing military applications in at least 500 different languages and dialects. This is not a joke.

Since then, programming languages have come into more quiet waters, and the rate at which new languages are proposed has dropped to somewhere between one and five per month. One of the reasons for this is that it has increasingly been realized that the mode of thinking a programming language induces, its paradigm, is more important and has more lasting value than the language itself.

Therefore, paradigms are explained early in this chapter, after a historical introduction. Two sections deal with common aspects of programming languages: their general structure and their processing. Two further sections cover the communication aspect and ways in which to handle the main obstacle to this communication, complexity. Not all important notions in programming languages have been gathered together in this chapter. A number of them are examined in the text at the points where they become relevant. This may occasionally interrupt the flow of the argument, but it has the advantage of making it eminently clear why a notion is important.

No programming language is covered in depth in this book, but a few are dealt with in some detail, and many more are mentioned in passing.

Literature references to programming languages have been collected in Appendix A.

As in all fields of knowledge, programming languages have their own terminology, but as is usual in young fields, the terminology is not always consistent. What one author or manual calls 'semantics' and 'run-time behaviour', another calls 'context' and 'semantics'; words like 'aggregate' or 'heap' may mean vastly different things to different people; and the different definitions of 'declaration' and 'definition' have confused many. The bottom line of this is that anyone who reads books, articles and manuals about programming languages is advised to look carefully at the meaning an author attaches to a term, and not to jump to conclusions at the mere sight of a familiar word.

1.1 Why programming languages?

The primary purpose of a programming language is to enable the user to enlist the help of a computer in solving problems in the domain of interest. This places the problem at one end and the machine at the other. The user would probably like to be isolated completely from the influence of the machine, but, if possible at all, this can only be done at great expense. The second purpose of a programming language is to enable the user to bridge the gap between problem and machine domain.

To understand better some of the features found in programming languages, and some of the issues in programming language design, it is useful to summarize here some well-known aspects of the machine. Very broadly, a computer consists of

- a memory, which includes registers, an instruction pointer, main memory (RAM – Random Access Memory) and file system;

- a Central Processing Unit (CPU), which can inspect and modify the memory; and

- peripheral equipment (for human interaction), which may include keyboard, display, mouse and printer.

The memory contains machine instructions and data, both represented as sequences of bits, generally grouped into bytes of 8 bits each; on most machines each byte has an address. The machine instructions constitute the program. At any point in time, the computer is in a certain **state**, determined by the contents of its memory and the state of the peripherals. A central item in the state is the **instruction pointer** (IP), which points to the next machine instruction in memory to be executed. The series of successive values of the instruction pointer is called the **flow of control**; manipulating it is a main issue for many programming languages.

A machine of this type is called a **von Neumann machine**, although the principles were probably first developed by Atanasoff and by Eckert and Mauchly. Other machine types exist, for example the dataflow machine (described in Section 7.2.1), but the von Neumann type is still predominant.

The fundamentals of a computer have not changed since its conception in the early 1940s. A program running on a computer was, and is, a sequence of machine instructions, and thus a sequence of bits. Programming the computer by writing this sequence of bits by hand was necessary in the very early days, but it was abandoned as soon as possible, for obvious reasons. Soon a notation was invented that was more palatable to humans: **assembly language**, in which names were given to machine instructions, data and positions in the program. As an example, Figure 1.1 shows a short program fragment which counts from 1 to 10. The fragment is in machine code in hexadecimal notation and in assembly language. The code is for the Motorola MC 68000 series.

```
Machine code (hex):                    Assembly language:
23fc 0000 0001 0000 0040                 movl     #0x1,n
                                       compare:
0cb9 0000 000a 0000 0040                 cmpl     #0xa,n
6e0c                                     bgt      end_of_loop
06b9 0000 0001 0000 0040                 addl     #0x1,n
60e8                                     bra      compare
                                       end_of_loop:
```

Figure 1.1 Sample machine code and assembly language texts.

We shall first consider the assembly language column in Figure 1.1. The program fragment addresses a memory location called n, initializes its value to 1 using the assembler instruction 'move long number 1 to location n' (movl #0x1,n) and then enters a program loop which repeatedly increases the value in n by 1 until it becomes greater than 10. The loop consists of four instructions and starts by comparing n to the number 10, using the instruction cmpl #0xa,n; the 0xa is the hexadecimal notation for decimal 10. If the result of this comparison is 'greater' the program branches to the location named end_of_loop, which means that the instruction pointer is set to the address of that location. Otherwise the instruction pointer is not affected and now points to addl #0x1,n which adds 1 to n. A branch instruction bra compare sets the instruction pointer to the address of the location labelled compare, causing the loop body to be repeated.

The left column in Figure 1.1 shows the corresponding machine code, but we will not analyse that here.

Although assembly languages were a big step forward, the written text was completely machine-specific, and a more machine-independent notation was desired. This coincided with an increased demand for a more problem-oriented notation and led to the development of the *high(er)-level languages*. Examples of early higher-level languages are FORTRAN and COBOL, modern representatives are (ANSI) C and Ada.

```
    FORTRAN code:              COBOL code:

    DO 2 N = 1,10              MOVE 1 TO N.
  2 CONTINUE                 AGAIN.
                               IF N IS EQUAL TO 10
                                 GOTO END-DEMO.
                               ADD 1 TO N.
                               GOTO AGAIN.
                             END-DEMO.
```

Figure 1.2 The loop from Figure 1.1 in FORTRAN and COBOL.

Figure 1.2 shows code for the loop in FORTRAN and COBOL, and Figure 1.3 shows it in C and Ada.

```
        C code:                    Ada code:

  for (n = 1; n <= 10; n++) {   for N in 1..10 loop
                                   null;
  }                              end loop;
```

Figure 1.3 The loop from Figure 1.1 in C and Ada.

1.2 Some history

Just as fashions and life-styles can be labelled by decades, the history of programming languages can be divided into a series of decades, each with a more or less clear theme.

The late 1940s can be characterized as the *prelingual stage*: programs for the very early computers looked roughly like pages from a railway timetable. Also, machines were often not programmed exclusively by the internal program: console buttons, switches and plugs influenced the behaviour of the computer enough to be called part of the program.

A notable exception was the work of the German engineer Zuse (1989) who, in exile in Switzerland, in 1944 designed his Plankalkül, which is a programming language by any definition. This language already featured variables, structured values and procedures with parameters; moreover, it emphasized structure over efficiency. Historical events prevented Zuse's work from becoming known to the rest of the world until the early 1970s, or present-day programming languages might have looked different.

The 1950s were concerned with *exploiting machine power*. Computers were programmed in assembly language, and since their main application was in numerical calculation, much of the programmers' work consisted of converting numerical formulas to assembler instructions. The first higher-level programming languages, the Autocodes, emerged from the automation of this process. Most Autocodes featured only 26 identifiers, named A to Z, and allowed only very simple formulas to be converted. FORTRAN mitigated both limitations and added procedures and some other flow-of-control features. Emphasis remained on numerical formulas; after all, the name FORTRAN is an abbreviation of 'IBM Mathematical FORmula TRANslating System' (Sammet, 1969).

During the 1960s, *increasing the expressive power* was given much attention, resulting in a plethora of languages: COBOL, Lisp, Algol 60, BASIC, PL/I, to name a few. Programming languages grew in many directions, offering new ideas like structured data (for example, COBOL and PL/I), recursion (Lisp and Algol 60), user interaction (BASIC) and big-is-beautiful (COBOL and PL/I). Often these languages were considered luxuries, though. Most 'serious' programming was still done in assembly languages.

Reducing machine dependency was a main theme of the 1970s, with the keyword 'portability'. A second important issue was *increasing program correctness* (fighting the software crisis). The tool for this was 'structured programming', a set of guidelines for improved program structure. Fortunately, both goals reinforced each other: a well-structured program will be more machine-independent, since its machine dependencies are more localized. Structured languages like Pascal, Algol 68 (finished in 1975!) and C achieved a considerable measure of portability by offering an increasingly more abstract view of the computation process. In the end, portability was achieved through three independent factors: a decreasing variety in hardware, operating systems and character codes; improved compiler technology; and a better programming style resulting from structured programming. Given a present-day environment (compiler and operating system), a good program in FORTRAN is just as portable as a good program in C. And assemblers lived quietly on.

During the 1980s the emphasis was on *reducing the complexity*, both of the programming task and of the program management task. For decades, people had recognized and accepted the complexity of programming as an inherent but minor nuisance, to be abated by cleverness or some strict programming discipline. But as programs grew into thousands of subprograms expressed in millions of lines, it became the major obstacle to getting a working system. To overcome or at least reduce the problem, new traditional languages like Ada and Modula-2 were supplemented by program management systems like *Make* (Oram and Talbott, 1993) and *APSE* (Ada Programming Support Environment) (IEEE, 1985). In addition, new ways of thinking about programming were introduced, resulting in, for example, the object-oriented language Smalltalk-80 and the functional language Miranda. These languages were designed to be directly integrated with the programming environment. Assembly languages were not forgotten, though: much of the code inside the Giotto probe that scouted Halley's comet on March 14, 1986 was written in assembly language.

Turning to our crystal ball, we suggest that the 1990s will be the decade of *exploiting parallel and distributed hardware*. *Ad hoc* means of exploiting parallel and distributed hardware have been known since the 1960s, but their systematic inclusion in a language had to wait until the advent of occam (notice that the name occam does not begin with a capital). Languages emerging at present are Hermes, Linda, Orca, SR and Ada 9X, as well as various parallel extension of C++ (Grimshaw, 1993; Bershad *et al.*, 1988). Such languages allow problems to be solved efficiently by splitting them up into subproblems that can be worked on in parallel, by different machines. It is widely believed that the speed of sequential computers will eventually reach a limit, and that parallelism must be used to obtain performance beyond this limit. At the moment this seems difficult, but then, so was achieving machine independency in the 1970s.

The introduction of RISC (Reduced Instruction Set Computer) hardware, which has a number of very unintuitive properties, may finally spell the end of the use of assembly language by human programmers.

Figure 1.4 shows a one-liner history of programming languages.

1940s	Any program that runs is a good program
1950s	Any program can be done in one instruction less
1960s	'Look what this one-line program can do!'
1970s	Algol 60 was a considerable improvement over all its successors
1980s	Ada is a language that is doomed to succeed
1990s	It's not easy to make ten computers do the work of one

Figure 1.4 A one-liner history of programming languages.

1.3 Paradigms and the structure of this book

One common and useful way of classifying programming languages is according to the programming paradigm they support. To understand this classification, we have to take a closer look at what a paradigm is.

The history of the word 'paradigm' is long and varied. Its meaning has changed considerably over the last 2500 years and depends on the field of knowledge in which it is applied. The word derives from two Greek words, **para**, 'side-by-side' and **deigma**, 'that which is shown'. It was originally used in ancient Greece for articles displayed (side-by-side) in the marketplace. From there it acquired the meaning of 'sample' and, still in antiquity, 'example'. Since much teaching is done by showing examples, the meaning then changed to 'fixed example used in teaching', and that is still its meaning in the humanities.

In the sciences, its meaning took quite a different turn. Rather than designating an example for teaching, it began to designate a standard example for testing theories. The motions of the planets was *the* paradigm used to develop our knowledge of the laws of mechanics. Since such a paradigm (well-chosen example) usually led to a successful theory or method, the meaning of the word was then transferred to that theory and/or method, and it is this latter meaning that has been elaborated by T.S. Kuhn in his book *The Structure of Scientific Revolutions* (Kuhn, 1970). We can now come to the definition of paradigm as it concerns us.

In computer science, as in most of the sciences, a **paradigm** is a coherent set of methods that have been found to be (more or less) effective in handling a given type of problems, the *problem domain*. For example, democracy, oligarchy and dictatorship may be called paradigms for governing.

A paradigm can usually be characterized by a single principle, simple to formulate, and this fact is a major source of its effectiveness. In terms of our example, in a dictatorship all power resides with one person, in an oligarchy power is in the hands of a small élite class, and in a democracy power ultimately rests with everybody.

Three points have to be made here. The first is that the definition of a paradigm involves judgement, in that it requires the set of methods to be perceived as effective to a certain extent. A paradigm should have at least some followers or it isn't a paradigm. The second is that the principle, though useful and catchy, is an oversimplification, as our example amply shows.

The third point is that to apply the principle in practice, a number of *methods* and/or techniques are required. To continue with our example, a democracy needs an electoral system to guide the flow of power from the bottom to the top and an administration to administer its flow down again. Each of these methods must be supported by a number of *concepts* in order to function properly. The electoral system requires the concepts of election, representation, ballot, and so on. It is important to note that these are concepts rather than the actual items. An actual election will often involve many ballots, each of which is an instantiation (realization, actualization) of the concept (calque) of 'ballot'. Like the methods, the concepts have their roots in the principle of the paradigm.

1.3.1 Programming paradigms

Figure 1.5 shows how paradigms, concepts and methods apply to programming. We consider the problem of sorting a list of words alphabetically, and we decide to use the so-called 'imperative' paradigm. As will be explained in Chapter 2, this paradigm is characterized by the principle of 'fully specified and fully controlled manipulation of named data in a stepwise fashion'. For our problem it suggests several methods, one being the use of linked lists. The method of linked lists rests on the concepts of allocatable data (for example, records), reference to data (for example, pointers) and repetition (for example, loops). It also uses some other concepts for manipulating and controlling the above, which are not shown in Figure 1.5. The program itself may also use additional methods, for example one for input/output, which rests on the concept of external data (for example, files). The bottom three layers support the program, which then serves as a tool to solve the problem.

A number of paradigms have been developed for the programming problem. The most prominent ones are

- the imperative paradigm,
- the object-oriented paradigm,
- the functional paradigm and
- the logic paradigm.

Other paradigms exist, and indeed new paradigms are being proposed more or less regularly.

The four major paradigms are dealt with in Chapters 2–5, respectively, and the structure of these chapters reflects that of a paradigm. Section 1 of each chapter explains the principles of the paradigm, including possible problems. Section 2 and following each describe a concept, often with some of the methods it helps to support. Examples of representative languages, a summary, literature references and exercises conclude each chapter.

The methods of a paradigm are not discussed exhaustively in this book, but only in as far as they are relevant to explain the concepts. There are two reasons for this. The first is that the number of concepts involved in a paradigm is relatively small and fixed (certainly the number of concepts available in a given programming language is fixed!), whereas the number of methods is extended every time somebody invents a new technique or data structure. An arbitrary number of methods can be implemented using a fixed number of concepts. The second reason is that covering the known methods in any depth would be tantamount to teaching programming in the given paradigm, a task better left to the many good books available on any of the paradigms. References to those can be found at the end of each chapter.

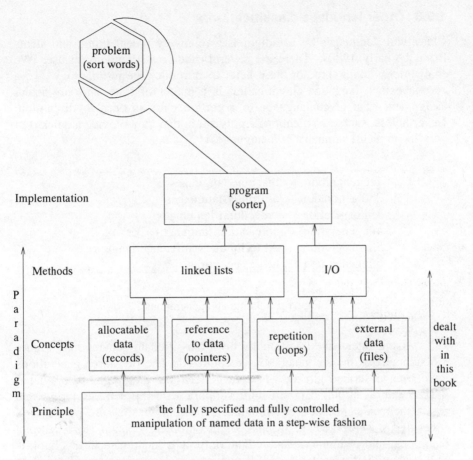

Figure 1.5 The relationships between the components of a paradigm.

1.3.2 Programming models

The four major paradigms aim at solving general programming problems, but in some situations the programming problem has additional aspects that have to be taken into account. An important example is parallel and distributed programming; here the additional aspect is the requirement to utilize optimally the available multiple processors, data storage and their connections.

It will not come as a surprise that the standard paradigms are not fully capable of handling these additional aspects, so new paradigms or extensions to the existing paradigms are needed. For parallel and distributed programming, additional paradigms such as distributed data structures are being researched. Programming paradigms for subproblems are often called **programming models**. The parallel and distributed programming problem is discussed in Chapter 6, where some models are presented. Other paradigms and programming models are covered in Chapter 7.

1.3.3 Other language classifications

Classifying languages by paradigm is a relatively recent thing, and stems from the early 1980s. There are several other classifications in use. We shall briefly cover three of these here, to introduce the terminology. To a certain extent, language classification is a matter of taste, and any actual assignment of a given language to a certain class is open to discussion. Nevertheless, such classifications are useful in that they provide a quick (but very incomplete) summary of a language.

1st generation	machine languages
2nd generation	assembly languages
3rd generation	procedural languages
4th generation	application languages
5th generation	AI techniques, inference languages
6th generation	neural networks

Figure 1.6 Language generations.

Languages have traditionally been classified in generations. Figure 1.6 summarizes the six generations recognized. The first three generations have been described already. **Fourth-generation languages** (abbreviated **4GLs**) exhibit strong data structure support: data are self-describing and retain their existence between program calls (that is, they are **persistent**). Most 4GLs incorporate knowledge of the problem domain (for example, databases) and of user interfaces. The only 4GL mentioned in this book is SQL, covered in Chapter 7. **Fifth-generation languages** are intended to allow non-specialist users to use artificial intelligence techniques; many are based on logical inference. Prolog can be considered a (simple) fifth-generation language. **Sixth-generation languages** are based on neural networks and sixth-generation programs exhibit learning behaviour. Whereas most 4GLs are pretty well established, fifth- and sixth-generation languages are at present experimental.

Another classification is shown in Figure 1.7; it is based on the degree of abstraction from the machine. The figure shows the degree of abstraction from two machine features, instructions and memory allocation.

Languages can also be classified by the measure of emphasis they put on *what* is to be achieved compared to *how* it must be achieved. A language that expresses what must be achieved and leaves it up to the system to figure out how to achieve it is called **definitional** or **declarative**. A language that expresses how something is achieved and leaves it up to the reader to figure out what is being achieved is called **operational** or **non-declarative**.

Level	Instructions	Memory handling	Examples
Low Level Languages (LLLs)	simple machine-like instructions	direct memory access and allocation	assembly languages, Autocode
High Level Languages (HLLs)	expressions and explicit flow of control	memory access and allocation through operators (for example, **new**)	FORTRAN, the Algols, Pascal, C, Ada
Very High Level Languages (VHLLs)	fully abstract machine	fully hidden memory access and automatic allocation	SETL, Prolog, Miranda

Figure 1.7 Language levels.

1.4 The structure of programs

Sentences in a natural language are traditionally analysed on three levels. The lexical level is concerned with the set of words in a language, its vocabulary, and tells us that fox is a noun and that no English word can start with bz. The syntactic level describes how sentences are constructed from words and opposes the English word order to the French in I love you versus Je t'aime. Finally, the semantic level addresses the issue of the meaning of a sentence. Although there are strong parallels between natural and programming languages, this division does not carry over exactly to programming languages, and it is instructive to see why.

That the lexical level is there is immediately obvious to the eye: program text naturally breaks up into wordlike units such as begin, end and ;. The syntactic level is very similar to that of natural languages, and is indeed often modelled vaguely on standard phrases from natural languages. A typical example is the conditional statement if ... then ... else ... .

In programming languages, there is an additional level between the syntactic and semantic levels, the contextual level. Its existence derives from the fact that programs, especially imperative and object-oriented programs, consist mainly of instructions to be obeyed, unlike most text in natural languages. The contextual level is concerned with the feasibility of instructions and indicates which actions can be performed on a given object. The semantic level describes what the permissible actions mean. On closer examination we find that this distinction is also present in natural languages. Suppose we ask instructions on how to find the post office on foot. An answer that requires us to go through a car tunnel is an infeasible order and therefore constitutes a contextual error, but if we get the answer 'Straight on and then to the right after the cinema' and then find that there is no cinema, we have a semantic error. The distinction between contextual and semantic levels is less pronounced in functional and logic languages, which is not surprising, since these languages are less instruction-oriented. We shall now deal with each of the four levels in more detail; they are summarized in Figure 1.8.

Level	Sample unit
lexical	begin
syntactic	if ... then ... else ... end if
contextual	a variable with its type, name, declaration and uses
semantic	flow of control during procedure call and return

Figure 1.8 Summary of the structure level of programs.

1.4.1 Lexical structure

Just as the building blocks of a natural language are lexical items called *words*, the building blocks of a programming language are lexical items called **lexical symbols**, **lexical units** or **tokens**. The lexical structure of different programming languages is reasonably uniform. The lexical symbols of almost all programming languages can be classified as identifiers, keywords, operators, separators, literals and comments. In addition to these symbols, the layout may play a role. We shall now briefly describe each of these items.

Identifiers are names, chosen by the programmer to identify objects of interest. Examples are x_prime, number_of_employees and Z80. Although the exact admissible form of an identifier depends on the programming language, an identifier generally starts with a letter and can contain letters, digits and a few other characters such as underscore (_) or apostrophe ('). Some languages differentiate between upper-case and lower-case letters, making x_prime and X_prime two different identifiers (for example, C), some do not (for example, Ada). In the latter case, the language may allow both cases to be used indiscriminately, or may insist that one case be used exclusively.

Keywords are names chosen by the language designer to help determine the syntactic structure. Examples are begin, if, else and procedure. With few exceptions they consist of letters only, and their rules for case significance are related to the rules for identifiers. Programs in languages that do not distinguish between upper and lower case may traditionally be written with lower-case keywords and upper-case identifiers (as in Ada) or the other way round. Since words in lower-case letters are often felt to be easier to read than words in upper case, and since identifiers are more crucial to the understanding of a program than keywords, the second approach seems to be preferable. If keywords are constructed according to the same rules as identifiers, they are called **reserved words**.

Operators serve to identify actions on **operands**. Examples are +, − and ÷. Operators may be composite: +=, << or *%. Some operators have the form of an identifier: in Modula-2, 7 div 3 yields the integer result (2) of the division of 7 by 3. Such operators are reserved words in most languages.

Separators, like keywords, support the syntactic structure, but consist of punctuation marks. Examples are the comma ',', the colon ':', the semicolon ';' and the open and close parentheses '(' and ')'. Separators may also be composite: an example is the '..' in a range indication such as 1..10.

Literals denote values directly. Numeric examples are 1, −123, 3.14 and 6.02e23, the latter representing 6.02×10^{23}. Examples of non-numeric literals are 'a' and "Virtual Reality". The literal 'a' represents the character *a*, as opposed to the identifier a. The demarcating marks ('...') are called **apostrophes**. The last example is called a **string**, consists of 15 characters and represents the text *Virtual Reality*. The demarcating marks ("...") are called **quotes**, and are not part of the string. Some languages, for example SETL, use apostrophes for strings as well: 'Virtual Reality'.

Ways to specify a quote in a string include doubling it and using an escape character. In the doubling method a quote inside a string is represented by "" and the text *"Yes," he said* corresponds to the string """Yes,"" he said". In the escape method, an **escape character** is defined in the language, often the backslash (\), which has the property that it takes away any special interpretation of the character that follows it. So the quote can be represented as \" and the backslash itself as \\. In this style, the above string is rendered as "\"Yes,\" he said". Neither method is very attractive, but no better format seems possible. Once an escape character has been introduced, it can also be used to solve some other minor problems with strings. Well-known conventions are the use of \n for the newline character (in those systems in which it is a character) and that of the escape character followed by digits in octal or hexadecimal notation, to place an arbitrary character in a string. Ada uses the doubling method and C (and many UNIX programs) use the escape method.

A **comment** embeds some explanatory text in a program, but is otherwise ignored. It starts with a keyword (for example comment), or a separator like /*, −− or #. It may end with a separator (for example ; or */), or at the end of the line on which it started. However minor the issue may seem, the proper design of the format of comments is important, since an awkward comment format is a constant source of nasty errors and a real nuisance in programming. A comment starter that is at least two characters long may prevent the accidental start of a comment. On the other hand, inadvertent layout between the two characters may cause an intended comment to be missed. Having the comment stop at the end of the line will prevent unterminated, 'run-away' comments. If a language has an explicit comment terminator different from the comment starter, it is possible to have nested comments, as in Modula-2.

Layout, important as it may be for the human understanding of a program text, plays a minor role in the syntax of most programming languages: **white space** (spaces, tabs, new lines) may be inserted or omitted at will. The role is not zero, though; some white space is required to separate reserved words, and to separate reserved words from identifiers. A few languages try to exploit the natural indentation of a well-written program and make the indentation part of the syntax: indentation indicates nesting. Examples of such languages are occam and ABC. This approach is attractive since it does away with **begin** and **end** keywords around blocks, and makes for a cleaner program appearance. It has the disadvantage that it runs into trouble when program lines are longer than the medium (screen, printer paper) allows. Also, the loss of redundancy may lead to more programming errors.

1.4.2 Syntactic structure

The syntactic structure of a programming language is often described precisely by a context-free grammar, usually in Backus Naur Form (BNF) or Extended Backus Naur Form (EBNF). An example is given in Figure 1.9. It describes a very simple language; Figure 1.10 shows a program in that language. The first rule in the EBNF grammar should be read as: a <program> is defined as (::=) the keyword **program** followed by a <statement>, zero or more times repeated (this is what the superscript * means), followed by the keyword **end**. The second rule says that a statement is defined as an <assignment> or (|) a <loop>. The third and fourth rules define the assignment and the loop. The <statement>$^+$ in the fourth rule means a statement repeated *one* or more times (indicated by the superscript +). The notion of <expression>, used in the above rules is defined as either a <value> or the sum of two <value>s or the comparison of two <value>s. <value> is defined in rule six to be either an <identifier> or a <number>. The latter are not defined in the EBNF grammar since they are lexical rather than syntactic notions.

The reader will note that the character < occurs in the grammar both as an open angle bracket to demarcate the notion names and as part of a <=-sign. We agree that this is slightly confusing but it is not unusual for grammars in EBNF notation to require some cooperation from the reader.

We can now use this grammar to produce the program of Figure 1.10 starting from the notion <program>; see Figure 1.11. We replace **program** by its definition (line 2) and then decide to have two statements for our

```
<program>          ::=    program <statement>* end
<statement>        ::=    <assignment> | <loop>
<assignment>       ::=    <identifier> := <expression> ;
<loop>             ::=    while <expression> do <statement>+ done
<expression>       ::=    <value> | <value> + <value>
                                | <value> <= <value>
<value>            ::=    <identifier> | <number>
```

Figure 1.9 A sample grammar in EBNF notation.

```
program
  n := 1;
  while n <= 10 do
    n := n + 1;
  done
end
```

Figure 1.10 A simple program from the grammar in Figure 1.9.

```
<program>
program <statement>* end
program <statement> <statement> end
program <assignment> <loop> end
program <identifier> := <expression>; while <expression> do <statement>+ done end
program n := <value>; while <value> <= <value> do <statement> done end
program n := <number>; while <identifier> <= <number> do <assignment> done end
program n := 1; while n <= 10 do <identifier> := <expression>; done end
program n := 1; while n <= 10 do n := <value> + <value>; done end
program n := 1; while n <= 10 do n := <identifier> + <number>; done end
program n := 1; while n <= 10 do n := n + 1; done end
```

Figure 1.11 Producing the program from Figure 1.10.

<statement>* (line 3). We continue replacing each notion by one of its definitions, making choices along the way, until all notions have been fully developed into lexical symbols.

The relationship between grammar and program works two ways. We can use the grammar to produce a sequence of lexical symbols which is a program, but given this sequence of lexical symbols, we can use the grammar in a process called **parsing** to structure the sequence into meaningful units. Parsing will, for example, tell us that the n+1 in n := n+1 is an <expression>.

Using a context-free grammar rather than text in a natural language to define the form of programs has two advantages. It facilitates answering certain detailed questions about the language ('Can I have a loop with no statement in it?'), and it serves as a basis to derive language processors semi-automatically. Examples of the latter are compilers, interpreters and editors.

The syntactic structure of different programming languages differs greatly. No general classification like that for lexical symbols can be made.

1.4.3 Context and semantics

The identification of named notions in the program such as <expression> or <loop> through parsing is important, since language definitions describe the properties and meaning of a program by describing the properties and meaning of these named notions. For our example, the language definition would probably state that for an expression of the form <value> + <value>, both values must be integers, and if either value is an identifier, it must have a value, that is, it must have been initialized. The former condition forbids expressions like 1 + 'a' and the latter forbids a program like **program** n := n + 1; **end.** Such conditions in the language definition concerning entities in the program are called **context conditions**. The first condition in our example will probably be checked by the compiler, the second probably will not.

The language definition will also specify what notions mean; for example, it will state what will happen when the value of an **expression** is calculated. This is called the **semantics of the expression**, and the semantics of the various notions in the program combine into the semantics of the whole program.

There are some formal methods to describe the context conditions and semantics of a programming language with the same rigour as its syntax is described by a context-free grammar, but these methods are much more difficult and arcane than context-free grammars. They are used only to a limited extent in language definition, and are not normally found in user manuals. Notable exceptions are the Algol 68 report (van Wijngaarden *et al.*, 1975), which uses a two-level grammar, and the Turing manual (Holt *et al.*, 1988), which uses denotational semantics.

1.5 Programming languages as communication media

Like a natural language, a programming language can be viewed as a means of communication. The most common mode of communication is that from human to machine, but other modes are not unusual:

- from human to human, where text in a programming language serves to convey an algorithm, approach or technique;
- from machine to machine, in the not at all uncommon situation in which a program generates a second program, thus achieving results often hard to obtain by other means.

The nature of what is communicated depends on the paradigm the language supports. The code written in imperative and object-oriented programming languages communicates a set of instructions; the logic programming languages communicate relations between entities; and the functional programming languages communicate definitions of entities in terms of other entities. Languages that concentrate on sets of instructions are sometimes called **algorithmic**.

Each form of communication has a speaker and a listener, a writer and a reader. In the early days of programming, it was already difficult enough to express one's wishes in a computer-acceptable form, and writeability, often called 'ease of use' in those days, had a high priority in the design of programming languages. Writeability reached its peak with languages like APL. The APL statement $I \leftarrow (1 \downarrow \rho A) \rho \Diamond [1] A$ can serve as an example. In it, A is an array of complex numbers, possibly multi-dimensional, in which each complex number is modelled as an array of two elements. The statement assigns to I an array of the same shape consisting of the imaginary parts of the complex numbers in A. One can be impressed by the extreme conciseness of APL and still regret its lack of readability.

As the art of programming matured, designers realized that, since any serious program is read many more times during its lifetime than it is written, readability is the more important aspect. Languages like Modula-2 and Ada reflect this attitude. It should be noted, though, that the designers of COBOL already emphasized readability in 1959.

There is one fundamental difference between natural-language communication and human–machine communication: the lack of feedback in the latter. Humans, if of good will, are very fault-tolerant in their communications, but a computer requires every detail to be spelled out with little room for error. This makes human–machine communication unexpectedly more difficult and taxing than human–human communication, a phenomenon that was not recognized in the 1950s and 1960s and that was at least partially responsible for the software crisis of the 1970s.

Providing support for managing and reducing the unexpected and unfamiliar complexity of ultra-precise communication has been *the* challenge of programming language design for more than two decades. Dozens of concepts have been proposed, in equally many programming languages, and most of them have been found wanting. Among the few survivors are *procedures*, *modules* and *abstract data types* in various guises.

Some programming languages provide advanced programming support at the expense of a considerable loss of run-time efficiency. Imperative examples are SETL and ABC. These languages are examples of VHLLs (Very High Level Languages). They are very suitable for prototyping, since they allow complex processes to be specified relatively simply and reliably, but the loss of efficiency precludes wider usage.

Some designers try to improve programming by removing those features that are found to be most dangerous in the face of complexity. A well-known slogan of this approach is 'Feature X considered harmful'. This may result in a loss of expressivity, and may even reduce it to a level that the programmer finds unacceptable; some argue that functional languages come into this category, notably Backus' FP. The successful exorcism of the goto statement has shown, however, that a restriction that is unacceptable to one generation of programmers may very well go unnoticed by the next. (Goto statements and their problems are discussed in Chapter 2.)

In summary, it is the task of a modern programming language to assist the user in managing and reducing the complexity of the programming task, without unduly restricting expressivity, and without causing undue loss of efficiency.

1.6 Managing and reducing complexity

All known techniques for handling complex problems successfully seem to fall into one of three classes: subdividing the problem (decomposition), ignoring irrelevant detail in a safe way (abstraction), and having an independent agent check the internal consistency (contextual checking). The first two provide guidelines for solving the problem; the third serves to provide early warnings. A good programming language supports all three.

In computer science, the phrase 'to abstract from X' is used in the sense of 'to ignore X judiciously as being irrelevant to the present level of discussion' rather than in the possibly more common sense of 'to excerpt'. The term is not synonymous with 'to generalize' either. If irrelevant details are ignored, an idea may be more generally applicable, which shows that generality is not equivalent to, but can result from, abstraction.

Various collections of complexity-reducing techniques have been called **structured programming** over the years, but the term has been abused so often that it is virtually meaningless now.

1.6.1 Problem decomposition

The technique of decomposing a problem into two or more smaller problems that it is hoped are easier to solve was already known in antiquity: 'Divide et impera', which is Latin for 'Divide and rule'. It is known in English as 'divide and conquer'.

Some of the subproblems may be similar to the original problem, in which case the problem decomposition leads us to a **recursive solution**. This recursive solution is viable provided each of the subproblems is easier to solve than the original problem.

The traditional example of a problem that yields easily and in many ways to decomposition is that of sorting the items in a list. If we call the list L and the number of items in it N, the technique shown in Figure 1.12 will sort the list.

sort the list L with length N:
  case 1: $N < 2$:
    □ do nothing (a list of fewer than two items is already sorted)
  case 2: $N \geq 2$:
    □ split the list in two sublists, L_1 with length N_1 and
      L_2 with length N_2, such that $N_1 > 0$ and $N_2 > 0$
      (this can always be done since there are at least two items)
    □ sort the list L_1 with length N_1 and sort the list L_2 with length N_2
      (both problems are guaranteed to be easier to solve
      than the original since $N_1 < N$ and $N_2 < N$)
    □ merge L_1 and L_2, preserving the sorted order.

Figure 1.12 Decomposing the problem of sorting a list.

This example shows several features of problem decomposition. First, there must always be at least one alternative that does not define the problem in terms of itself: the **escape hatch**. This non-recursive alternative is often the trivial case, as it is in the above example (case 1: do nothing).

Second, one has to be careful to ensure that the subproblems are indeed easier to solve. If one of them is not, subdivision continues but no real progress is made.

Third, the details of the subdivision can be chosen independently, yielding different algorithms for different choices. If N_1 is always 1, the above example describes a variant of insertion sort. If N_1 and N_2 are chosen as close together as possible, binary sort-merge results. And if L_1 is chosen to contain all items below a certain threshold and L_2 the rest, a variant of quicksort results.

Problem decomposition hinges on procedures, recursion and parameter passing, and can be applied in almost all high-level and assembly languages.

1.6.2 Abstraction

The desire to 'ignore irrelevant detail in a safe way' immediately raises two questions: what is 'irrelevant detail' and what is 'in a safe way'?

Irrelevant detail is detail that is of no concern to a user in solving the problem. It is of no concern to the user who deals with calendar dates in a program whether these dates are represented internally in the form of triplets (year, month, day) or as a single integer (for example, the number of days since January 1, 1900). All that is required is that the operations on them work properly. Note that this introduces a 'user' and consequently a 'used': the set of dates implemented in a particular way. The user can apply a number of operations on the 'used' and expect them to work properly, but the user is not supposed to look inside the used object to see its internal structure, let alone modify it. Such a formalized access to an object, with the user on one side and the object on the other, is called an **interface**.

The interface for calendar dates may include such operations as: create a date variable; add a date and a number to yield the resulting date; and determine whether a given date is the last of the month. Each of these operations can be implemented using the triplet or the single-integer representation, although the efficiency will differ: adding a number to a date, for example, is trivial in the single-integer representation but requires some calculation in the triplet representation.

An interface allows the user of a feature to abstract from the internal details of that feature, and it allows the implementer of that feature to change those details of the implementation that do not affect the interface, without having to bother or even notify the user. The interface veils the secret of the implementation.

Such interfaces can exist entirely in the mind of the user, who restricts him- or herself, through disciplined programming, to the 'published' facilities the implementation supplies, and who, through sheer will-power, resists the temptation to go around the interface and gain efficiency. Since no special support is required, interfaces can be used in any language.

'Ignoring irrelevant details *in a safe way*' implies that the secret hidden by the interface must indeed be impenetrable. Users should be not so much *allowed* to abstract from the underlying implementation, they should have *no choice but* to abstract from it. Only then can the implementer of the feature be sure that users cannot, by accident or intent, write code that is dependent on implementation details. The interface hides the secret of the implementation completely.

Such interfaces do not exist exclusively in the mind of the user; they show up in the program code, and are known to the compiler and to other program-processing programs. Safe abstraction by information hiding requires the support of the programming environment, most often of the compiler/linker. Such an abstraction then takes the form of a **package** or **module**, an encapsulated implementation of a set of services, encapsulated in that it allows the user only a restricted number of well-defined actions on the internal data; all the rest is inaccessible.

The technique the compiler uses to guard the implementation secret is very simple: since all directly accessible objects are accessible only through names that refer to them, the compiler just makes sure that names which refer to secret objects on the implementer's side of the interface are unknown or refer to some other object on the user's side of the interface. Information hiding is done entirely by name manipulation.

Packages and modules, as they are called in Ada and Modula-2 respectively, can be seen as implementations of the concept of *abstract data types*. For a somewhat different approach, see the chapter on object-oriented programming, Chapter 3. Packages, modules and abstract data types are discussed in Chapter 2.

1.6.3 Contextual checking

Text, both in natural languages and in programming languages, can suffer from lexical, syntactic, contextual or semantic errors. Lexical and syntactic errors will confuse neither human nor machine: 'Him of quickly five' will be rejected as readily as 'begin) end', since the first does not conform to the grammar of English as native speakers know it, and the second cannot be generated by the context-free grammar of a (normal) programming language. Contextual errors are different, however. Children can be confused by questions like: 'What colour are elephants' eggs?' and even adults can have trouble answering intelligently the rather more vicious variant: 'When did you stop beating your partner?'. Given the total lack of understanding on the part of the computer, it is not surprising that computers are even more prone to contextual confusion than humans. It would be nice to have reliable formal methods for checking contextual errors that possess the same power as those we have for lexical and syntactic checking. Unfortunately, only a few very simple contextual checks can be done properly. Most of the more comprehensive contextual correctness tests have been proved to be **recursively unsolvable**, which means that no algorithm can exist, even in theory, that does them properly. So we shall have to be satisfied with less.

The simple contextual checks routinely done by a compiler include such things as checking for undeclared identifiers and checking the number of parameters in a procedure call. At the other end of the spectrum, recursively unsolvable contextual checks include those for termination, integer overflow and many others. Only one advanced contextual check has proved its value through the years: strong type checking. Furthermore, there are a number of heuristic contextual checks that are helpful.

Ideally, one would like it to be impossible for semantic (that is, run-time) errors to occur, but since not all context conditions can be checked properly by the compiler, we know that we cannot attain this ideal even in theory. Run-time error testing is the safety net for semantic errors not caught by context condition testing in the compiler. Like most safety measures, such tests are awkward and carry a performance penalty, and there is an understandable tendency to avoid them and run the corresponding risk.

Strong type checking

The instructions on data in an imperative programming language fall under one of two categories: built-in actions and programmer-defined actions. The built-in actions generally require the values of their operands to belong to certain domains. For example, an if-statement needs the condition it tests to be a value from the domain {true, false} and the plus operator may require both operands to be a value in the range {−32768..32767}. Many programming languages require programmers to specify the domains of the operands of the actions they define. The compiler can then analyse the program to check whether any action can ever be presented with a value that is not in the expected domain, and if so, give an error message and prevent the program from being run, thus preventing the semantic error. The domains are called **data types** or simply **types**. If the domain consistency checking will signal *all* domain inconsistencies, it is called **strong type checking**, otherwise it is called **weak type checking**.

Strong type checking is useful in that it provides programmers with early warnings about possible semantic errors in their programs. This protection is, however, partial: a type-consistent program can still be semantically incorrect. For example, the second operand of a division operation may be of the correct type integer, but the actual value may be zero at run time. Or an array variable may be of the correct type, but the value used to index it may be out of range. Also, a type-inconsistent program need not always come to harm when run, since the offending code may never be reached. Still, the general experience with strong type checking is very favourable, and modern imperative programming languages like Ada and Modula-2 support it.

In the above, strong type checking was explained in the context of imperative languages. The idea can also be applied reasonably well to object-oriented and functional languages, but this is not always done. The reason for this may be that object-oriented and functional languages have traditionally been implemented using interpreters, and strong type checking is very much a compilation issue. Languages like Eiffel (object-oriented) and Miranda (functional) show, however, that it can be done. Logic languages usually do not have strong type checking.

Heuristic contextual checks

In an attempt to supply additional contextual checking, some compilers perform **heuristic checks** on the program. A heuristic test or technique is a test or technique based on intuitively reasonable ideas rather than on a well-founded theory. Such a test or technique will work often but not always. Since it will fail occasionally, it is necessary to get a clear idea of the cases in which that happens. A good heuristic check has the property that if it identifies an error, the error is certain to occur at run time, provided the code concerned is executed at all. If the heuristic check does not find the error, the error may still be there, though. An example could be the test whether a recursive routine has an escape hatch, as explained in the section on program decomposition: if each invocation of a routine will inevitably result in another invocation of that same routine, the program is certainly erroneous. If the escape hatch is there but will never be reached, the test will not find an error, but the program is erroneous nevertheless.

We are now reaching the outskirts of programming methodology, however, and shall not pursue the subject any further.

1.7 Program processing

Writing a program is not enough, the program must also be run on a computer. The hardware of the computer is unable to execute, say, Ada commands directly, but it can execute machine instructions directly. There are basically two ways to run programs in a high-level language, called **source programs**, on a computer: interpretation and compilation.

1.7.1 Interpretation versus compilation

In interpretation, we have a special program, consisting of machine instructions and running directly on the hardware, which is capable of reading, analysing and executing, for example, Ada commands. Such a program is called an **interpreter**, in this case an Ada-interpreter. To run our source program using an interpreter, we call the interpreter and pass it the name of the source program (see Figure 1.13). The interpreter then reads and analyses the source program, may give warnings or error messages, and starts performing the instructions contained in the source program. While it is running, the interpreter has access to the complete text of the source program. This enables it to formulate possible error messages or statistics in terms of the source program.

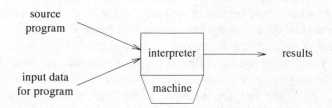

Figure 1.13 Interpretation.

In compilation, we have a different special program, also consisting of machine instructions and running directly on the hardware, which is also capable of reading and analysing commands in a high-level language, but which translates them to equivalent machine instructions rather than executing them. Such a program is called a **compiler**.

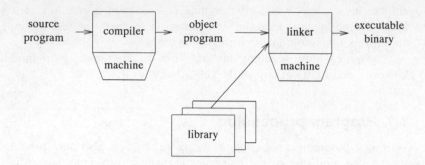

Figure 1.14 Compilation.

To run our source program using a compiler, we call the compiler and pass it the name of the source program (see Figure 1.14). From this source program, the compiler produces an **object program**, which consists mainly of machine instructions and some administration. In a sense, the source program and object program are semantically equivalent. Contrary to expectations, the object program cannot be run directly. The reason for this is that complicated source code commands, for example the Pascal write command or the Ada tasking commands, are often not translated to the full required sets of machine instructions but rather to references to these sets. The actual sets of instructions are stored in **libraries**, where they are identified by **external names**. The actual code for the Pascal write command may, for example, be stored in a library pascal.lib under the name write_cmd. When a reference to such a set occurs in an object file, it is called an **unsatisfied (external) reference**; it contains the external name.

To satisfy these references, we have to call a second special program, called a **linker**, which searches some run-time libraries for sets of code identified by the external names in the unsatisfied references. The linker then combines the object program and the code from the libraries into an **executable binary program**, also called **binary** for short. As the name says, this program is executable on the hardware.

To actually run our original program, we call the equivalent binary program, supplying our input data as shown in Figure 1.15. We can, of course, repeat the last step as often as we want with different input data, without having to repeat the compilation process.

Figure 1.16 shows how this two-stage compile-and-link scenario enables programmers to split their source programs into manageable chunks, compile them separately and combine them using the linker. The mechanism used here is the same as that for identifying and adding library code. An object file A can use code from an object file B if that code is

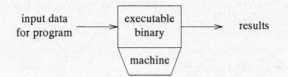

Figure 1.15 Calling a compiled program.

identified by an external name, say N, and A refers to that name. Object file A will then contain an unsatisfied reference to N, which will be resolved by the linker, connecting it to the code named N in B.

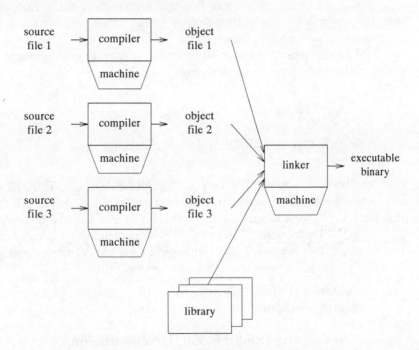

Figure 1.16 Separate compilation of three source files.

The advantage of compilation over interpretation is that execution of a binary program can easily be a hundred times faster than execution through an interpreter. A disadvantage is that in most compilers, most of the original source code structure is lost in the binary program, so run-time error messages can be given only in terms of the machine code instructions and are often next to meaningless to the user.

At the beginning of this section we assumed for simplicity that both the interpreter and compiler consist of machine instructions, that is, result from compilation. Indeed, both could again be interpreted (by an interpreter that could be interpreted or compiled), but it will be clear that this stacking of interpreters must end somewhere in an interpreter that does consist of machine instructions.

1.7.2 Macro preprocessing

We have already mentioned the possibility that the input to the compiler is generated by a program rather than written by a human. The simplest technique that employs this possibility is **macro preprocessing**. A macro is a pair consisting of a name and a string, with the understanding that the string is intended as a replacement for the name. A macro preprocessor first reads the (user-written) macro definitions. It then reads the program text and creates from it a new program text, in which each occurrence of each macro name is replaced by the corresponding string. This second text is then presented as source code to the compiler.

Macro preprocessing can, for example, be used to give names to constants. Using the C macro preprocessor, we can generate the C code from Figure 1.3 by writing:

```
#define  NUMBER_OF_TURNS  10

for (n = 1; n <= NUMBER_OF_TURNS; n++) {
}
```

The #define line defines a macro named NUMBER_OF_TURNS with substitution string 10. Such naming of constants improves the readability of program text. Also, it localizes the actual value of a conceptual quantity.

The C preprocessor allows macros with parameters. We can use this feature to replace the awkward notation n++, which means that n is increased by 1, by the more attractive notation INCR(n):

```
#define  NUMBER_OF_TURNS  10
#define  INCR(a)                 a++

for (n = 1; n <= NUMBER_OF_TURNS; INCR(n)) {
}
```

With four more macro definitions, we can even 'customize' the C compiler to seemingly accept for-statements in a pseudo-Ada notation, as shown in Figure 1.17 (compare this to the Ada code in Figure 1.3). Such an approach may be appealing to the Ada programmer who has to work with C programs, but we can see that the simulation is far from perfect. The result of the macro expansion will contain semicolons where the original had none; as it happens, these superfluous semicolons do not matter in this case, however. In general, a macro processor will very easily get us almost what we want; getting exactly what we want by macro processing is very difficult and often impossible.

Many language designers feel that the above examples demonstrate

```
#define  NUMBER_OF_TURNS  10

#define  For(var,from,to)   for (var = from; var <= to; var++)
#define  loop               {
#define  end_loop           }
#define  null

For (n, 1, NUMBER_OF_TURNS) loop
   null;
end_loop;
```

Figure 1.17 Implementing an Ada-like for-loop in C by macro preprocessing.

less the usefulness of macro preprocessing than the inadequacy of C. A well-designed language should have built-in means to name constants, and should not feature notations that are so awkward that users want to change them. Also, the 'cute' customization shown above results in program texts that are hard to maintain by a professional C programmer, and that do not respond well to other C-processing software, for example prettyprinters. Another problem is that a macro preprocessor manipulates strings only, has no notion of the data types in the language, and consequently cannot do any type checking. For example, in

```
#define  NUMBER_OF_TURNS  10
```

the 10 is considered as a string rather than as an integer. This causes a discrepancy between the perception of the programmer and that of the compiler, which can easily lead to errors.

In summary, macro preprocessors are very powerful low-level tools, but their proper use requires considerable restraint from the user, more than most language designers credit the average programmer with. Pascal, Modula-2 and Ada do not have standard macro preprocessors, but C and C++ do. Most language designers feel that a well-designed language does not need a macro preprocessor, but many users find a macro preprocessor to be a very effective tool when the situation is less than ideal.

1.7.3 Debugging tools

The incomprehensibility of run-time error messages produced by compiled programs has led to the development of various debugging tools. The simplest of these read the machine error message, which often takes the form of a so-called 'core dump', and try to display information and answer questions about it. They make a mediocre job of it at best, but are better than nothing. Much of today's debugging is still done at the Stone-Age level.

Modern systems keep the entire source code in the binary program and use it to display the information in a form relevant to the user. The best of them enable the user to navigate through various states of the running program. These debuggers approach the reporting capabilities of interpreting systems.

1.7.4 Programming environments

In practice, compiling a program is often more complicated than described above, especially during the development phase. In a well-organized large program, the program text is spread out over many files. Each file can be compiled separately to produce the corresponding object file. The linker gathers all these object files and composes one executable binary program from it, the runnable program. When a program under development is run, more often than not an error shows up, the correction of which necessitates the modification of a small number of the program files, followed by a recompilation. It would be foolish and wasteful to recompile all program files. Recreating only the object files that are affected by the modifications suffices. The linker then constructs a new executable binary program and the development cycle continues.

Keeping track of which files have been modified and finding out which object files and/or executable binaries should be reconstructed after a modification can be a major effort in a fair-sized project, but fortunately the activity can be automated to a large extent. Software for that purpose is called a **program management system**, and it comes in two varieties: general and integrated.

A general program management system is an independent program or set of programs that can, in principle, manage programs in any language, including natural languages. It can, in some way, be parametrized with knowledge about the programs it should manage, available compilers, program dependencies, user wishes, and so on. Examples are the UNIX program Make or the VMS program MMS.

An integrated program management system is built in or around a programming language. Often the language cannot be used outside the program management system: the programs are not available as separate files to the user, and all code is under control of the program management system. In exchange, the system can give much relevant support. Program management systems are appreciated differently by different people. Some like them for the support they give, some hate them for the freedom they take away. The imperative language ABC and the functional language Miranda supply a largely integrated programming environment, and the object-oriented programming language Smalltalk-80 comes as a fully integrated program management system. Program composition and the possibilities of programming management systems are dealt with further in Section 2.5.5.

Summary

- Programming languages can be classified according to the programming paradigm they support.
- A paradigm is a coherent set of methods for handling a given type of problems, the problem domain. It is a mode of thinking and moulds the design process.
- There are at present four major programming paradigms: imperative, object-oriented, functional and logic. There are also a number of minor ones.
- Additional problem domains require additional paradigms. One such problem domain in programming is parallel and distributed programming. A paradigm for a specific problem domain is called a model.
- Communication with a machine requires extreme precision, is unfamiliar and is unexpectedly difficult.
- It is the task of a modern programming language to assist the user in managing and reducing the complexity of the programming task, without unduly restricting expressivity, and without causing undue loss of efficiency.
- Techniques for handling complex problems successfully are: subdividing the problem (decomposition), ignoring irrelevant detail in a safe way (abstraction), and having an independent agent check the internal consistency (context checking).
- An interface is a formalized way of accessing an object, with the user on one side and the object on the other.
- A type is a set of values with operations on them. In a slightly different view it is a set of operations with their domains.
- Strong type checking will signal all domain inconsistencies, weak type checking will only signal some.
- Since any serious program is read many more times during its lifetime than it is written, readability is more important than writeability.
- An interpreter is a program that can read, analyse and execute commands of a high-level language. A compiler translates these commands into machine instructions, rather than executing them.
- A macro preprocessor produces compiler input by scanning a program text and replacing specified names in it by specified strings. Macro preprocessors can simplify programming but are easily abused.

Bibliographical notes

The full width of the programming language terrain, from paradigms to structure to semantics to compiler construction, is covered by Watt's trilogy (1990, 1991, 1993). Almost all present-day books on the principles of programming languages are of excellent quality, and it is impossible to mention a limited number of them without omitting equally good ones. The books by Appleby (1991), Wilson and Clark (1993), and Ghezzi and Jazayeri (1987) span a range from easy-going to technical. The philosophically inclined reader may enjoy the book by Abelson, Sussman and Sussman (1985). A review by Owens (1992) compares nine recent books on principles of programming languages.

Very detailed information can be gathered from journals, for example *Computer Languages* (Elmsford, NY) (there is a second journal called *Computer Languages*, which is published in San Francisco), *ACM Transactions on Programming Languages and Systems*, and *ACM SIGPLAN Notices*. The latter also publishes descriptions of newly proposed languages. Some important general conferences on programming languages are: the ACM Symposium on Principles of Programming Languages, the ACM SIGPLAN Conference on Programming Language Design and Implementation, and the IEEE CS International Conference on Computer Languages. Much historical information about programming languages can be found in the proceedings of two conferences on the history of programming languages, HOPL (Sammet *et al.*, 1978) and HOPL-II (Lee and Sammet, 1993).

Exercises

1.1   Take two or three pages of an existing Ada or Modula-2 program and make the capitalization consistent: all keywords lower-case and all identifiers upper-case, or vice versa. Compare this text to the same text with the reverse convention, both on screen and on paper. Add to your comparison an all lower-case version (like C), an all upper-case version (like FORTRAN) and a mixed-case version (like Ada). Compare them, as far as possible, for aesthetic satisfaction, for the speed with which you can find a given identifier and for eye strain. Equipment allowing, make printouts in a monospace serif font (Courier), a proportional sans-serif font (Helvetica) and a proportional serif font (Times Roman, Schoolbook). In short, find a representation style that you are comfortable with.

1.2   Read Zuse (1989) about Plankalkül, or Bauer and Wössner's (1972) introduction to it, and speculate about differences, had this work been known earlier.

1.3   List advantages and disadvantages of nested comments.

1.4

a.   A young and inexperienced language designer (the worst kind) wants to generalize the notation for real numbers and proposes to introduce the dot (.) as an operator, allowing people to write expressions such as a.b in which a is the integral part and b the decimal part. Explain why this does not work.

b. Undaunted by this failure, the designer now proposes to have the exponent marker e as an operator, allowing people to write expressions such as a e b, which evaluates to $a \times 10^b$. Will this work?

1.5 List perceptible differences between implementations which use triplets for calendar dates and those which use single integers.

1.6 A programmer is to write code to determine if a string B consists of zero or more repetitions of string A. In a divide-and-conquer approach, the programmer writes:

B is a repetition of As:
  case 1: B is empty:
    □ succeed
  case 2: B is not empty:
    □ cut B in two parts, B_1 and B_2, such that B_1 is as long as possible but not longer than A.
      (this can always be done, regardless of the lengths of A and B)
    □ test if A equals B_1.
      (this test is not recursive)
    □ test if B_2 is a repetition of As.
      (this problem is guaranteed to be easier to solve than the original since B_2 is shorter than B)
    □ if both tests succeed, B is a repetition of As; otherwise, it is not.

In spite of the 'proof' given above, the programmer's code fails for some values of A and B. Why?

1.7 Why should heuristic tests test conservatively rather than aggressively?

1.8 In one or more languages you know (C, Ada, Modula-2, Pascal or others), think which features make automatic program management easy/difficult.

1.9 [Requires some knowledge of Pascal] Suppose we have a macro preprocessor that will substitute macro parameters even inside strings, and we use this preprocessor for Pascal. We can then define a macro show that will generate code to print, for example, a variable or expression, both as text and as a value:

    #define show(expr)   write 'expr =', expr; writeln

Now, show(a[i]); will generate write 'a[i] =', a[i]; writeln; which prints something like a[i] = 5, followed by a new line. In what situation will this macro fail?

2

Imperative Languages

In the early years, programming languages were designed by abstracting more and more from the hardware; in a sense virtual hardware of a higher level was created. Then the emphasis shifted to the algorithmic, the recipe-like nature of a program. This resulted, among other things, in a better understanding of data types and flow of control, and allowed the level of the virtual hardware to be raised even more.

We have seen that in reaction to these automaton-flavoured, if not machine-oriented languages, some designers set out from the other end, basing their design on different paradigms such as functional programming or logic programming, and leaving it to the compiler writer community to reach the hardware level from there.

These developments did not mark the end of the imperative paradigm. On the contrary, imperative languages have continued to grow and to be used. The reason for this may be twofold. First, on present-day hardware, programs in imperative languages will often be ten to a hundred times faster than those in other types of languages, and they are certainly not ten to a hundred times more difficult to write. Second, the imperative paradigm is fairly congenial to the present-day Western mind, often more so than the other paradigms are. Both effects may change, though, as hardware is developed and culture changes.

Most serious programming today is done in imperative languages. Attempts to change this situation by using a variant of Prolog, KL1, in the Japanese Fifth Generation Computer Systems project have not met with the success some had hoped for. The most prominent imperative languages at the moment are Ada, ANSI C, C++, Pascal and Modula-2, although FORTRAN and COBOL may still be more widely used.

Most imperative languages are designed explicitly for compilation. The designer expects the programmer to be willing to sacrifice some advanced features and programming convenience in exchange for speed of execution. A program in these languages shows in many details that it is running on a machine. In particular, memory allocation, initialization and deallocation is generally explicit.

Some designers concentrate completely on the level and convenience of programming and allow the programmer to abstract to a large extent from the fact that the program still runs on a machine. In particular, memory manipulation is automatic and invisible. Present state-of-the-art compiler construction, however, cannot really produce reasonable translations for such very high-level imperative programs, although progress in this direction is being made. Therefore, it is often preferred to run such programs by the use of an interpreter, as explained in Chapter 1. This approach has the additional advantage that it provides the language designer with great freedom in choosing the proper concepts and primitives; the price is a considerable loss of speed.

The bottom line is that there are two kinds of imperative languages, one designed with compilation in mind, the other with interpretation in mind. Given the great difference in emphasis, no fair comparison between the two is possible; both types are successful in their fields. Most examples in this chapter are from compilation-oriented languages; interpretation-oriented languages mentioned here are Icon, ABC and PostScript.

Characteristic features of imperative languages will be illustrated below using two languages, C and Ada. There are several reasons for this choice. Both languages are good representatives of their species; there is ample literature on both; and together they exhibit most imperative language features.

More than one version exists of both of these languages. C, which existed in many variants, was standardized in 1988 to ANSI C. With one or two important exceptions the differences are minor, and we will not use old C in our examples. The case with Ada is different. There are only two main versions of Ada, the original Ada 83, as defined by the US Department of Defense (1983), and its successor, Ada 9X, which is in the last stages of design at the time of writing this book. Ada 9X extends Ada 83 considerably but has not yet been standardized. The Ada 9X standard is described in the Reference Manual by Intermetrics, Inc. (1993), and Barnes's book (1994). For most of our examples the difference between Ada 83 and Ada 9X does not matter, and we just use the name Ada. When the difference is significant, we use the specific names **Ada 9X** and **Ada 83**.

2.1 Principles

The basis of the **imperative paradigm** is the fully specified and fully controlled manipulation of named data in a step-wise fashion. This paradigm fits comfortably in the human mind, which is already used to cooking from recipes or to following instructions for changing brake linings on a car. It also fits in well with the hardware, which already manipulates data in a step-wise fashion. All we have to do in an imperative program is to specify the named data and the manipulations, and to control the stepping. Imperative languages have a clear 'do this, then do that' structure, a fact which lends them their name. A disadvantage of the imperative paradigm is that it tends to bog down the programmer with large amounts of detail. Assembly languages are the archetypal imperative languages.

Specifying the named data is done through data declarations, data manipulation is done through state-changing commands, and controlling the stepping is called flow of control. Each of these will be covered in a main section in this chapter. Through historical accident, commands in a programming language have come to be called **statements**.

The language constructs will be illustrated with examples from (ANSI) C in the left column and Ada (9X) in the right column. Program text will be in a **sans serif** font. Case differences are significant in C and are ignored in Ada. Both languages use lower-case letters for the keywords. We will use identifiers in lower-case letters in C. Traditionally, identifiers were in upper case in Ada 83, but the Ada 9X Reference Manual uses mixed case, and we will follow that suggestion. To avoid duplication, we use lower-case letters in the running text, thus: 'cost_of_living' where the C text has lower-case cost_of_living and the Ada text has mixed-case Cost_Of_Living.

2.2 Data

Data, a Latin plural noun meaning 'things that have been given' but generally used as a singular collective noun in English, is the carrier of information. Every data item in a computer has a representation and a number of properties collectively known as its 'type'. Most data items have **names**, used for manipulating them. Anonymous data items exist but have to be used right where they are produced; the 5×6 in 4+5×6 is an example of anonymous data. The relationships between data items, names, types and representations are specified by the programmer in data declarations.

2.2.1 Data declarations

A data item in memory has the form of a number of bits, without any hints as to what these bits represent. In order to manipulate a data item meaningfully, structure has to be imposed on it and for many purposes it has to be given a name. A **data declaration** does both; it binds a name to the data item and to a structure. The imposed structure is specified as a type and the name is an identifier. The bit pattern combined with the imposed structure determines the value of the data item. Since the hardware can modify or replace the bit pattern in response to machine instructions, the value of the data item can in principle be changed. If the programming language indeed allows such a change, the combination of name, type and value is called a **variable.** Note that the data item exists in the machine, while its structure and its name exist only in the program.

Data declarations look slightly different in C and Ada:

int i, j;   I, J: Integer;

Both declare two variables, named i and j respectively, both represented by bit patterns that are to be interpreted as integers. Note that the data type is also indicated by a name: int and Integer. Figure 2.1 summarizes the interrelationships between type names, types, imposed structure, variable names, memory locations, bit patterns and interpreted value.

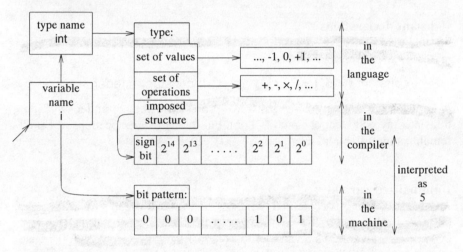

Figure 2.1 The interrelationships between names, structure and values.

Some languages have the possibility to **initialize** the data items upon declaration:

int i = 5, j = 5;   I, J: Integer := 5;

Unlike Ada, C has the facility to initialize each identifier in a declaration to a different value. Multiple initializations raise a question in languages in which expressions can have side-effects. Suppose two variables are declared and initialized in one multiple declaration. Will the expression that yields the initial value be calculated once or twice? Both answers are reasonable: the expression is written once, so it should be calculated once; and: it is used twice, so it should be calculated twice. But if the expression has side-effects (it may, for example, print something), the difference is noticeable. This is a question the language definition must answer. In Ada the expression is evaluated twice in the above example; C has no multiple initializations.

As said at the beginning of this section, the data declaration performs two tasks: it creates and if necessary allocates a typed data item, and it binds a name to it. At least one language, Algol 68, separates these two functions. To obtain the effect of the C declaration int i = 5;, one can write:

ref int i = (**loc int** := 5);

if one wants to be explicit. The '**loc int**' allocates room for one **int** value and the ':= 5' fills it with the value 5. The parenthesized part yields a reference to a data item of type **int** and with value 5, and the '**ref int** i =' binds the name i to it. When there is no need for such emphasis on the structure of the declaration, the above 'identity declaration' for **ref int** i can be replaced by the more convenient 'variable declaration' **int** i := 5;.

Constant declarations

Some languages have **constant declarations**: the bit pattern cannot be modified after initialization:

const int i = 5, j = 5;   I, J: constant Integer := 5;

In almost all cases, this is software protection: the compiler will not translate any code that can modify i or j, but the hardware locations of i and j remain as modifiable as ever.

Uninitialized variables

A non-initializing declaration creates an **uninitialized variable**: the memory is allocated, but it will contain an arbitrary bit pattern that may not even be interpretable as a value of the type of the object declared. The use of such an uninitialized value produces unpredictable and, in the worst case, seemingly correct results, and is to be avoided.

There are a number of approaches languages can take towards this problem.

- The problem is ignored and it is considered the responsibility of the programmer not to use uninitialized values. This is inelegant.
- The use of an uninitialized value is declared erroneous and it is left up to the compiler writer to make sure this is checked. This may be expensive in terms of processing speed and/or compiler complexity.
- All non-initializing declarations silently initialize the allocated memory to an appropriate value, defined for each basic type. Pointers may be set to null and numerical values to zero, for example. This works, but it may give the programmer a false sense of security.
- There are no non-initializing declarations. This forces the programmer to think about a proper initialization value for each declared item.
- For each type, have a special value, traditionally called omega or om, which represents the property of being uninitialized. This omega pro-

pagates (omega + 3 yields omega), except when it is used in an equality test: omega = 3 is false, omega = omega is true. This allows programmers to check dynamically whether a variable is initialized or not, but puts the entire concept 'uninitialized' in doubt.

In addition, other more complicated schemes are possible. Most languages, among them Modula-2, ignore the problem. Others use combinations of techniques, depending on the exact type of the object declared. Ada initializes pointers to null and ignores the problem for other types, and C initializes global variables to an appropriate form of zero and further ignores the problem.

Renaming and aliasing

There is a second type of declaration, the **renaming** or **aliasing declaration**. It binds a name to an already existing data item, thus providing a second access path to that item. The Ada declaration

K: Integer renames I;

binds the name K to the integer data item to which I was already bound. The old binding between I and the data item remains intact. C has no renaming declaration.

Renaming is useful to give simple names to objects that have more complicated names. The Ada declaration

Middle_Element: Integer renames A((N+M)/2);

gives the name Middle_Element to the middle element of the array A, where the lower and upper bounds of A are N and M, respectively.

In principle, renaming can be applied to any named item in a language, types, constants, variables, procedures, modules, and so on, but most languages that have renaming restrict its use. For example, types cannot be renamed in Ada. When renaming, or aliasing, is applied to variables, problems can arise. After the aliasing of I by K in the example above, assigning a new value to K will change the value of I. Thus this form of aliasing carries in it the seeds for many surprises, and this is why the concept of aliasing has a moderately bad reputation. Some parameter transfer mechanisms, however, give rise to a form of variable aliasing that is hard to avoid, as we shall see in the section on parameter transfer.

Overloading

Overloading is the counterpart of aliasing. Whereas aliasing binds more than one name to one object, **overloading** binds one name to more than one object. Since names are used to identify objects, this will, in principle, cause an ambiguity. For overloading to be feasible, the context in which the overloaded name is used must provide enough information to resolve the ambiguity. Presented this way, overloading may seem more of a liability than an asset, but it is an important ingredient in efficient communication. In natural languages, it allows one to speak about a *foot* and be understood, without having to specify each and every time if a body part or a unit of length is meant: the word 'foot' is overloaded with two related meanings. Likewise, thanks to overloading we can write expressions like 3+5 and 3.14+2.72, although the pluses identify different operations, both formally (one works on two integer values, the other on two real values) and in hardware. The + is overloaded with two similar and conceptually identical operations. But for this overloading, we would have to write something like add_int(3, 5) and add_real(3.14, 2.72), as we actually have to do in some languages.

Natural languages often overload a word with unrelated meanings (compare 'He took the plane to Amsterdam' with 'He took the plane off the carpenter's bench'), but such overloading is to be avoided in programming languages. Unfortunately there is no known method to enforce this rule.

Ada uses overloading extensively, with elaborate rules for overloading resolution. C uses overloading for some built-in operators only.

2.2.2 Types and type constructors

From a hardware point of view, a type is a method for interpreting data bits in a computer; and from a programming language point of view, it is a set of values and a set of operations defined on those values. It is the task of the compiler writer to find the most appropriate hardware representation for a given programming language type. Generally, the hardware supplies three data types:

- **characters**, which are actually integers in the range $\{0..255\}$;
- **integer numbers** of various sizes, with common ranges $\{-32768..+32767\}$ for signed 16-bit integers, $\{0..65535\}$ for unsigned 16-bit integers and $\{-2147483648..+2147483647\}$ for signed 32-bit integers; and
- **real numbers** (also called **floating point numbers**) of various sizes and precisions.

These form the **basic types** in many programming languages. Sample declarations involving basic types are shown in Figure 2.2. The way in which the range or precision can be specified by the user differs from language to language. Some languages have no provisions at all. C provides five 'adjectives', short, long, signed, unsigned and double, to indicate classes roughly. Ada takes the most high-level approach by allowing the user to specify the range or precision explicitly. It will be clear that infinite-sized integers or infinite-precision real numbers cannot be stored in

```
                               type Small_Int is
                                  range 0 .. 255;
char c;                        C: Character;
int i;                         I: Integer;
unsigned int n;                N: Natural;
float d;  /* a real number */  D: Float;  -- a real number
unsigned char s;               S: Small_Int;
```

Figure 2.2 Some declarations involving basic types.

a finite computer. The mathematical objects $\mathbb{N}$ and $\mathbb{R}$ cannot be faithfully modelled on a computer, common intuition notwithstanding.

Values of the basic types can be obtained by writing them down literally in a program. Examples of such literals are 'a' for the character a, -123 for the integer -123 and 6.02e23 for the real number 6.02×10^{23}.

Since a type is, among other things, a set of values, the empty set also corresponds to a type. It corresponds to zero bits in memory and is known as **void** in some languages, but it is conspicuously absent from many others.

The above types and their names are generally built into the language. The programmer can extend the set of available types in his program by using **type constructors**, which construct new types out of zero or more old types. The thus constructed types can be used directly and anonymously in a declaration:

```
int ia[10];                    IA: array (Integer range 1..10)
                                  of Integer;
```

or be bound to a name first, in a type definition:

```
typedef                        type Int10_Array is
   int int10_array[10];          array (Integer range 1..10)
                                  of Integer;
int10_array ia;                IA: Int10_Array;
```

Each of these four declarations of ia involves a type 'array of 10 integers indexed by integers', but that fact is more obvious from some declarations than from others. The named type definition plus variable declaration in Ada is the easiest to read. In it, the type name Int10_Array is bound to the type array (Integer range 1..10) of Integer. It now has the same status as built-in type names and can thus be used in a variable declaration IA: Int10_Array to declare IA. The other Ada declaration involves the same type array (Integer range 1..10) of Integer but now no name is bound to it. It is used immediately to declare the variable IA, but since it has no name it cannot be used elsewhere in the program. The subtle consequences of this are explained in more detail in Section 2.2.5 on type equivalence. Note that in Ada the syntactic structure of a definition (... is ...), which binds a name to an entity, differs from that of a declaration (... : ...), which binds a name to a type and a location; the name that is being introduced comes first in both forms.

The C declarations are much less readable, since they are based on the following clever but unintuitive and somewhat shaky analogy. When we see the declaration int i; we may conclude that i is of type int. So by some stretch of imagination, we could conclude from the declaration int ia[10]; that ia[10] is an integer, and from this we can infer that ia must be an array of integers. The latter inference is correct, but the conclusion that ia[10] corresponds to an integer is not: the array is made up of the integers ia[0], ia[1], ..., ia[9], since all arrays in C start at 0. On similar grounds, typedef int int10_array[10]; defines int10_array as a type rather than as a variable of type array of integer.

The following description of type constructors is simplified. Most type constructors have strange quirks and unexpected limitations in specific languages, generally for implementation reasons. Data types that are composed of other data types are called compound types.

Enumeration types

The simplest type constructor is the enumeration; it does not build upon other types, but rather defines a set of names to be the values of the new data type. The type definition

```
typedef enum {              type Traffic_Light_Colour is
  red, amber, green           (Red, Amber, Green);
} traffic_light_colour;
```

defines a new type traffic_light_colour with three enumeration values: red, amber and green. We can use this type in defining the lights at a crossing:

```
traffic_light_colour        N, E, S, W:
  n, e, s, w;                 Traffic_Light_Colour;
```

There is a fundamental difference between the names red, amber and green, and the names n, e, s and w. The first are names of (unchangeable) values of type traffic_light_colour and the second are names of variables that can hold these values.

A well-known enumeration type is often not recognized as such:

```
typedef enum {              type Boolean is
  false, true                 (False, True);
} boolean;
```

Boolean is a built-in enumeration type in Ada.

One would expect the only operations allowed on values of an enumeration type to be copying and comparison for equality, but most programming languages also allow comparing them (for greater/smaller) or even incrementing them (finding successors). As a result of this, after the declaration

```
typedef enum {                 type Continent is
    africa, europe,            (Africa, Europe,
    australia, asia,           Australia, Asia,
    america, antarctica        America, Antarctica);
} continent;
```

which lists the continents in random order, we have america < antarctica and the successor of europe is australia, which is clearly nonsensical. Some enumeration types, however, have a natural order, for example the days of the week. For such types, comparison and successor are useful operators.

It is also possible to consider a character set as an enumeration type. We then imagine a type definition for the ASCII character set:

```
type ASCII is ( ..., ' ', '!', '"', '#', ..., 'A', ..., '~');
```

which make the characters into enumeration values.

Arrays

The simplest type constructor that builds on another type is the **array**. An array is a series of a known number of items, all of the same type. An item in the array, called an **element**, can be accessed by specifying its ordinal number, called its **index**, through an indexing operation. An array represents a **mapping** from values of some type, typically integers, on values of the element type. There are often operators to determine the index of the first element (the **lower bound**), the index of the last element (the **upper bound**) and the number of elements in the array. Given the array variable declaration

```
int ia[10];                    IA: array (Integer range 1..10)
                                   of Integer;
```

the first element can be accessed as

```
ia[0]                          IA(1)
```

and the lower and upper bounds and size of the array can be found as

```
always zero in C               IA'First
not available in C             IA'Last
sizeof ia                      IA'Length
```

In Ada, the lower bound is defined by the programmer; in C, it is always zero. C has no single operator for obtaining the upper bound. The C expression sizeof ia gives the size of the array in bytes rather than the

number of elements. Consequently, the artifact (sizeof ia)/(sizeof ia[0])
can be used to obtain the number of elements in the array, from which the
upper bound follows. The Ada forms are straightforward. Trying to access
a non-existing element, for example ia[11], is erroneous and the attempt
may or may not be caught in an actual system.

The initialization of an array requires a compound value (called
aggregate in Ada):

    int ia[3] = {3, 5, 8};   IA: array (Integer range 1..3)
                                           of Integer := (3, 5, 8);

In the above examples, the bounds of the arrays were given as constants, which makes them known at compile time; such bounds are called
static. It is often useful not to specify the size of the array until the program
is run, by writing non-constant expressions for the bounds; such bounds are
called dynamic. This is possible in Ada though not in C:

    not available in C   IA: array (Integer range M..N−1)
                                           of Integer;

An even more powerful feature is the ability to resize the array after it has
already been declared; arrays with this property are called flexible. Neither
Ada nor C has flexible arrays, but Algol 68, Orca and Icon have. In C flexible arrays can be simulated reasonably efficiently by using the library routines malloc and realloc, though.

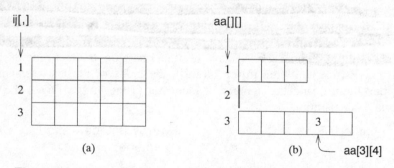

Figure 2.3 A two-dimensional array (a) and an array of arrays (b).

The arrays described above are one-dimensional; one can also have
multi-dimensional arrays and some languages feature arrays of arrays. An
N-dimensional array is a rectangular block of elements in which N indices
are required to access an element. A usual notation to access an element in
a two-dimensional array ij is ij[3, 5]; its structure is shown in Figure 2.3 (a).
A possible array of arrays is depicted in Figure 2.3 (b), which shows an
array aa of three elements. aa[1] is an array of three elements, aa[2] is an
array of zero elements and aa[3] is an array of five elements. The marked

element can be accessed as **aa[3][4]**, assuming that all indices start at 1. Not all languages allow arrays with zero elements.

Ada has multi-dimensional arrays and arrays of arrays, with notations similar to those used above. The usefulness of Ada's array of arrays, however, is restricted by the fact that all arrays in an array must have the same bounds. C has no arrays of arrays and uses forms like **ia[2][3]** to index multi-dimensional arrays.

Slicing is similar to indexing, but accesses a subarray rather than a single element. In Ada, the slice consisting of the elements **IA(3)** through **IA(6)** can be accessed as **IA(3..6)**. C has no slicing. A slice from a multi-dimensional array, if allowed by the language, accesses a rectangular block inside the multi-dimensional array.

Although it is natural to use integers for indexing an array, values of other types can often be used. Both C and Ada allow indexing with characters and enumeration values, and at least one language, ABC, has gone to the extreme of allowing values of any type as indices. Given an arbitrary complex variable **book**, we may issue the command **PUT 17.95 IN price[book]** and expect the command **WRITE price[book]** to reproduce the value 17.95. An array with an index type that does not allow simple linear addressing of the elements is called an **associative array**.

Sequences

A second type constructor that builds a new type using only one type is the **sequence** or **list**. A sequence is a series of an unknown number of elements, all of the same type; elements in a sequence cannot be reached by indexing. The first element can be accessed through a **head** operator, the rest of the sequence through a **tail** operator. There is definitely no simple operator to determine the size of the sequence (the length of the list). If there were, the number of elements would be known and it would be an array in disguise. Given the implementation problems of dealing with an unknown number of items, hardly any imperative language supports the sequence as a type constructor, although a sequential file may be viewed as an example.

Sequences and arrays are often confused, and although strings are generally used as sequences, most languages model them as arrays, at the cost of much messy programming.

Sets and bags

A third type constructor that builds a new type using only one type is the **set**. A set over a type *T* with a set of values *V* is a type the values of which are sets of the elements of *V*. Neither C nor Ada feature sets, but Modula-2 does. The Modula-2 code

```
TYPE CharSetType = SET OF CHAR;
VAR ChSet: CharSetType;
```

defines a set type CharSetType over the characters and a variable ChSet of that type. The language has a set constructor consisting of the type name followed by {}; operations for set union, difference and intersection; and a checking operator IN:

```
ChSet := CharSetType { 'q', 'w', 'e' };
IF 'z' IN ChSet THEN ...
```

The number of elements in a set is known as its **cardinality**. An interesting operator on sets is the **powerset** operator; powerset S yields the set of all subsets of S.

Bags are a variant of sets; they differ from sets in that they can contain a value more than once, and record how many times a value has been inserted. The primary operations on them are 'insert value' and 'remove value', rather than union and intersection. Bags are also called **multisets**. C, Ada and Modula-2 do not feature bags, but ABC does. SETL has powersets.

Records and pointers

Often the need arises to group together a fixed number of data items of differing types into one data item. The type of this item can be constructed as a **record**, also called a **structure**. The record definition in Figure 2.4 describes a car; it assumes a type brand_type has been defined before. The items in a record are called **fields** or **components**; they can be accessed by using their names, which in this case are called **selectors**. Given a variable new_car of type car_type, its brand can be accessed as

new_car.brand   New_Car.Brand

The dot (.) for selecting from a record serves a purpose similar to that of the square brackets or parentheses for indexing an array.

```
typedef struct {              type Car_Type is
                              record
    brand_type brand;             Brand: Brand_Type;
    unsigned int                  Number_Of_Doors:
      number_of_doors;              Natural;
    int price;                    Price: Integer;
} car_type;                   end record;
```

Figure 2.4 A record definition describing a car.

Unlike the basic and constructed types discussed earlier, records can be recursive: a record can, in a sense, contain an item of the same type. This is very convenient in programming. Suppose we have a collection of items, for example pairs consisting of a name and a telephone number, and want to represent this collection as a tree-like structure that contains one of the items and two new trees which together hold the other items. Such a structure is called a **binary tree**. Given this simple structure, one is tempted to declare its type as

```
typedef struct {              type Bin_Tree_Type is record
  bin_tree_type                 Left, Right:
   left, right;                   Bin_Tree_Type;
  item_type value;              Value: Item_Type;
} bin_tree_type;              end record;
```

but it is immediately clear that this has a problem: a data item of say N bytes cannot contain $2N$-plus bytes, and the above declaration is in effect incorrect. The problem is solved by storing the internal nodes left and right elsewhere as independent nodes, and replacing them inside the record by the machine addresses of those nodes. The machine addresses have a fixed size, regardless of the size of the item they address, and thus the size of a node is kept finite. This trick also supplies the escape hatch needed in any form of recursion: if the left or right node is absent, the corresponding machine address is a special value which does not, actually or by convention, address any node. The correct definition of bin_tree_type is given below.

The administrative task of declaring, manipulating and checking these machine addresses rests on the programmer's shoulders, even in high-level languages. The machine addresses are known as **pointers**, which are said to *point to* or to *refer to* the addressed item. The special value indicating the absence of an item is called a **null pointer**, since it points nowhere.

Given a pointer pntr to an object, we can access the object by **dereferencing** the pointer:

        *pntr   Pntr.all

To access a field field in the record under the pointer pntr, one would expect to use forms like

        (*pntr).field   Pntr.all.Field

These forms are correct, but they are awkward, and many languages have an abbreviated form for selection under a pointer:

        pntr->field   Pntr.Field

We have seen that the record declarations for bin_tree_type given above are incorrect; both require the use of a pointer. Obtaining a pointer to type My_Type in Ada is straightforward: one defines a type **access**

My_Type and declares the pointer to be of that type. Although the same method is possible in C, it is much more usual to use an anonymous, inferred type as we did with the array. To obtain a pointer pntr to a type my_type in C, we declare pntr using the declaration

        my_type *pntr;

As before, this actually declares *pntr to be of type my_type, from which the compiler infers that pntr must be a pointer to an object of type my_type.

```
                                type Bin_Tree_Type;
                                type Bin_Tree_Access_Type is
                                    access Bin_Tree_Type;

typedef struct _bin_tree_type {     type Bin_Tree_Type is record
    struct _bin_tree_type               Left, Right:
        *left, *right;                      Bin_Tree_Access_Type;
    item_type value;                    Value: Item_Type;
} bin_tree_type;                    end record;
```

Figure 2.5 The correct definition for bin_tree_type.

The requirement to use the name of a type T in a declaration of a pointer to T, natural as it may be, immediately causes another problem: to define the record type bin_tree_type we need a name, say bin_tree_access_type, and to define this pointer type name we need the name bin_tree_type. The two types are **mutually recursive**. Both languages employ a different mechanism to deal with the mutual dependency of names. Again Ada has the more understandable notation. It allows a name to be declared as a type name, without specifying the type. Such incompletely defined types can be used in pointer type definitions only. In C, the user can specify a name right after the keyword struct which can then be used inside the structure declaration. We shall not investigate this mechanism further. The correct definition of the record bin_tree_type is given in Figure 2.5. A value of a given pointer type can be obtained by using an **allocator**; the forms

```
    (bin_tree_type *)              new Bin_Tree_Type
        malloc(sizeof
            (bin_tree_type))
```

allocate memory for one record of type bin_tree_type and yield a pointer to it. The Ada facility is built into the language; the C construction is a properly packed call of the standard library routine malloc.

Pointers are also used to make data manipulation more efficient. Copying a pointer pointing to a large item is much more efficient than copying the item itself. To assist in exploiting this possibility, some languages allow a pointer to be created to an existing object, for example to a local variable. If used properly this feature can simplify some details of a few algorithms, but since it may involve pointers to local, short-lived items, which can be carried around and stored anywhere, its use is not entirely without danger. In C, given an item x of any type, &x denotes the pointer to it, subject to a number of restrictions. In Ada 9X, a pointer to an item X can be obtained as the expression X'Access, subject to the restriction that the item be declared as aliased. Ada 83 had no way to obtain a pointer to a local item.

Although pointers are introduced here as pointing to records, they need not do so and can point to objects of any data type. The code fragment in Figure 2.6 declares an integer i and a pointer to integer ip which is initialized with a pointer to i. Next, the value 7 is assigned under the pointer ip, that is, to the variable i. The output command (printf/Put) prints 7, although no explicit assignment to i has occurred. (The meaning of printf and the string "%d\n" are explained in the section on output statements.)

```
int i;                          I: aliased Integer;
                                type Int_Access is access Integer;
int *ip = &i;                   IP: Int_Access := I'Access;

*ip = 7;                        IP.all := 7;
printf("%d\n", i);              Put(I);
```

Figure 2.6 Implicit assignment through a pointer.

Some languages (for example, C++ and Ada) make a distinction between pointers and references. In these languages, a pointer to an object of type T is of type 'pointer to T' and accessing the object requires dereferencing. A reference to an object of type T is itself of type T and is just another way of accessing the object. In Ada, a renaming declaration creates a reference to the renamed object. The code fragment in Figure 2.7 (the text on the left is in C++) first declares an integer i. The C++ version then declares a reference to integer ir, which is initialized to be identical to i, and the Ada version declares just an integer IR, which renames I. Next, the value 7 is assigned to ir, which act is identical to an assignment to the variable i. Again the output command will print 7.

It is unfortunate that the term 'reference' is used in two different but closely related meanings. The fact that a pointer is 'dereferenced' and that references in the above sense are often implemented using pointers adds to the confusion.

Pointers are a constant source of programming errors. They have to be checked almost every time they are used to avoid following a null

```
int i;                          I: Integer;
int &ir = i;                    IR: Integer renames I;

ir = 7;                         IR := 7;
printf("%d\n", i);              Put(I);
```

Figure 2.7 Implicit assignment through a reference (alias).

pointer. In some languages, the memory segment obtained for a pointer through the use of an allocator may be deallocated explicitly by the programmer; any pointers to it will, however, continue to exist. Such pointers are termed **dangling references**, and if one of them is used subsequently owing to a programming error, the results are unpredictable. Section 2.5.2 on subprograms discusses a second source of dangling references. Also, pointers are not valid across networks (as explained in Chapter 6). Yet the efficiency and convenience of their use is so great that hardly any imperative language has dared to abolish the pointer, although most take some measures to tame it. Examples of imperative languages without pointers are ABC, SETL and Orca. They obviate the need for pointers by supplying those data structures that need pointers (for example lists, tables, sets and graphs) as built-in features. Such languages either do not emphasize efficiency or require strong optimizing compilers.

Unions

As we have seen, a record of a type with N fields contains field 1 *and* field 2 *and* ... *and* field N. Occasionally, it is useful to have a data type the values of which are *either* field 1 *or* field 2 *or* ... *or* field N. Such a type is called a **union**. To model a garage that can house either one car or a number of bicycles we can use the union **garage** shown in Figure 2.8.

The field holding the number of bicycles in a variable **my_garage** of type **garage** can be accessed as if **my_garage** was a normal record:

my_garage.nmb_of_bicycles   My_Garage.Nmb_Of_Bicycles

In C, the burden of remembering which of the fields in the union is present rests on the programmer; the union is **undiscriminated**. In Ada, there is a special field in the record (**Status** in this example) that records the nature of the active field: the union is **discriminated**. As usual, Ada requires more code from the programmer, but gives more support than C does. In C, both fields **car** and **nmb_of_bicycles** can be accessed at any moment, regardless of what was last stored there. Since the compiler will probably use the same memory space for all fields of a union, this can have dire consequences: if the last store was to **my_garage.car**, then **my_garage.nmb_of_bicycles** will blithely interpret the bit pattern of type

```
                                       type Contents is
                                         (Has_Car, Has_Bicycles);
typedef union {                        type Garage(Status: Contents) is
                                         record
                                           case Status is
                                             when Has_Car =>
  car_type car;                              Car: Car_Type;
                                             when Has_Bicycles =>
  unsigned int nmb_of_bicycles;            Nmb_Of_Bicycles:
                                             Natural;
                                           end case;
} garage;                              end record;
```

Figure 2.8 A union declaration for a dual-purpose garage.

car_type as an integer. Suppose the car_type in the above example is an enumeration type and the enumeration value Trabant happens to be represented internally by the number 13. Then the C code fragment

```
my_garage.car = Trabant;
printf("%d\n", my_garage.nmb_of_bicycles);
```

will compile without errors and print 13 or any other number, depending on compiler properties. In fact, strong type checking is not possible in the presence of undiscriminated unions.

In Ada, each access is checked for consistency; moreover, the present contents of My_Garage can be found out by examining My_Garage.Status:

```
if My_Garage.Status = Has_Car then
  Put(My_Garage.Car);
else
  Put(My_Garage.Nmb_Of_Bicycles);
end if;
```

Changing the type inside a union is also more restricted in Ada and depends among other things on the way in which the union was declared.

Routines as data types
Some imperative languages allow routines (procedures and functions) to be manipulated and used as ordinary values, though often with restrictions of some sort. This feature is useful for many purposes. For one thing, we can use it to declare arrays of procedures. In the design of a text editor we can then have an array of 256 procedures, called handle_key, so that handle_key[key_ch]() performs the code for keystroke key_ch. Many

designers of imperative languages, however, feel that having routines as values constitutes an undesirable mixing of data and flow of control. Both C and Ada 9X have pointers to routines as data. (Ada 83 did not allow any data involving routines.)

If routines are accepted as data, they will have to have types. **Routine types are obtained from a type constructor which combines the types of the parameters and that of the routine result into one routine type.** The declaration

```
                              type R2I_Access_Type is access
                                 function (F: Float) return Integer;
int (*convert_to_int)(float);    Convert_To_Int: R2I_Access_Type;
```

declares a variable convert_to_int of type 'pointer to a routine with one floating point parameter (named F in the Ada 9X case), which yields an integer'. Once the pointer convert_to_int has been initialized with a proper value (the address of a routine of the correct type), it can be used in a call:

```
    i = convert_to_int(3.14);        I = Convert_To_Int(3.14);
```

This implicitly dereferences convert_to_int to obtain the routine, which is then called with one parameter, 3.14. Both ANSI C and Ada 9X allow the dereferencing to be implicit (one could not supply parameters to a pointer anyway), but explicit dereferencing is also allowed:

```
    i = (*convert_to_int)(3.14);        I = Convert_To_Int.all(3.14);
```

Routines as a flow-of-control issue are discussed in Section 2.4.3, and their use as a structuring mechanism is discussed in Section 2.5.2.

2.2.3 Orthogonality of data types and declarations

In principle, all of the above type constructors can be combined and applied in any combination. We can have arrays of records, records containing arrays, or sets of sets of pointers to unions, to give a few examples. In practice, though, each language has its own set of restrictions, mostly dictated by implementation considerations. For example, most imperative languages which have sets at all allow them only for enumeration types.

Two features in a language which can be combined freely without in any way restricting each other are said to be **orthogonal**. The word, whose Greek components mean 'perpendicular', derives from a metaphor in which the two features are viewed as operating along two independent perpendicular axes: motion along one axis does not result in motion along the other.

It is useful to distinguish three kinds of orthogonality: combination orthogonality, sort orthogonality and number orthogonality.

Combination orthogonality states that if one member of a sort S_1

can be combined meaningfully with one member of a sort S_2, then any member of a sort S_1 can be combined meaningfully with any member of a sort S_2. For example, there are three kinds of declarations: plain declarations, initializing declarations and initializing constant declarations; and there are many kinds of types: basic, array, record, and so on. Combination orthogonality for declarations and types states that any kind of declaration can be used for any kind of type. More particularly, one can have plain declarations of arrays, initializing declarations of arrays and initializing constant declarations of arrays. This orthogonality is violated in a number of places in C (for example, one cannot have initializing declarations of unions) and is upheld quite well in Ada.

Sort orthogonality states that in any circumstance in which one member of sort S is allowed meaningfully, any member of sort S is allowed meaningfully. It is a special case of combination orthogonality, in which one axis is kept constant. Sort orthogonality for types implies, for example, that if a language has records containing basic types, it should also have records containing arrays, records containing records, and so on. Both C and Ada follow this principle faithfully.

Number orthogonality states that in any circumstance in which one member of sort S is allowed meaningfully, zero or more members of sort S are allowed meaningfully. This implies, for example, that where one declaration is allowed, zero or more declarations should be allowed. Number orthogonality often requires syntactic support: to allow more than one statement where one is expected, they have to be syntactically grouped into a block in many languages. In particular the zero version, if allowed at all, often requires a special notation. Ada has a special notation for a record of zero fields:

```
record
  null;
end record;
```

and treats procedures with zero parameters differently from those with one or more parameters. C has an explicit type void, with zero values; Ada has no type void, although the type of the above null record can serve.

Orthogonality is a very strong guiding principle in language design. Its immediate usefulness is obvious: it forbids unexpected exceptions ('WHAT? No two-dimensional array parameters?!?'), but it also has an indirect value. Since cleaner features are easier to combine, the orthogonality requirement will pressure the language designer to make the language features as clean as possible. Orthogonality was first used explicitly in the design of Algol 68.

2.2.4 Restricted types

Sometimes types are used in situations in which the fit is less than perfect.
An example is the use of integer variables as array indexes. Being of type
integer, the variable has a large range of values but being an array index,
only a small subrange is actually acceptable. This discrepancy leads to the
necessity of array bound checking. Some languages try to remedy this by
having mechanisms to restrict the value set of a type. In Ada, the declarations

> subtype Card_Index_Type is Integer range 1..13;
> Card_Index: Card_Index_Type;

declare a variable Card_Index of type Integer whose value set has been
restricted to the range 1 to 13. After the declaration

> Hand: array (Card_Index_Type) of Card_Type;

the expression Hand(Card_Index) will not require an array bound check,
since the value of Card_Index is guaranteed to be in range. Note that this
does not solve the problem, it just moves it to where Card_Index got its
value. The range check will now have to be done there. This has the advantage that it uncovers a possible error where it is made rather than where it
becomes apparent; and, with some luck, the range test will have to be done
less often.

Languages that have value-restricted types allow only the simplest
restrictions, generally to a single continuous range. The only way to enforce
more complex restrictions on the set of values, for example to prevent Feb.
29, 1993 from occurring as a value representing a calendar date, is to
implement the type as an abstract data type, as explained further on.

It is occasionally useful to restrict the set of operations of a type. If
real numbers are used to represent temperature values in centigrade, the
multiplication operator × should be disallowed: neither multiplying a temperature by a temperature nor by a number is a meaningful operation. No
language allows a type to be restricted with respect to its operations. Again,
the only methodologically sound way to do so is to implement the type as an
abstract data type.

2.2.5 Type equivalence

Strong type checking raises the question of exactly when two types are
equivalent. The question is subtler than it would seem. Is the type of an
array of integers with bounds 1 to 12 equivalent to that of a (shorter) array
of integers with bounds 1 to 11? Or to that of an array of integers with
bounds 2 to 13 perhaps? If they are not, programming becomes very awkward; if they are, there are operations that will succeed on values of one
type but fail on the other. Is a type apples defined as integer equivalent to a

type **pickles** also defined as integer? If so, would the programmer really want to be able to mix them in arithmetic expressions? If not, what is the difference between them? Is a union of an integer and a real equivalent to a union of a real and an integer?

There are two main answers to these questions: structural equivalence and name equivalence. Two types are **structurally equivalent** if their value sets and operators are the same. This makes the types **apples** and **pickles** equivalent. Also the order of the member types in a union becomes immaterial. In Algol 68, which adheres strictly to structural equivalence, it even makes the following two record types **t1** and **t2** equivalent:

> **mode t1** = **struct**(**int** value; **ref mode t1** link);
> **mode t2** = **struct**(**int** value; **ref mode t2** link);

where **mode** means 'type' and **ref** introduces a pointer type. Worse even, both are equivalent to

> **mode t3** =
> **struct**(**int** value; **ref struct**(**int** value; **ref mode t3** link));

And indeed, any code that will work on an object of type **t1** will work on an object of type **t3**, and vice versa. Structural equivalence, although intuitively appealing, has surprises for the programmer and is also difficult to implement.

Name equivalence requires that every type has a name. The rule is simple: two types are equivalent if and only if they have the same name. This is surprise-free[†], easy to understand and implement and keeps the pickles and apples apart. But what about anonymous types, as in

> IA: array (Integer range 1..10) of Integer;   ?

In Ada, which adheres strictly to name equivalence, each anonymous type has an implicit name that differs from any other name in the program, and the above declaration of IA is equivalent to something like

> type Anonymous_0001 is array (Integer range 1..10)
>   of Integer;
> IA: Anonymous_0001;

A surprising[‡] consequence of this is that in

> IA: array (Integer range 1..10) of Integer;
> JA: array (Integer range 1..10) of Integer;

the arrays IA and JA are of different types, since their anonymous type names differ.

It is generally agreed that name equivalence is to be preferred over

---

[†] and [‡]: Contradiction intended.

structural equivalence. Both Algol 68 and Ada are pure in their attitudes to type equivalence, but some languages take a hybrid point of view. In C, name equivalence is used for records and unions, and structural equivalence for the rest.

Whether array types that differ only in the range of the index are different is an issue that can be decided by the language designer independently from the above. The crucial question here is whether the values of lower and upper bound are part of the type. If they are, different ranges will introduce different types; if they are not, the normal rules for structural or name equivalence apply.

2.2.6 Coercions, contexts, casts and conversions

Actually, the question asked by strong type checking is the following. In a given grammatical position in the program, we require an object of type T_1 and we find an object of type T_2; is that acceptable? This question differs from that answered by type equivalence: if T_1 and T_2 *are* equivalent, the object of type T_2 is certainly acceptable, but if they are not, the answer should not always be no. For example, we would like the expression 3.14+5 to work even if after 3.14+ we expect a real value and we find an integer value.

Suppose, for a simpler example, that x is a variable of type real. Then in the right-hand side of the assignment x := 5 we expect a value of type real and we find an integer value. Yet we would not want to reject the assignment. What is missing here is a data conversion from integer to real, to bridge a small gap in the type system. The language designer can require such conversions to be explicit, thus forcing the programmer to write something like x := 5.0 or x := real(5), or can allow the compiler to insert conversions like these implicitly, if the context is clear enough.

Implicit conversions, inserted by the compiler to fulfil minor requirements of the type system, are called **coercions**. Exactly which coercions are allowed depends on the context. Although C has coercions both from integer to real and from real to integer, in the expression 3.14 + 5 we want to have the 5 converted to real rather than the 3.14 converted to integer. A coercion system requires the definition of a set of syntactically or contextually defined contexts, together with the coercions allowed in each of them. For example, in C the coercion from real to integer is not allowed in the context of operands. The design of a coercion system is difficult and no general theory for it is available. The most elaborate coercion system in existence, that of Algol 68, was designed by trial and error. C has a simple coercion system with a few not explicitly defined contexts; Ada has no coercions. The coercion system of a language is generally complicated greatly by the possibility of overloading of operator and function names.

If the context is not strong enough to imply the coercion unambiguously, the context can in some languages be strengthened by specifying the required type explicitly, using a **cast**. In the C assignment (int)3.14 + 5, the 3.14 is cast to int and *will* be coerced to integer before being added to the 5. Casts give the programmer considerable power over the coercion system. C has casts in the above form; they do not apply to Ada.

A cast differs from an explicit conversion in that it just names the type of the end product and relies on the coercion system to get there; a conversion is a function that does the data and type transformation. Ada uses conversions extensively and we are required to write Float(I) to obtain the floating point equivalent of I.

One coercion that deserves special attention is the **voiding** coercion. It takes an arbitrary value and converts it to void, that is, throws it away. This effectively allows using expressions as statements, which is useful in languages in which expressions can have side-effects. In C, the printing routine printf is actually a function, and a call to it is an expression which yields the number of characters written. Yet a call to printf can be used as a normal statement, thus greatly extending the usefulness of the printf routine. Ada has no coercions, no type void and no voiding coercion.

Since coercions cause actions to be performed that are not directly apparent from the program code, they are not without danger. After the C statement sequence

    x = 3.3;
    y = x + 2.7;

the programmer probably expects y to have the value 6.0, but if x happened to be declared as an integer, the actual value would be 5.7, due to truncation of the 3.3 to 3. Also, coercions can obscure errors; if Ada had a voiding coercion, the statement

    I = 5;

would compile without error, since the = would be taken as the Boolean equality comparison operator. At run time the value of I would be compared to 5 and the resulting Boolean would be discarded. Most probably, however, it was a typing error for I := 5;, in which the := indicates assignment.

2.3 State

An important activity of a program in an imperative language is changing the **internal state** of the machine as represented by the values of its variables, and the **external state** as stored in its input/output devices. The state of some output devices can be observed, for example as print-out on paper, and is then called the **result** of the program.

2.3.1 Assignments

The value of a variable can be modified by executing an **assignment statement**:

$$i = (x+y) / 2; \qquad\qquad I := (X+Y) / 2;$$

will calculate the value of the expression $(x+y)/2$ and assign the result as the new value to i. The expression is called the **source** of the assignment and the left-hand side is called its **destination**. Note that the assignment differs fundamentally from the equality in mathematics in that it does not set up a permanent relation: i will keep its new value only until the next assignment to it. This makes assignments like $i = i + 1$; legal and meaningful, as shown below.

The value transferred in an assignment is the result of evaluating an **expression**. Expressions have a form similar to those in mathematics, linearized and extended with notations for access to elements of constructed types. The type of the resulting value can normally be derived from the expression alone, without having to run the program: the type is known *statically* and strong type checking can be applied. Examples are:

$$i * j + 3 \qquad\qquad I * J + 3$$

which yields an integer if i and j are integers;

$$\text{car.number\_of\_doors} == 4 \qquad \text{Car.Number\_Of\_Doors} = 4$$

which yields a Boolean value; and

$$(\text{ia}[0] + \text{ia}[1]) / 2 \qquad\qquad (\text{IA}(1) + \text{IA}(2)) / 2$$

which requires ia to be an array of some type T on which arithmetic operations are allowed. The latter expression yields a value of some arithmetic type, probably T, depending on the definitions of the + and the / operators.

It is important to note that the actual transfer of data is not performed until the source expression has been evaluated completely:

$$i = i + 1; \qquad\qquad I := I + 1;$$

will increase the value of i by one. More particularly, the old value of i is taken, 1 is added to it and the result is made to be the new value of i; the latter act obliterates the old value of i. Contrast this to the expression

$$i == i + 1 \qquad\qquad I = I + 1$$

which will yield 0 in C and **false** in Ada, regardless of the value of i.

The above examples show that there is a certain confusion in notation between assignment and test for equality. C uses = for assignment and == for test for equality; Ada and many other languages use := and =, respectively; and other notations can be found, as in the ABC assignment PUT 17.95 IN price[book] shown above.

The rule that the source of an assignment be calculated in full before being assigned to the destination takes on a special significance for overlapping slice assignments. More particularly, given a variable S: array (Integer range 1..7) of Character which contains the string goblets, the result of the assignment S(4..6) := S(3..5); is that S now holds the string gobbles. The assignment is performed using a temporary character array T and is decomposed into T := S(3..5); S(4..6) := T;, as shown in Figure 2.9.

Figure 2.9 The assignment S(4..6) := S(3..5);.

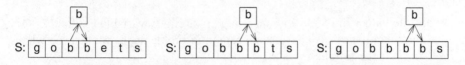

Figure 2.10 Incorrect interpretation of S(4..6) := S(3..5);.

A naive and incorrect interpretation would be to copy the characters one by one, thereby effectively decomposing the assignment into S(4) := S(3); S(5) := S(4); S(6) := S(5);. The result would be the string gobbbbs and the first b would gobble up all its successors, as shown in Figure 2.10.

Assignment operators

There are two important variants to the assignment statement. The first is based on the observation that many assignment statements have the form

<destination> := <destination> <operator> <something>

Examples are i := i + 1; and a[n*k+j+1] := a[n*k+j+1] * 2;. To simplify such statements, many languages feature combined **assignment operators**, generally consisting of the operator and the assignment symbol. The above examples can then be written i +:= 1; and a[n*k+j+1] *:= 2;. C has gone further than that and has introduced a single postfix operator ++ for increment by 1: the expression i++ increases i by 1. In an effect peculiar to C, it also returns the *old* value of i. This operator is called **post-increment**; its counterpart **pre-decrement**, --i, which decreases i by 1 and yields the *new* value of i, also exists in C, in addition to other combinations.

The combined assignment operators have several advantages. Not only do they reduce the work in writing the program, they also facilitate the translation into efficient code. In addition, they ease the task of reading and understanding the program: when confronted with the assignment a[n*k+j+1] := a[n*k+j+1] * 2; the reader has to convince him- or herself that both array indices are indeed equal; with the form a[n*k+j+1] *:= 2; no such worries arise. C has an ample array of combined assignment operators; Ada does not have this feature.

Simultaneous assignments

The second variant is the **simultaneous assignment**, in which more than one value is transferred simultaneously. The simultaneous assignment

> i, j := 3, 5;

assigns 3 to i and 5 to j. Simultaneous assignments have their uses. For example, the form

> i, j := j, i;

swaps the values of i and j without using an auxiliary variable explicitly. On the other hand, they also have some semantic problems, as we can see when we consider the simultaneous assignment

> a[i], a[j] := 3, 5;

What should this do when i and j happen to be equal? Not many languages feature simultaneous assignments; neither C nor Ada has them, but ABC does.

2.3.2 Expressions

The source of the value in an assignment is an expression. Expressions are very similar in shape to normal mathematical formulas, with some means of linearization to fit computer input requirements: a_k is rendered as a[k], for example.

Infix notation

Although expressions look like uniform streams of items and operators, we have all been taught in elementary school that operators have precedences: 4+5*6 is to be interpreted as 4+(5*6) rather than as (4+5)*6, because multiplication has precedence over addition. Programming languages have many more operators than the elementary +, −, × and ÷ and it is usual to divide them into levels. Lower-level operators have precedence over higher-level operators, which means that they bind their operands more strongly. Some levels contain forms that one would not normally view as operators. A typical set of operators with their levels is shown in Figure 2.11. At level 0 we find the names, literals and parenthesized expressions. A parenthesized expression serves to start a top level expression at any position and so provides a way to override the precedence regime. The level arrangement in Figure 2.11 implies, for example, that a < b ↑ c * d means a < ((b ↑ c) * d).

Level	Operators	
0	names, literals, parenthesized expressions	
1	(), [], .	(function call, subscripting, selection)
2	+, −	(unary plus and minus)
3	↑	(exponentiation)
4	*, /, mod, div	(standard arithmetic)
5	+, −	(binary plus and minus)
6	<, >, <=, >=, =, ≠	(comparison)
7	¬	(logical NOT)
8	&, |	(logical AND and OR)
9	:=	(assignment)

Figure 2.11 A simple set of operators with their levels.

The order of execution of operators on the same level is controlled by their **associativity**. **Left-associative** operators are executed from left to right. Most operators are left-associative and examples are + and −: a−b−c−d means ((a−b)−c)−d. An example of a **right-associative** operator is the assignment operator. The **multiple assignment** a := b := c := 3 means a := (b := (c := 3)), which works correctly provided the assignment operator yields the value that is being transferred. In C, the assignment operator = is a right-associative level 14 operator; the top level expression is on level 16. In Ada, the := is not an operator at all and assignment is a separate syntactic entity, not allowed inside expressions. Operators can also be **non-associative**; such operators cannot be used together in a sequence: if = is non-associative, the expression a = b = c is erroneous.

Operators with one operand are called **monadic** or **unary**, operators with two operands are called **dyadic** or **binary**. Monadic operators have precedences too: a monadic level N operator is not executed until the operators of lower levels on its right have been executed. Almost all monadic operators precede their operands; such operators are called **prefix**. Likewise, dyadic operators are called **infix**. An operator that follows its operand is called, quite logically, **postfix**. An example is the post-increment operator ++ in C. Such a notation is especially useful to express physical units: 3" (read: 'three inches') yields $3 \times 25.4 = 76.2$ (millimetres), where " is the postfix operator. (One inch equals 25.4 millimetres.) An example from mathematics is the use of ! for 'factorial'.

Difficult cases for language designers are a/b*c, which is often intended by the programmer as a/(b*c) but is interpreted as (a/b)*c, and −a↑b (with ↑ for exponentiation), with two reasonable interpretations:

(−a)↑b and −(a↑b). One would also want multiple comparisons like 0<=ch<=9 to work, but this is difficult to arrange; for the way in which Icon allows this, see Section 2.6.1.

The above considered only monadic and dyadic operators. Some languages feature a small number of other expression forms, the main example being the **conditional expression**:

q := IF x /= 0 THEN 1/x ELSE 0;

C incorporates this form in the normal precedence hierarchy, as a **ternary operator** consisting of two parts: a question mark (**?**) for the **then** and a colon (:) for the **else**:

q = x != 0 ? 1/x : 0;

The precedences of the operators ensure that this is interpreted as

q = ((x != 0) ? (1/x) : 0);

Also, it is possible to consider constants and enumeration values as **zeroadic**, operators with zero operands: pi, amber, asia, and so on. The degree of an operator (the number of operands it requires) is sometimes called its **arity** or its **adicity**.

Operator overloading and mixed-mode arithmetic

Traditionally, operators have been overloaded heavily. People have been writing forms like 2 × 12.5 and 1.07 × 370.18 for many years, often without realizing that two different ×-operators are involved. To cater for this so-called mixed-mode arithmetic, even early languages, which had no explicit overloading, allowed some *ad hoc* overloading of the operators. Once it was understood that operators were not so different from other names in the language, and that overloading could be profitably applied to other classes of language entities as well, operators lost their special status as 'the' overloaded items. In Ada, the output procedure Put is more heavily overloaded than any operator.

Prefix and postfix notations

The 'classical' expressions described in the previous section consist of a mixture of infix, prefix and possibly postfix operators. It is also possible to use prefix or postfix operators exclusively. In prefix notation, the operator always comes first and is followed by zero or more operands:

```
<expression>    ::=    <0-operand operator>
                |      <1-operand operator> <expression>
                |      <2-operand operator> <expression> <expression>
                |      ...
```

The arity of each operator determines how many of the following expressions it absorbs. The notation requires no parentheses, no precedences and no associativity, but is less readable than infix notation.

Postfix notation is the syntactic mirror image of prefix notation:

```
<expression>    ::=    <0-operand operator>
                |      <expression> <1-operand operator>
                |      <expression> <expression> <2-operand operator>
                |      ...
```

Since the order of the operands is not mirrored, prefix and postfix notations of the same expression need not be each other's mirror image, though. Postfix notation corresponds closely to the order of the machine instructions for expressions in the computer.

infix	prefix	postfix
3 + 4	+ 3 4	3 4 +
3 + 4 * 5	+ 3 * 4 5	3 4 5 * +
(3 + 4) * 5	* + 3 4 5	3 4 + 5 *

Figure 2.12 Some expressions in infix, prefix and postfix notations.

Prefix notation is used extensively in some functional languages and postfix notation is used in some imperative languages, especially those used in process control (Forth, PostScript). Figure 2.12 shows a few expressions in the three notations.

Lazy evaluation

For reasons that are much more obvious in functional languages than in imperative languages, it is often desirable that an operand be evaluated only when its value is needed. Suppose we have an array a[1..10]; then in the test

IF i <= 10 AND a[i] > 0 THEN ...

we do not want *both* operands of the AND operator to be evaluated if i > 10. In that case, i <= 10 is false and we know the result of the AND already: false. Moreover, evaluating a[i] for i > 10 would cause precisely the index overflow the test was designed to avoid. Operators with this lazy evaluation semantics are called **short-cut operators** or **short-circuit operators** in the imperative languages. Lazy evaluation is covered much more extensively in Chapter 4 on functional languages.

The logical operators and the conditional expression in C are short-cut operators. Ada has no conditional expressions but has logical short-cut operators. The correct Ada version of the above if-statement uses the **and then** short-cut operator:

> if I <= 10 and then A[I] > 0 then ... end if;

2.3.3 External state

Whereas assignment statements use the internal state to modify the internal state, output statements use the internal state to modify the external state, and input statements use the external state to modify the internal state.

Output

The external state can be changed with an **output statement**:

> printf("%d", (x+y)/2);   Put((X+Y)/2);

will evaluate the expression and display its result on some output device. Changing the external state differs from changing the internal state in that the result will probably be examined by a human and must be readable. This means that the value supplied by the expression must somehow be converted to a string in a readable format: outputting a value thus decomposes into converting the value to a string and outputting that string. For reasons of history and efficiency, most languages do not properly separate these two phases, a good example of unorthogonality. Such languages have only one output primitive: output to a file while formatting. Many languages then re-establish the separation after the fact, by allowing the user to do output to a faked file that is actually a string.

The desired conversion format may differ with the application and the intended audience, and may specify details like the suppression of leading zeros in numbers, the use of a dot or a comma for the decimal point in real numbers, the use of a 12-hour or 24-hour clock in printing the time, or even the typefont and screen position of the displayed information. In principle, all these conversions can be programmed by the user, but most languages supply some simple set of predefined conversions, either built in or through library routines. C's printf is an example of a routine that combines conversion and output; the string "%d" specifies that the output should be in decimal. Such strings that specify conversions are called **format strings** or **formats** and in some languages (for example, Algol 68) they are a separate data type, which in fact they are.

If the output mechanism is supplied through library routines, there is a second fundamental difference between assignment and output statements. Since the assignment is built in, it can work without problems on data of any type, including types defined by the user; such a feature that spans many different types is called 'polymorphic'. Strong type checking, however, prevents us from duplicating this very convenient feature for library routines: hardly any imperative language has more than marginal polymorphism (ABC is one exception). In principle, a different output routine must be provided for each basic type. This is indeed the approach taken by, for example, Modula-2 and Ada, although in Ada the problem is almost overcome by overloading one routine name with many different routines for different types; this simulates a finite form of polymorphism. C chooses to give up strong type checking for output (and input): the parameters of printf can be of any type, and it is quite possible to print an integer using a format for real numbers. If that happens, the bits of the integer (and probably some bits outside it!) will be interpreted as bits of a real number, and chaos results.

Even abandoning strong type checking for output does not solve the problem of how to output values of a user-defined type. To do that, the user will have to write explicit code to do the conversion. In short, built-in formats are good only for simple conversions on the basic data types; Ada and Modula-2 do not feature them.

The above output in readable format is known as **character output**. **Binary output** routines write the bytes constituting the value to a file, without any conversion. The result is for computer rather than human consumption.

Input

Much of what has been said about output also applies to input. There is an additional complication, though. Since static type checking cannot ensure type-correct input, the input has to be checked dynamically.

The simplest approach to input is to hide it behind an interface and to have, for example, a function read_int, which reads one integer and yields its value. One can then do input by writing i := read_int(). Most languages prefer, however, to use a routine with an output parameter, since this allows the reporting of dynamic type mismatches. (Output parameters are explained in Section 2.5.2.) The C expression

    scanf("%d", &i)

reads one integer (specified by format "%d") and stores it under the pointer &i, thus effectively assigning it to i. The routine scanf returns the number of values stored successfully. Ada uses the statement Get(I) in which I is an output parameter, and does not use the possibility of returning a success/failure value; in the case of an error it raises an exception instead. Ada exceptions are explained in Section 2.4.5.

2.4 Flow of control

Imperative languages give the programmer extensive control over the order in which the statements in the program are executed or skipped: the flow of control. The usual mechanisms are sequencing, selection, repetition and routine invocation, in various varieties.

2.4.1 Sequencing

A **sequencer** tells which statement must be executed next. In the absence of an explicit sequencer the next statement to be executed is the textually following one:

        i = i + 1; j = j + 1;   I := I + 1; J := J + 1;

Explicit deviation from the in-line sequence can be achieved by the **goto statement**, which specifies a **label** that must label a statement elsewhere in the program. The flow of control then jumps to that position:

        goto bad_case;   goto Bad_Case;
        ...   ...
        ...   ...
        bad_case: ...   <<Bad_Case>> ...

The goto statement has had much deserved bad publicity and has disappeared almost completely from the programming scene. It should be pointed out, though, that the actual culprit is the label. To understand an imperative program, one must at all times know what the state of the machine means, as expressed by the values of all visible variables. Arriving at a label, however, one can no longer know this, unless one checks the meaning of the state of the machine at all places from which the flow of control can reach the label; and that is an unattractive and error-prone task.

   Some modern imperative languages, for example Modula-2, have abandoned the goto statement altogether, while others, for example C and Ada, retain it, mainly to cater for computer-generated programs. A possibly legitimate use of the goto statement is for bailing out of a piece of code when an irreparable error has been encountered. This use, however, suffers from the same problems as any exception handling mechanism (for which see Section 2.4.5).

2.4.2 Selection

A simple form of selection, the **if-statement**, causes one of two pieces of code to be selected for execution, depending on the value of a Boolean expression, the **condition**. The if-statement

```
if (x < 0) {                    if X < 0 then
    y = -x;                         Y := -X;
} else {                        else
    y = x;                          Y := X;
}                               end if;
```

will set y to the absolute value of x. In an even simpler form, the else alternative may be omitted:

```
if (x > x_max) {                if X > X_Max then
    x = x_max;                      X := X_Max;
}                               end if;
```

Many languages allow a list of condition-action pairs to be specified in an **if ... then ... elsif ... then ... elsif ... then ... else ... end if** construction, thereby avoiding the need for nesting for the second and further condition-action pairs.

 Selection among a number of pieces of code, based on an integer or enumeration value, can be expressed by a **selection statement**, also called a **switch statement** or **case statement**; an example of a selection statement is shown in Figure 2.13. The syntax of the C switch statement can only be called bizarre, but, to be fair, the use of the keyword **is** in the Ada notation **case N is** is not very intuitive either. (The C break statement is explained in the subsection on exits from loops in Section 2.4.4.) The selection statement should not be confused with the Ada 'select statement', which is concerned with the selection of entries in tasks, and which is explained in Section 6.3.2.

```
switch (n) {                    case N is
case 0:                             when 0 =>
    printf("empty set");                Put("empty set");
    break;
case 1:                             when 1 =>
    printf("singleton");                Put("singleton");
    break;
default:                            when others =>
    printf("multiple");                 Put("multiple");
    break;
}                               end case;
```

Figure 2.13 A selection statement.

The selection statement specifies an expression and a list of value-action pairs. The expression in the head of the selection statement is evaluated, the resulting value is looked up in the list of choice values, and the attached action is performed. If the resulting value is not in the list, the default action is taken.

The manual of a programming language with a selection statement should at least clear up these questions:

- Can an action be labelled with more than one choice value? (Yes, both in C and in Ada, though in different ways.)
- Can an action be labelled with a range of choice values? (Yes in Ada; no in C.)
- Are there any restrictions on the expressions in the choice value list? There usually are, for efficiency reasons and also sometimes on metho- dological grounds, to increase the semantic distance between a selection statement and a list of if-statements. (It must be possible to evaluate the choice expressions at compile-time, both in C and Ada.)
- What happens if a value occurs twice in the list of choice values? This is usually an error. (It is a compile-time error in both C and Ada.)
- What happens if the expression value is not found in the list of value- action pairs and there is no default action? (In C nothing happens. In Ada it must be possible to see at compile time that this cannot happen: either actions for all values must be specified or a default action (when others =>) must appear.)

A natural application of the selection statement is in the analysis of union values, although of course its field of application is much wider than that. Ada emphasizes this relationship by having very similar syntax for the selection statement and the union declaration. The effect of the if-statement at the end of the section about unions can be obtained more elegantly using a selection statement, as shown in Figure 2.14. Compare this to the Ada union declaration in Figure 2.8.

```
case My_Garage.Status is
   when Has_Car =>
      Put(My_Garage.Car);
   when Has_Bicycles =>
      Put(My_Garage.Nmb_Of_Bicycles);
end case;
```

Figure 2.14 Ada selection statement is similar to a union declaration.

2.4.3 Routine invocation

When a sequence of statements forms a conceptual unit about which it is possible and useful to think and reason in isolation, it is convenient to encapsulate the sequence in a named procedure and to replace it by a procedure call in the original code. The procedure call names the procedure; its execution transfers the flow of control to the beginning of the procedure, but, unlike the goto, it guarantees that the flow of control will eventually return here, just after the procedure call. An example of a delegating procedure call is:

      read_next_line();   Read_Next_Line;

which delegates the work of reading the next line, presumably into a variable with a known name, to the procedure read_next_line. (Parameterless routines are called with an empty parameter list in C and without parentheses in Ada.)

It has long been recognized that the procedure call mechanism is capable of much more than simple flow of control for the benefit of delegating. It is a very powerful abstraction mechanism, and is discussed in more detail in Section 2.5.2.

2.4.4 Repetition

There are two main forms of repetition: repetition over a precalculated (finite) set and repetition as long as a given condition is met. The first is embodied in the for-statement and the second in the while statement. There is a valid third alternative, infinite repetition, used in programs that, in principle, have to run for ever. Examples of such programs are operating systems and the driver programs in printers and telephone exchanges. Infinite repetition is generally implemented as a while statement with a missing or trivially true condition.

For loops

A sequence of statements can be repeated a precalculated number of times by using a **for-statement**. The for-statement also features a **controlled variable**, which serves as a repetition counter and which is available to the sequence of statements to be repeated. Since the for-statement repeats its action a known number of times and an array has a known number of elements, the for-statement is used quite often, though by no means exclusively, to iterate over the elements of an array. For example, the code fragment in Figure 2.15 will sum the values of the elements of the n-element array a into the variable sum; i is the controlled variable.

The C syntax is again bizarre: i = 0; initializes the control variable,

```
int sum;                    Sum: Integer;
int i;                      -- No declaration of I needed

sum = 0;                    Sum := 0;
for (i = 0; i < n; i++) {   for I in 1..N loop
   sum += a[i];                Sum := Sum + A(I);
}                           end loop;
```

Figure 2.15 Using a for-statement to iterate over an array.

the check i < n is performed before each repetition and the increment operation i++ is performed after each repetition. It can even be argued that the C
for-statement is not a for-statement at all, but rather a dressed-up while
statement. For example, the initializing, checking and incrementing code in
the for-statement header can each be replaced by arbitrary expressions,
resulting in effects that no longer have anything to do with repeating some
action a precalculated number of times.

Most languages associate with the for-statement a range over which
the controlled variable runs. The range is specified by giving its bounds,
and often the direction of traversal can be chosen: the construction

for I in reverse 1..N loop

will run I from N to 1 in Ada. Occasionally the step size in the range is also
under the programmer's control (1 to 10 by 2 for the sequence 1, 3, 5, 7, 9),
but this raises questions about the meaning of the upper bound and also may
be of limited usefulness. Ada has no step control.

C has explicit dynamic initialization, limit testing before each iteration and recalculation of the controlled variable after each iteration, thus
allowing the user great freedom of expression and great opportunities to
make mistakes.

Like the selection statement, the for-statement raises a number of
questions that should be addressed in the manual.

- Who declares the controlled variable and what is its scope? (The
  'scope' of a variable is the region of the program in which it is known,
  as explained further on in this chapter.) (In C, the controlled variable is
  a normal variable to be declared explicitly by the programmer in any
  surrounding block, and its scope is that block. In Ada, the controlled
  variable is declared implicitly by its occurrence in the for-statement
  and its scope is the action in the for-statement.)
- If the scope of the controlled variable is larger than the for-statement
  itself, what is its value after the loop has finished? (In C, it is the value
  on which the test failed. In Ada, the controlled variable is no longer
  accessible.)

- If the controlled variable is declared implicitly, how is its type determined? (Ada has a complex set of rules for this, which primarily try to derive the type from the apparent type of the range; not applicable to C.)
- Can the value of the controlled variable be modified from inside the loop body? (In Ada no, in C yes.)
- Can the range over which the controlled variable will run be empty? What happens if it is? (Yes; the action in the for-statement will be performed zero times, both in C and in Ada.)
- Can the range over which the controlled variable will run be modified from inside the loop, for example by modifying the variables of values used in the expressions for the limits of the range? (C: yes; there are no explicit limits, only a dynamic test to be performed before each iteration. Ada: no; the range is determined once, during loop start-up.)

While loops

A sequence of statements can be repeated an indeterminate number of times by using a **while statement**: repetition continues as long as a given condition remains fulfilled. An example is:

```
while (!end_of_file()) {          while not End_Of_File loop
    read_next_line();                Read_Next_Line;
    process_line();                  Process_Line;
}                                 end loop;
```

which continues to call end_of_file, read_next_line and process_line, until end_of_file succeeds. (The ! is the Boolean negation operator in C, corresponding to not in Ada.) If the condition never fails, the while statement loops until interrupted externally. To achieve the normal situation in which the condition first succeeds a number of times and then fails, the code in the body of the while statement has to make changes to the variables accessed by the condition: the proper functioning of the while statement depends on side-effects.

Many languages feature, in addition to the while statement, a **repeat-until statement**, which continues to repeat the enclosed sequence of statements until a given condition is met. The repeat-until statement is written do ... while ... in C. The loop

```
do {
    read_next_line();
    process_line();                 not available in Ada
} while (!end_of_file());
```

reads and processes lines from a file until the file is exhausted. Ada has no repeat-until statement, although the effect can be achieved by using an exit statement (see below).

The repeat-until statement is probably to be avoided, since it embodies the misconception that a set or sequence cannot be empty: the above code crashes abysmally when presented with an empty input file.

Exits from loops

The while statement provides a testing point at the top of the loop and the repeat-until statement provides one at the bottom. Often the need is felt to terminate the loop somewhere in the middle. Some methodologists object to such a facility, on the grounds that it destroys the suggested all-or-nothing semantics of the loop body. Without going into this issue, we only note that many language designers have judged that the continuation condition of a loop is often more complicated than can be expressed conveniently by a simple Boolean expression; they therefore supply a form of **exit** or **break statement**. The code in Figure 2.16 has two continuation conditions, !end_of_file() and !line_is_empty(), which cannot easily be combined into a single Boolean expression since an action must be performed between the first and the second. We see that these two conditions are in no way treated on equal footing, but in spite of considerable research on this problem in the 1970s, no convincingly better notation has been found.

```
while (!end_of_file()) {          while not End_Of_File loop
    read_next_line();                 Read_Next_Line;
    if (line_is_empty())              if Line_Is_Empty then
        break;                            exit;
                                      end if;
    process_line();                   Process_Line;
}                                 end loop;
```

Figure 2.16 A loop with two continuation conditions.

In C, the break statement is also used to exit from a switch statement after an alternative has finished, as we saw in Figure 2.13.

In some languages the exit statement can effect an exit from more than one nested loop in one action. This feature has even more enemies than the simple exit statement.

2.4.5 Run-time error handling

The above sections paint a smooth picture of the flow of control in a program, but the nasty truth is that a program can get into difficulties that cannot be handled reasonably by the above flow-controlling mechanisms. We shall first consider the main causes of such mishaps and then see what constructs programming languages provide to cope with them.

There are three main causes of a program getting into trouble:

- domain/data errors (synchronous);
- resource exhaustion (synchronous/asynchronous);
- loss of facilities (asynchronous);

Examples of these situations are given below.

Run-time problems are often classified as either **synchronous** or **asynchronous**, but actually there is a double dichotomy:

- caused internally or externally;
- reproducing or non-reproducing (that is, intermittent).

Problems caused internally (that is, by the program itself) include integer overflow and running out of memory; examples of external errors are the user interrupt and power failure. Almost all internal problems will reproduce and are thus synchronous, and all external problems will not reproduce and are therefore asynchronous, which is why a simple dichotomy almost always works. There are, however, program-triggered problems that will not necessarily reproduce; running out of memory is one example.

If the programmer takes no special measures, most or all of the above problems will result in the termination of the program, hopefully with a reasonable error message. Sometimes this may be adequate but often it is not. A program that has brought a database into an inconsistent state will definitely have to restore that database to its proper state before terminating, regardless of any errors; and the internal control program of a moonlander should not come to a grinding halt under any circumstances. It is therefore imperative that the programmer has the option of regaining control after an error. The two main concepts for providing the programmer with the power to do so are **signals** and **exceptions**.

Domain/data errors

A domain (or data) error occurs when an operation is called with data values that cannot be handled by that operation. Prime examples are division by zero and integer overflow. Since such errors are caused directly by the program, they are synchronous errors: they will occur every time the program is run with the same data. It would seem to be the responsibility of the programmer to see to it that such errors cannot occur, but that is easier said than done. Testing for zero before a division operation is easy enough, but devising a machine-independent addition overflow check that does not in itself cause overflow is much harder. For many operations such a test is not feasible: a singular matrix cannot be inverted and thus should not be given to a procedure to do so, but checking whether a matrix is singular is about as difficult as inverting it.

Resource exhaustion

Most resources are requested explicitly: memory to store a record, disk space when writing a file, the exclusive use of a video screen. Some of these requests may return a condition code upon failure but some do not, depending on language design. For example, the memory allocator new in Ada will fail rather than return a null pointer (or error code) when the requested memory is not available. There are, however, two resources that are requested implicitly: stack space and CPU (processor) time; both can run out. Both types of errors are synchronous in that they coincide with (and are caused by) a specific action in the program, and asynchronous in that they will not necessarily occur again when the program is run a second time.

Running out of CPU time is caused by a time limit set by the caller, the operating system or the program itself. Even if a program has used up all its CPU time, it may need a short reprieve in order to reconsolidate its permanent data or to save some results.

Loss of facilities

Loss of facilities comprises a host of unpleasantries that can befall a program: a network connection may break, an open file may be removed, a disk head may crash, memory may fail, or the electric power may drop below a threshold. Also, the user or operator may break off the program externally, by sending an interrupt. All these errors are asynchronous, since they are unrelated to any action of the program.

Signals

To enable the programmer to say something about error handling, errors are grouped into named classes, **error conditions**. Examples are Constraint_Error in Ada for any result that is out of bounds with respect to its type, and SIGFPE in C on UNIX-like systems for any error in a floating point operation (FPE – Floating Point Exception). A **signal statement** names an error condition and a procedure; when the named error occurs, the procedure is called. The idea is that this procedure, which is generally required to be declared on the outermost level, cleans up and then terminates the program. In UNIX C, the statement

signal(SIGFPE, close_down);

will cause the procedure close_down to be called whenever a floating point operation goes awry. The administration needed for this is kept by the run-time system or the operating system. Signals can be used to handle both synchronous and asynchronous errors. In some systems, the signal statement also doubles as the inter-process communication primitive; generally, this use of it is packed away in library routines.

The main problem with the signal statement is that the procedure, when called, has no access to the local variables of the routine that was active at the moment of the error. In a normal program, these variables would contain the most recent and probably most relevant information for a sudden close-down. The use of signals forces the programmer to make global all the information that might be necessary for a proper close-down, allowing less program structure than would otherwise be possible.

A minor problem concerns the question of what happens if the called procedure chooses not to terminate the program but returns instead. Depending on language specification and implementation, various undesirable things may happen. The same error may occur again, causing an infinite loop of errors and signals. The interrupted sequence of statement may be continued after the error, generally with faulty data. Or the run-time system may consider this an error and terminate the program anyway.

A possible advantage of the signal statement is that it can be implemented as a library routine and can thus be added to any language that can have procedures as parameters. In UNIX C, signal is indeed a library routine. Ada 9X uses this mechanism to handle external interrupts. Under certain circumstances, the Ada 9X form

Attach_Handler(Close_Down, Control_C_Hit)

will cause the parameterless procedure Close_Down to be called whenever a Control_C_Hit interrupt arrives. Attach_Handler is a library procedure from a language-defined package and Control_C_Hit must be a value of the type Interrupt_Id from that same package.

Exceptions

A more integrated feature which avoids the above problems to some extent is the **exception handler**. An exception handler consists of an error condition and a set of statements and can be attached to a block of statements. If one of the statements in the block fails with the error condition specified in the exception handler, the set of statements in it will be executed as a replacement for the rest of the statements in the block. Figure 2.17 shows a block with an appended exception handler. The arrow on the left represents normal execution, the arrow on the right shows what happens when statement *m* causes an error.

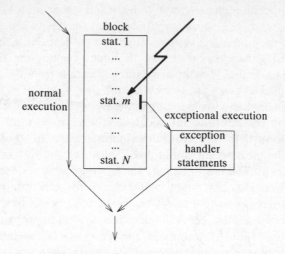

Figure 2.17 Block with normal and exceptional execution.

In Ada, exception handlers can be inserted before the **end** keyword in a **begin** ... **end** block. The Ada code in Figure 2.18 will normally execute the statement Put(1/X);, but in the exceptional case that this causes a division by zero, it will execute the statement Put("Division by zero!"); instead.

```
begin
   Put(1/X);
exception
   when Constraint_Error =>
      Put("Division by zero!");
end;
```

Figure 2.18 A block with a simple exception handler in Ada.

Since the clean-up code is in the same block as the offending statement, it has access to all names the offending statement could access. This solves the major problem of the signal statement for the most part. If, however, the same error can originate in more than one statement in the block, the code in the exception handler cannot know how far execution has progressed in the block, and thus cannot know what the values of the variables mean, nor which statement caused the error. The problem is exacerbated in

Ada by the coarse grouping of errors in only four exception names:

Constraint_Error for values that are out of bounds;
Program_Error for problems with the flow of control;
Storage_Error for storage allocation problems; and
Tasking_Error for problems with parallel processes.

These broad categories increase the chance that a given exception can originate from more than one statement in the block. On the other hand, the broad Ada exception classes are more operating-system independent than the UNIX C signal numbers.

In addition to the above predefined exception names, Ada programmers can define their own exception names, which are treated on par with the built-in ones. Programmer-defined and system exceptions can be caused explicitly by using the name in a **raise statement**: the command raise Storage_Error; simulates a storage problem.

Ada 9X distinguishes between an *exception*, which is the name of an error condition, and an **exception occurrence**. The latter is a value of type Exception_Occurrence, which is generated by the actual occurrence of an error. It contains the name of the exception and information about where and exactly why the exception occurred. An exception occurrence is a normal value which can be manipulated by the programmer like any other value. Some operations are defined on it, to extract printable information from it. An exception occurrence value can be obtained by using an extended form of the exception handler, as shown in Figure 2.19. This form of the exception handler declares a constant EO of type Exception_Occurrence (the declaration and the type are implicit in the syntax). When the exception Constraint_Error occurs, EO is initialized with the information about the exception occurrence, and is then available inside the handler. The library function Exception_Message converts the message part of EO to a string, which is then printed.

The manual of any programming language with an exception handling facility should at least answer these questions:

- How are exceptions represented? (C: as integers; Ada: as declared names.)
- Can exceptions be declared by the programmer? (C: no; Ada: yes.)
- Can additional information about the exception be obtained? (C: no; Ada 9X: yes, through exception occurrence values.)
- What happens if an exception is not caught? (C: depending on the signal, the program is aborted or the signal is ignored. Ada: the exception propagates to the dynamically enclosing unit, following special rules; ultimately the program may be aborted.)

```
begin
  Put(1/X);
exception
  when EO: Constraint_Error =>
    Put("Division by zero!");
    Put("Details follow.");
    Put(Exception_Message(EO));
end;
```

Figure 2.19 An exception handler which analyses the exception occurrence.

- Can multiple exceptions be caught by the same exception handler? (C: yes; Ada: yes.)
- In a multiple exception handler, can the current exception be determined? (C: yes; the signal number is passed as a parameter to the handler routine. Ada 9X: yes, by using a library routine on the exception occurrence value.)
- Can a catch-all exception handler be written? (C: only by explicitly catching all exceptions; Ada: yes.)
- Can exceptions be passed as parameters? Stored in variables or record fields? (C: yes, since they are just integers; Ada: no, but exception occurrences can.)
- Can the programmer cause a given exception to occur? (C: yes; Ada: yes.)

In addition, exceptions occurring in some language contexts may be handled differently from those in other contexts. For example, Ada has special rules for exceptions occurring in declarations and during parallel task initialization.

Although the above mechanisms are no doubt better than nothing, it will be clear that run-time error handling is still one of the least understood areas in programming language design.

2.4.6 Orthogonality of statements

Sort orthogonality of statements implies that in any position in which a statement is allowed, any statement is allowed. Although early programming languages had restrictions in this respect, modern languages are almost completely orthogonal as to statements. The fact that exception handlers in Ada can be attached only to begin-end sequences and not to single statements is an interesting but minor deviation from this rule.

Number orthogonality of statements means that wherever one statement is allowed, zero or more statements should be allowed. Since the matter is clearly related to the syntax of the rest of the language, languages differ in this respect. The more-than-one case is fulfilled in Ada, but generally requires the introduction of a block enclosed in { and } in C. The zero case is covered by the **null statement**, which consists of a single semicolon in C and has the form null; in Ada.

2.5 Program composition

To be effective, the above declarations and statements must somehow be grouped into complete programs. Four levels of hierarchy can be distinguished here:

- blocks;
- routines (procedures, functions and operators);
- modules/packages/tasks; and
- programs.

Two other important ingredients of program composition are abstract data types and generics. Generics are discussed in Section 2.5.4; abstract data types are introduced in a subsection of Section 2.5.3 and are covered in full in Chapter 3.

Historically, the routine and program levels have been recognized from the earliest days of programming, although the program level has for a long time been accepted as a fact of life rather than being recognized as a separate entity. Blocks were first introduced around 1960 in Algol 60. Modules are relative newcomers on the scene, appearing first in the mid-1970s in experimental languages like Alphard and CLU. The need for modules did not arise until programs became so large that blocks and routines began to fail as structuring tools. Before, people had thought that structuring by routines would scale to arbitrary program size, and it came as a surprise that 'programming-in-the-large' is fundamentally different from and requires other tools than 'programming-in-the-small'. The breaking point occurs when the forced nesting inherent in blocks and routines becomes a hindrance rather than a help in creating interfaces. Modules supply nesting-independent structure and increased control over the name space. The latter is important in formulating interfaces and in information hiding.

The imperative languages are characterized by a strict nesting of the flow of control. At any one moment, only one routine R is active, which was called by exactly one routine S, which is suspended in the call for R; S was called by exactly one routine T, which was calling exactly one routine, S; and so on, until the top-most call by the program proper. This simple chain of one-to-one caller/callee relations is implemented very efficiently by using a stack of **activation records**, in which each activation record holds the local data and linkage information for one routine call. Consequently, the only time a routine has an activation record and therefore a place to store local data, is when it is in the direct path of activation records from the active routine to the main program. This makes it difficult for a routine to remember values from one call to the next, without making these values more public than the routine itself. This is one problem that is solved by modules.

In time, modules too will begin to fail as structuring tools for some – very large – programs. In fact, this may already be happening (Wiederholt *et al.*, 1992).

2.5.1 Blocks

A **block** is the smallest grouping of declarations and statements. It is generally delimited by keywords like **begin** and **end** or by separators like { and } and is itself a statement. Syntactically, it allows a set of declarations and statements in a context in which one statement is expected. Contextually, its main feature is that it defines a local **scope**, a set of names that are known only within the block. These names originate in local declarations and generally refer to temporary (auxiliary) variables. The block shown in Figure 2.20 swaps the values of the non-local integer variables x and y, using a temporary variable t. The flow of control enters the block at the top and leaves it at the bottom. Entities declared in the block can no longer be accessed after the flow of control has left the block and can then be removed by the system.

```
{                              declare
    int t;                         T: Integer;
                               begin
    /* swap x and y */             -- swap x and y
    t = x; x = y; y = t;           T := X; X := Y; Y := T;
}                              end;
```

Figure 2.20 The use of a block to declare a temporary variable.

Although some languages (for example, Algol 68) allow declarations and statements to be interspersed arbitrarily in a block, most languages require all declarations to precede all statements. Ada makes this very explicit by having a three-keyword notation for blocks: **declare** ... **begin** ... **end**. Some languages impose even more structure on the sequence of declarations. For example, in Pascal we first have constant definitions, then type definitions, then variable declarations, and finally, routine declarations. One reason for this is that this is the order in which the information is normally used: type definitions use constant declarations (for example, in array bounds) but not vice versa. So, presenting the material to the reader in this order will increase readability; it also simplifies compilation.

Of course, a block does not have to have declarations in it. Some languages distinguish blocks that carry declarations from those that do not. A block that does carry one or more declarations is sometimes called a **locale**.

Most programming languages have an outermost level of declarations, the **global scope**. Variables declared on this level remain in existence and accessible throughout the entire program run. A few experimental languages have a **persistent** or **permanent scope**. Variables declared as persistent remain in existence even between runs of the program. The run-time system of such languages squirrels their names and values away somewhere in the file system between runs. This very useful feature may become standard in future languages. All global data in ABC is persistent.

Block structure and nested local declarations were first introduced in Algol 60. Earlier languages had no local variables (for example, COBOL) or only one level of them (for example, FORTRAN).

Scope rules

A direct consequence of the fact that a block is composed of statements and is itself a statement is the possibility of having nested blocks. Each such block defines its own local scope and the same name may be declared in more than one nested block. The rules that determine which names from surrounding blocks are accessible in a given block are known as the **scope rules**; they differ from language to language.

Nested blocks with declarations result in a situation in which for a given name there may exist several **defining occurrences** in declarations and several **applied occurrences** in other contexts. It is the task of the scope rules to determine for each applied occurrence of a name its defining occurrence. This process is called *binding* and, since it is performed at compile time, more specifically *static binding*. The general principle of static binding scope rules is that the defining occurrence of a name is found in the same block or in the nearest surrounding block that has a defining occurrence for the name. Figure 2.21 shows a nest of blocks; the x and y swapped in the innermost block are identified in the outermost and middle block, respectively. (It should be pointed out here that this use of nesting has its opponents as well as its proponents, and this and the following examples are given for explanatory purposes only.)

The situation is complicated by overloading in many languages; overloading can be resolved only by considering the context. Consequently, there are syntactic scope rules, which determine the set of eligible declarations for a given name, and contextual scope rules, which select the pertinent declaration from this set.

Some imperative languages, especially those that are normally

```
{                              declare
    int x;                         X: Integer;
                               begin
    ...                            ...
    {                              declare
        int y;                         Y: Integer;
                                   begin
        ...                            ...
        {                              declare
            int t;                         T: Integer;
                                       begin
            /* swap x and y */             -- swap x and y
            t = x; x = y;                  T := X; X := Y;
            y = t;                         Y := T;
        }                              end;
        ...                            ...
    }                              end;
}                              end;
```

Figure 2.21 Identification in nested blocks.

interpreted rather than compiled, delay the binding until the program is run, resulting in *dynamic binding*. Since this has been found to be confusing, dynamic binding has lost most of its support in imperative languages. A slightly different form of dynamic binding is essential, though, in object-oriented languages.

To answer detailed questions about name binding, we have to distinguish three notions:

- the *block* of a name: the block in which it was declared;
- the *scope* of a declaration and of the name in it: that part of the block over which the declaration extends;
- the *visibility range* of a declaration and of the name in it (generally called the *visibility*): those parts of the scope in which the name can indeed lead to a binding.

These notions are static in that they pertain to the text of the program. A fourth, related, notion is:

- the **lifetime** of an entity: the period of the running time of the program during which the programmer can count on the entity to exist.

'Lifetime' is a dynamic notion in that it pertains to the running program.

The definition involves the programmer's view of it, because the entity may not really exist during part of its lifetime, owing to compiler optimizations.

There is, unfortunately, some disagreement over the definitions of scope and visibility among authors. The above definitions are from the Ada Reference Manual, and are in our opinion the most useful. The definitions of block and lifetime are more stable.

Scope

In most languages, the scope of a declaration starts at the end of the declaration and extends to the end of the block. This has two immediate consequences. The first is that a name cannot be used before it has been declared: the language requires **declaration-before-use**. The second is that if the language allows initializing declarations, a data name declared in one declaration can be used in the initialization part of the next one, as shown in Figure 2.22.

```
{                                 declare
   int height = 6;                  Height: Integer := 6;
   int width = 7;                   Width: Integer := 7;
   int area =                       Area: Integer :=
      height*width;                    Height*Width;
                                  begin
   ...                               ...
}                                 end;
```

Figure 2.22 Immediate use of declared names.

Declaration-before-use causes a problem with mutually recursive items. There is no way to declare two mutually recursive functions F and G (F calls G and G calls F) and still have declaration-before-use for both names. This is solved by **forward declarations**. A forward declaration of name N says that name N exists and that a genuine declaration for it will follow. It may supply some additional information about N, for example that it is a procedure name rather than a function name or a type name. Now we can solve the mutual recursion problem by first giving a forward declaration for G, then the real declaration for F, which can now call G, and then the real declaration for G. Given the symmetry between F and G in the original problem, it is perhaps better to use forward declarations for both; see Figure 2.23.

```
    void f(void);                 procedure F;
    void g(void);                 procedure G;

    void f(void)                  procedure F is
    {                             begin
      ...                           ...
      g();   /* use g() */          G;      -- use G
      ...                           ...
    }                             end F;

    void g(void)                  procedure G is
    {                             begin
      ...                           ...
      f();   /* use f() */          F;      -- use F
      ...                           ...
    }                             end G;
```

Figure 2.23 The use of forward declarations.

Visibility

The **visibility** of a declaration of a given name is its scope minus the areas in which it is invisible. There are two main reasons for a declaration to become invisible: it may be hidden by another scope of a declaration for the same name, or the syntactic position may make it invisible. The first occurs in nested blocks, the second for example after the dot which separates a record name from a selector. Examples of both effects are shown in Figure 2.24, in which three defining occurrences of i appear: as a variable in the outer block A, as a selector in the record rec_ij in the outer block and as a variable in the inner block B. The scope of each i is the region from the end of its declaration to the end of its block in C and from the beginning of its declaration to the end of its block in Ada; these scopes overlap. The visibility of each i has been indicated in the figure by a letter under the program text. A small A beneath a lexical unit means that an i in that position would be (or is) identified in block A; likewise, a B signifies identification in block B and an R signifies identification in the record rec_ij. These visibilities are disjoint, allowing a unique identification of each i at each applied occurrence.

Contextual scope rules

The above scope rules are syntactic scope rules. In C, which has no overloading of identifiers, they are all that is necessary and available. To resolve overloading, the syntactic scope rules must be supplemented by **contextual scope rules**, which help to select the proper declaration from among

```
A: {                              A: declare
    int i, j;                         I, J: Integer;

    typedef struct {                  type Rec_IJ is record
        A        A                          A
        int i, j;                         I, J: Integer;
            A  R
    } rec_ij;                         end record;
      A
    rec_ij s;                         S: Rec_IJ;
    A      A                          A   A
                                  begin
    ...                               ...
    j = i;                            J := I;
    A   A                             A    A
    j = s.i;                          J := S.I;
    A   A R                           A    A R
    B: {                              B: declare
    A                                 A
        int i, j;                         I, J: Integer;
        A    B
        rec_ij t;                         T: Rec_IJ;
        B    B                            B  B
                                      begin
        ...                               ...
        j = i;                            J := I;
        B   B                             B    B
        j = s.i;                          J := S.I;
        B   B R                           B    B R
        j = t.i;                          J := T.I;
        B   B R                           B    B R
        ...                               ...
    }                                 end B;
    ...                               ...
}                                 end A;
```

Figure 2.24 Scope and visibility of the is.

the several declarations visible at a given point. These contextual rules are highly language-dependent. As an example, consider the Ada code of Figure 2.25, which contains two semantically similar declarations of the routine **Cents**, one working on floating point values and the other on strings. This overloads the name **Cents** in a permissible way in Ada. The context provided by the actual parameter in the call is strong enough to identify the correct function in each case. Contextual scope rules are also known as **semantic scope rules**.

The scope rules will also be called upon to handle names introduced by module declarations, as explained in the subsection about module use in Section 2.5.3.

```
declare
   -- Cents working on Float values:
   function Cents(V: Float) return Integer is
   begin
      return Integer(V*100.0);
   end Cents;

   -- Cents working on String values:
   function Cents(S: String) return Integer is
   begin
      -- convert a string like "$19.95" to
      -- 1995 and return that value
   end Cents;
   -- the name Cents is overloaded now
begin
   Put(Cents(18.95));
      -- identifies first Cents and prints 1895
   Put(Cents("$8.99"));
      -- identifies second Cents and prints 899
end;
```

Figure 2.25 Overloading resolution in Ada.

2.5.2 Subprograms

The term **subprogram** is the collective name for those groupings of statements and expressions that must be invoked explicitly and whose invocation is guaranteed to return the flow of control to the point right after the invocation. These two properties give the programmer a very convenient grip on the flow of control. The main examples are: *procedures*, which return no value; *functions*, which return a value; and *operators*, which are like functions but have a different notation.

The correct term for procedures and functions together is *routine*, but in practice the word 'procedure' is also used when it is immaterial to the discussion whether the subprogram returns a value or not. Another term for the same is *subroutine*, but strictly speaking there is little reason for the prefix 'sub-'. The term 'subprogram' stems from an era when modules did not yet exist and routines were the direct building blocks of programs. It is a misnomer now.

Routines

A **routine** is a named and parametrized block and originates from a **routine declaration**. A routine declaration consists of a **routine header**, which specifies the name of the routine and the names and types of its parameters, if any, followed by a block of statements, the **routine body**. A routine is activated by a **routine call**, which names the routine and supplies information about the parameters. The routine call starts by identifying the routine, transfers parameter information to the routine, causes the flow of control to enter the top of the body of the routine, waits until the body has finished and then leads the flow of control back to the statement after the call.

The parameters in a routine declaration are called **formal parameters**, those in a call **actual parameters**. The traditional way to supply the called routine with parameter information is by following the routine name by all actual parameters between parentheses, in the correct order. Such parameters are called **positional parameters**. When there are more than two or three of them, however, this scheme becomes awkward and error-prone, since the meaning of the call is no longer apparent. Even a call like Insert(A, B) is ambiguous, since it may insert A in B or B in A, depending on the declaration of the routine Insert.

There are two improvements over simple positional parameters: keyword parameters and default parameters. The meaning of a **keyword parameter** derives from a keyword attached to it, rather than from its position: the form

Insert(Source => A, Dest => B);

leaves no room for misunderstanding. Ada allows keyword parameters as an alternative to positional ones and has special rules for mixing both styles in one call. The keywords are equal to the names of the corresponding formal parameters. C has no keyword parameters.

Default parameters may be omitted in a call; an expression in the routine declaration then supplies a default value. Since they may be omitted, they are also called **optional parameters**. Suppose the routine Insert has an optional third parameter, called Mode, of an enumeration type with two values, Prepend and Append, which controls details of the insertion, and suppose Append is its default value. The above call will perform the insertion in Append mode, since the Mode parameter is missing and the default applies. A useful application of default parameters is in output routines, where they serve to avoid the repetitious mention of 'standard output' in most of the calls. Ada has optional parameters of the form described above. C has no optional parameters, although the C library contains some trickery ('varargs') that allows part of the above effect to be obtained.

Parameter passing mechanisms

In its simplest form, the value of the actual parameter is passed from the call to the routine, where it is used as the initial value of the corresponding formal parameter. This input parameter mechanism is called **call by value**. In some languages, the formal parameter is a variable, as in C, where its value can be changed from inside the routine body. It is important to note that this does not in any way affect the actual parameter: call by value transfers a copy of the value only. In other languages, among them Ada, the formal parameter is immutable, thus avoiding this somewhat surprising semantics. The C column of the code in Figure 2.26 prints a 1, a 3 and a 1, as follows. In the call to test_arg, the value of i, 1, is used to initialize the formal parameter n inside test_arg and this is the value which is printed. Next, a value 3 is assigned to n, which is again printed. Upon return from test_arg, i is printed, which still has its original value 1. The Ada code produces a contextual error message at compilation, caused by the attempt to use the formal parameter N as the left-hand side of an assignment.

```
int i;                          I: Integer;

test_arg(int n) {               procedure Test_Arg(N: Integer) is
                                begin
   printf("%d", n);               Put(N);
   n = 3;                         N := 3;        -- <<<< error
   printf("%d", n);               Put(N);
}                               end Test_Arg;

i = 1;                          I := 1;
test_arg(i);                    Test_Arg(I);
printf("%d", i);                Put(I);
```

Figure 2.26 Assigning to a formal parameter in C and Ada.

Most languages, but not C, have some form of output parameters: the routine can change the values of some of its actual parameters by assigning to the corresponding formal parameter. There are two choices for the moment the change is effected: immediately or upon return from the call. The former mechanism is called **call by reference** and the latter **call by result**.

Call by reference, represented for example by the Modula-2 or Pascal VAR parameter mechanism, establishes an alias for the actual parameter in the call: everything that happens to the formal parameter actually happens to the actual parameter. Although this is often convenient and efficient, it has all the dangers of aliasing. The two identical calls of WriteInt in the Modula-2 code shown in Figure 2.27 will print a 1 followed by a 3, in spite of the fact that both print the value of i and that no intervening modification of i is visible. Only upon close scrutiny will we discover that the x in x := 3; was an alias for i and that its effect was that of i := 3;.

```
VAR i: INTEGER;          (* declares i of type integer *)

PROCEDURE TestVar(VAR x: INTEGER);
    (* x is a call by reference parameter *)
BEGIN
   WriteInt(i, 1);          (* print i using 1 position *)
   x := 3;
   WriteInt(i, 1);          (* print i again *)
END TestVar;

i := 1;
TestVar(i);
```

Figure 2.27 An aliasing problem caused by a call by reference parameter.

Closely related to call by reference is the **call by copy-restore** mechanism, also called **call by value-result**. As the name says, the value of the actual parameter is copied to the formal parameter, which may then be modified by the routine. Upon completion of the routine, the value of the formal is copied back to the actual parameter. This achieves almost the same effect as call by reference and avoids the aliasing problem. It has, however, the disadvantage of requiring copying the value twice, which may be expensive if this value has a large size.

There are other parameter passing mechanisms of varying degrees of sophistication, but interest in clever parameter mechanisms has waned since the 1980s.

Procedures

A procedure without output parameters is useful only if it changes some state outside itself. The following procedure pr_sq prints the square of its integer parameter:

```
pr_sq(int n) {                procedure Pr_Sq(N: Integer) is
                              begin
   printf("%d", n*n);              Put(N*N);
}                             end Pr_Sq;
```

Note that the formal parameter n is declared *with* its type, but in a manner different from a local variable declaration. Calls can be pr_sq(-1); and pr_sq(i+j); in which -1 and i+j are the actual parameters.

An example of the use of an output parameter is the Ada call Get(l), which will read an integer value from the standard input and assign it to the variable I. The corresponding procedure header is

procedure Get(N: out Integer);

In C, an output variable can be simulated by passing a pointer to it as an input parameter. Rather than assigning to the parameter, the called procedure assigns to the item to which the pointer refers, as shown in Figure 2.28. The corresponding call is get(&i), in which get is passed the address of the variable i.

```
get(int *np) {
    ...
    some code to read an int value
    ...
    *np = the value read;    /* assignment under int pointer np */
}
```

Figure 2.28 Simulating an output parameter in C.

Functions

A **function** differs from a procedure in that it returns a value; its call must be used as an operand in an expression rather than as a statement. To specify and return the value, the function body must execute a **return statement** in most imperative languages. The function sq returns the square of its parameter:

```
int sq(int n) {                 function Sq(N: Integer)
                                    return Integer is
                                 begin
    return n*n;                     return N*N;
}                               end Sq;
```

Examples of calls are n = sq(n); which squares n, or p = sq(sq(n)); which sets p to the fourth power of n.

In some languages (for example, Pascal) the function value is returned by assigning it to the function identifier and then returning from the function in the normal fashion, by reaching its textual end.

Both procedure and function bodies can contain direct or indirect calls to themselves and are then called **recursive**. As we have seen in Chapter 1, recursive routines are very useful to implement certain programming techniques in an imperative language. They are exploited much more extensively in the functional languages, as described in Chapter 4.

Operators

There is no fundamental difference between operators and routines: operators are just a different syntactic notation for routines with one or two parameters. Intuitively one associates operators with being small, less heavy in some sense, and with in-line implementation, but this impression is far from accurate: real number exponentiation (x↑y) is heavy and will almost certainly be implemented as a routine call, and the Modula-2 ORD function, which yields the integer value of a character, may well correspond to no code at all.

Most imperative languages do not allow users to define their own operators: all existing operators are built in. In Ada, existing operator names can be overloaded with new definitions. Algol 68 features user-defined operators, which can also be overloaded. All user-defined operators in Algol 68 are left-associative and the user has to specify their precedences.

User-defined operators have their pros and cons. They increase the orthogonality of the language and allow the programmer to mesh in with the existing set of operators. Natural applications are the use of + for vector and matrix addition and that of * for string repetition (the expression 2 * "mur" yielding "murmur"). But new operators have to be given priorities and associativities, which has to be done very carefully or the resulting expressions will be unreadable. From the previous paragraph we can see that Ada avoids the problem and Algol 68 meets it head-on. Also, the programmer is easily tempted to formulate everything as an operator, thus putting a heavy burden on the reader.

User-defined operators are sometimes advertised as 'extending the language', but this is a misconception. New operator definitions extend the language as little or as much as new routine definitions. The impression of extending the language stems from the fact that operators have traditionally been built in and have thus been considered part of the language.

Rather than viewing operators as a special case of routines, one can also view routines as a special case of operators: a routine with, say, three parameters of types integer, character and Boolean, is then considered to be a monadic prefix operator with one operand, a record consisting of these three values. A language taking this view is ABC.

Refinements

A programmer may have several reasons to group a number of statements together:

- the statements have to be executed in more than one place in the program;
- the statements form a conceptual unit with a significance larger than the present problem;

- the code just gets too long and has to be chopped into named chunks.

If the first two reasons do not apply but the third does, it is often felt that the full routine mechanism is too heavy, the parameter list needed is too long and the ensuing creation of a new scope of names is more a hindrance than an aid.

The **refinement** is a lightweight routine designed to fill this niche. It just allows a set of statements to be named, to be moved to a nearby place in the code and to be invoked by that name; it involves no parameters and no new scope. It is used for structuring and increased readability only.

A language featuring refinements is ABC. The four lines following HOW TO PRINT.STOCK in Figure 2.29 show at a glance what the procedure PRINT.STOCK does, and will continue to do so even when the refinements PRINT.ENTRY and PRINT.TOTAL get much more complicated. (The backslash starts a comment, which ends at the end of the line; indentation replaces block demarcation in ABC; the PUT statements are examples of simultaneous assignments; and the / in the WRITE statements causes a new line to be appended to the output.)

```
HOW TO PRINT.STOCK book.list:
    PUT 0, 0 IN n.bks, s.val        \ number.of.books, sales.value
    FOR book IN book.list:
        PRINT.ENTRY
    PRINT.TOTAL
PRINT.ENTRY:
    PUT book IN number, title, quantity, price
    WRITE number, quantity, price, title /
    PUT n.bks + quantity, s.val + quantity*price IN n.bks, s.val
PRINT.TOTAL:
    WRITE "We have ", n.bks, " books, worth ", s.val /
```

Figure 2.29 A HOW TO unit with two refinements in ABC.

Anonymous subroutines

In a slightly different view, we can consider a procedure declaration as a constant declaration of the name of a value of some procedure type. We can emphasize the similarity by writing the declaration of the procedure Pr_Sq above as a constant declaration in an Ada-like notation:

```
Pr_Sq: constant procedure :=
  (N: Integer)
    begin
      Put(N*N);
    end;
```

This is the normal form in Algol 68, where we can write (Algol 68 allows spaces in names):

proc(**int**)**void** pr sq = (**int** n): **begin** print(n*n) **end**;

This suggests strongly that the part after the := or the =, which represents a routine except for its name, is an expression. In Algol 68, the form

(**int** n): **begin** print(n*n) **end**

is indeed an expression: it is a literal of type **proc**(**int**)**void**. Since literals are called **denotations** in Algol 68, this one is called a **routine denotation**; elsewhere it is known as an **anonymous subroutine**.

Anonymous subroutines are useful because they integrate routines as values in the language. This allows programmers to manipulate routines in much the same way as values. Anonymous subroutines can, for example, occur in conditional expressions; the Algol 68 declaration

proc(**int**)**void** pr sq =
  if debug
  then (**int** n): **begin** print(n); print(n*n) **end**
  else (**int** n): **begin** print(n*n) **end**
  fi;

declares pr sq as the first or the second routine denotation, depending on the value of debug at the moment the declaration is met during execution. Examples of imperative languages that feature anonymous subroutines are Algol 68 and PostScript.

Stack regime

An important point about a routine is that its local data exists only between the moment it is called and the moment it returns. This allows very efficient memory allocation for the local data, using a stack, but also involves some restrictions. For one thing, a routine cannot remember data locally between calls, making it impossible to write a routine that counts how many times it has been called without using non-local data. Since such data is conceptually local to the routine, Algol 60 had so-called **own variables**, which *would* survive between calls. C has **static locals**, which combine local scope with program-wide lifetime, and which can be used to much the same effect. The close relation between a routine and non-stacking data can be achieved in Ada by combining them in a package, as explained below.

A second consequence of the ephemerality of local data is that pointers to local data become dangling references upon routine exit. In C, we can write:

```
int *bad_ptr() {
    int i = 0;        /* local i */

    return &i;        /* &i is dangling outside bad_ptr() */
}
```

A call of **bad_ptr** will allocate memory for the local i, set i to zero, return a pointer to i and then remove the memory allocated for i, leaving the pointer dangling. Any subsequent use of the pointer will give unpredictable results.

The status of subprograms
Since there is considerable disagreement about the question of whether routines are data, the following issues are resolved differently in different languages:

- Can routine declarations nest? That is, can we have a routine declaration inside a routine declaration? (C: no; Ada: yes.)
- Can routine names be passed as parameters? (Both in C and in Ada 9X, pointers to routines can be passed as parameters.)
- Can routine names be stored in data structures? (Both in C and in Ada 9X, pointers to routines can be stored in data structures.)

These and similar decisions have subtle but profound consequences for the programming methodology supported by the language. The kind of compromise that language designers have struck on this subject is exemplified by Modula-2, in which routine declarations may nest, but only names of non-nested routines may be passed as parameters and assigned to variables. In a similar vein, Pascal and Modula-2 allow nested blocks inside routines, but the inner blocks cannot have local declarations.

2.5.3 Modules and packages

A number of related declarations of types, variables, routines, and so on, can be grouped together in a module, also called a package. Aside from the grouping, modules are characterized by restrictions on the access to their contents: anything still accessible is part of the interface the module provides. This grouping of items combined with restriction of access makes modules very helpful in hiding implementation details. We have seen in Chapter 1 that hiding of implementation details is an indispensable facility for writing large programs.

A module generally consists of a **specification part**, which contains a description of the interface that the module implements, and an **implementation part**, which contains the code that implements the interface. Module boundaries are explicit in Ada using the keyword **package** and coincide with file boundaries in C.

The specification part is accessible for the user of the module and contains the published interface. The implementation part and all the implementation details it contains are hidden from the module user, thus providing the desired information hiding. The implementation module *is* accessible for the module programmer, of course. But even if the module user and module programmer are one and the same person, the module mechanism keeps their responsibilities apart.

Module definition

Since even a very small module is already tens of lines long, we give here a very limited example, concerning the implementation of two operations on calendar dates: the function **create_date** which creates a date from integers indicating year, month and day, and a Boolean function **last_of_the_month**. Rather than showing the programs side by side in the usual two columns, we present them one after the other, starting with the Ada version.

```
package Date is

    type Date_Type is private;

    function Create_Date(Y, M, D: Integer)
        return Date_Type;
    function Last_Of_The_Month(Date: Date_Type)
        return Boolean;

private
    type Date_Type is record
        Year, Month, Day: Integer;
    end record;
end Date;
```

Figure 2.30 Package specification for handling calendar dates in Ada.

Our Ada version consists of two compilation units, the package specification and the package body; they are identified syntactically. The package specification is shown in Figure 2.30. It declares the named interface **Date** to consist of the names **Date_Type**, **Create_Date** and **Last_Of_The_Month**, with their properties. The bottom part starting with the keyword private, which shows the internal structure of Date_Type, is not part of the interface. Its presence here is explained in the subsection on representation parts in this section.

```
package body Date is

    Normal_Month_Length: constant array (1..12) of Integer :=
        (31, 28, 31, 30, 31, 30, 31, 31, 30, 31, 30, 31);

    function Is_Leap_Year(Y: Integer) return Boolean is
    begin
        return ((Y mod 4 = 0) and (Y mod 100 /= 0))
            or (Y mod 400 = 0);
    end Is_Leap_Year;

    function Month_Length(Y, M: Integer)
        return Integer is
    begin
        if M = 2 and Is_Leap_Year(Y) then return 29;
        else return Normal_Month_Length(M);
        end if;
    end Month_Length;

    function Create_Date(Y, M, D: Integer)
        return Date_Type is
    begin
        -- we should check the values of M and D here
        return (Year => Y, Month => M, Day => D);
    end Create_Date;

    function Last_Of_The_Month(Date: Date_Type)
        return Boolean is
    begin
        return Date.Day =
            Month_Length(Date.Year, Date.Month);
    end Last_Of_The_Month;

end Date;
```

Figure 2.31 Package body for handling calendar dates in Ada.

Figure 2.31 shows the package body. It starts by declaring three auxiliary items, the constant array Normal_Month_Length and the functions

Is_Leap_Year and Month_Length. It then gives the full definitions of the interface functions Create_Date and Last_Of_The_Month.

The C version consists of two files, date.h and date.c. The specification part date.h is traditionally a so-called **header file**. Any interpretation of it as a specification part is conventional rather than being enforced by the compiler. The file date.h is shown in Figure 2.32; we see that it has no syntactic demarcation. Also, the defined module has no explicit name. Its name is apparent from the file name date.h only.

```
typedef struct {
    int dt_year, dt_month, dt_day;
} date_type;

extern date_type create_date(int, int, int);
extern int last_of_the_month(date_type);
```

Figure 2.32 Header file date.h for handling calendar dates in C.

Figure 2.33 shows the implementation file date.c. It starts by including the header file date.h and then proceeds to define the other items in a way similar to that of the Ada package body in Figure 2.31.

There are two kinds of names in the implementation part, public and private. The public names are available to the user through the interface, the private ones are local to the module. Languages vary widely in the means by which the difference is indicated. C uses extern for public names and static for private names, supplemented by some trickery that we will not explain here. Ada distinguishes between public and private by syntactic means. Some languages, among which older versions of Modula-2 and some extensions of Pascal figure, use **export statements**. Other schemes can also be found.

Module use
The user of a module is concerned with the interface definition or specification part only. User programs that use the service supplied by a module must refer to the interface definition, in Ada through a **with clause** and in C through an **include compiler control line**. This reference introduces the names with their proper types, values, and so on, through which the service can be accessed. Figure 2.34 shows a small procedure in Ada, which declares one variable of type date, gives it a value and determines if that value is the last day of the month. The with Date; clause identifies the name of the module explicitly.

The C version is given in Figure 2.35. The name of the module used is apparent by convention from the #include "date.h" compiler control line.

```
#include  "date.h"

static int normal_month_length[12] =
  {31, 28, 31, 30, 31, 30, 31, 31, 30, 31, 30, 31};

static int is_leap_year(int y)
{
  return ((y % 4 == 0) && (y % 100 != 0))
    || (y % 400 == 0);
}

static int month_length(int y, int m)
{
  if (m == 2 && is_leap_year(y)) return 29;
  else return normal_month_length[m-1];
}

date_type create_date(int y, int m, int d)
{
  date_type dt;

  /* we should check the values of m and d here */
  dt.dt_year = y, dt.dt_month = m, dt.dt_day = d;
  return dt;
}

int last_of_the_month(date_type date)
{
  return date.dt_day ==
    month_length(date.dt_year, date.dt_month);
}
```

Figure 2.33 Implementation file date.c for handling calendar dates in C.

Module scope rules

Ada and some other languages base their access rules for module items upon an interesting property of record declarations. A record declaration groups a number of named items together in an enclosed form, such that the names are still available outside the enclosed form. This differs from what happens with the names in blocks. After the block

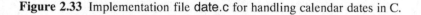

    declare Nm: Integer; begin ... end;

```
with Text_IO;    -- import package Text_IO
with Date;       -- import package Date
use Date;        -- make the names in it visible

procedure Use_Date is
  Date: Date_Type;
begin
  Date := Create_Date(1992, 2, 29);   -- Feb. 29, 1992
  if Last_Of_The_Month(Date) then
    Text_IO.Put("Pay day!");
  end if;
end Use_Date;
```

Figure 2.34 Use of the Date package in Ada.

```
#include   <stdio.h>
#include   "date.h"

use_date(void)
{
  date_type date;

  date = create_date(1992, 2, 29); /* Feb. 29, 1992 */
  if (last_of_the_month(date)) {
    printf("Pay day!");
  }
}
```

Figure 2.35 Use of the date package in C.

the name Nm is no longer available, but after the record declaration

    record Nm: Integer; ... end;

the name Nm is still available for use as a selector.

In Ada, defining a package only declares that package's name. Any public name in it will have to be accessed using the dot notation, as is the case with record fields. This is why we have to write Text_IO.Put in Figure 2.34, to reach the Put routine in the (standard) package Text_IO.

To avoid programs from being cluttered up by endless repetitions of prefixes like Popular_Package.⋯, Ada provides a **use clause**, which makes visible, on the present level, all public names in the package it mentions. The clause **use Date**; in Figure 2.34 adds all public names from the module **Date** to our visible names, thus relieving us of the duty to write forms like **Date.Create_Date**. The use clause may easily cause overloading and Ada has rules to deal with that.

There are ways to introduce names from a module in a more controlled way than Ada's all-or-nothing method. Modula-2 has an **import clause**

> FROM *Module* IMPORT *N1*, *N2*, ... ;

which makes available from *Module* only the names *N1*, *N2*, ... A usual example is:

> FROM InOut IMPORT WriteInt;

The above assumes that the name of the module has already appeared in a declaration, which is true for a module declared in-line. If the module has been compiled separately, though, the name has to be introduced first. In Ada, this is performed by the **with Date**; clause in Figure 2.34. The introduction of the name is implicit in the use of the import clause in Modula-2. C uses textual inclusion of the specification part, using a **#include** compiler control line, as in Figure 2.35.

Representation parts

It is disquieting to see the internal structure of the type **date_type** displayed openly in the specification part of the module **date**, both in Ada and in C. The internal structure is precisely the kind of detail we want to hide. For technical reasons, however, the compiler has to know the internal structure (or at least the size) of the type **date_type** when translating the allocation of the variable **date** and the call to **last_of_the_month**, if it wants to generate efficient code.

Such information obviously does not belong in the specification part but it does not properly belong in the implementation part either, for the following reason. Whenever code is compiled that uses the module **date**, the compiler has to consult the specification part of **date**, *and* it has to retrieve the size information of the data used. Suppose the information were stored in the implementation part. Then all implementation parts of all modules, with their implementation details, would have to be accessible in readable form all the time, a situation one would like to avoid. The size information, together with some other data, properly belongs in a third part, the **representation part**, which is in between the specification and implementation parts.

Very few languages have a separate representation part. As a compromise to efficiency, both Ada and C allow this information in the specification part. In Ada, the keyword **private** marks the start of a so-called **private part**, which holds information for the compiler but which the programmer cannot use: the names declared in it will be available in the implementation part only, and not in the code which uses the package. In C, the module system is a matter of convention rather than syntax. In one useful and rather common convention, private names start with two letters which abbreviate the name of the module, followed by an underscore, and such names should be used only in the corresponding implementation file. Examples are the **dt_year** and **dt_month** field selectors from Figure 2.32.

Modula-2 evades the problem by having **opaque types**. An opaque type is an abstract data type of which the only thing that is known externally about its implementation is that it is a pointer to something. This restriction solves most compiler problems, since all pointers have the same fixed size.

Abstract data types

A data type is a set of values, often available as literals, together with a set of operations for manipulating the values. An **abstract data type** (ADT) is a named data type defined solely through operations for creating and manipulating values of that data type. If values are available directly, they are known by name only. All internal structure is hidden from the user.

Strange as it may seem, many present-day programming languages do not have special language constructs for dealing with abstract data types. The reason is that modules/packages with private parts are reasonably suitable for the implementation of abstract data types: they provide about the right amount of abstraction and information hiding. It is clear that Figure 2.30 shows a usable representation of the abstract data type Date_Type.

Nevertheless, the module from Figure 2.30 is not a real ADT. The fundamental difference between a module and an ADT is that a module *contains* a type definition from which items can be declared and contains the tools to manipulate the items thus declared, whereas an ADT *is* a type that is used directly to declare items, and each item thus declared carries in it the tools to manipulate it. Since Ada has no abstract data types in this form, Figure 2.36 shows the ADT definition of Date_Type in an pseudo-Ada notation. It is true that Ada 9X does feature *protected types*, which have the proper syntactic form, but these are mainly concerned with parallel and distributed programming (protected types are explained in Section 6.5.3). We assume that the definitions of Month_Length and its auxiliaries are supplied from Figure 2.31.

The ADT Date_Type contains seven items: a public one, Last_Of_The_Month, and six private ones, Year, Month, Day, Normal_Month_Length, Is_Leap_Year and Month_Length. The type can be used to declare variables:

Date: Date_Type(1992, 2, 29);

```
abstract type Date_Type(Y, M, D: Integer) is
private Year, Month, Day: Integer;

-- private definitions of Normal_Month_Length,
-- Is_Leap_Year and Month_Length from the earlier
-- package Date

function Last_Of_The_Month return Boolean is
begin
  return Day = Month_Length(Year, Month);
end Last_Of_The_Month;

begin
  -- we should check the values of M and D here
  Year := Y, Month := M, Day := D;
end Date_Type;
```

Figure 2.36 An abstract data type for Date_Type in pseudo-Ada.

which declares a variable Date, initialized to Feb. 29, 1992. For comparison, the corresponding declaration using the package of Figure 2.30 would be:

Date: Date_Type := Create_Date(1992, 2, 29);

The ADT of Figure 2.36 knows only one operation:

if Date.Last_Of_The_Month then ...

which shows that the function Last_Of_The_Month is found inside the variable Date rather than in the module. It is up to the compiler to allocate the variable parts of Date_Type variables only (Year, Month, Day). Neither C nor Ada has genuine ADTs, but C++ and Orca do.

ADTs reach their full potential in the object-oriented languages, where they are supplemented by inheritance and dynamic binding, as will be described in Chapter 3.

2.5.4 Generics

Much of the code a programmer normally writes is more specific than is strictly necessary. For example, almost any implementation of a linked-list algorithm specifies the type of the items in the linked list together with the algorithm, the two melded together in an inseparable unit. Both structure and reusability would be gained if we could first write the algorithm and then specify the type of the manipulated items. With generics, we can do just this.

For each kind of named unit in the language (types, constants, variables, routines, modules) there exists, in principle, a corresponding **generic unit**. A generic unit can be seen as a template from which the actual unit or units can be created by a compile-time process called **instantiation**. The generic unit has one or more generic parameters. During instantiation, specific information about types, sizes, names, and so on can be supplied through instantiation parameters.

Ada has generic routines and modules; it also has generic types, though under a different name, **discriminated types,** and with a different notation. C has no generic facilities.

```
generic
   type Item_Type is private;
package Bin_Tree is
   type Bin_Tree_Type is private;
   function New_Bin_Tree return Bin_Tree_Type;
   function Add_Item(T: Bin_Tree_Type; I: Item_Type)
      return Bin_Tree_Type;
   procedure Print_Bin_Tree(T: Bin_Tree_Type);
   -- more Bin_Tree handling subprograms ...
private
   type Bin_Tree_Access_Type is access Bin_Tree_Type;

   type Bin_Tree_Type is record
      Left, Right: Bin_Tree_Access_Type;
      Value: Item_Type;
   end record;
end Bin_Tree;
```

Figure 2.37 An (incomplete) generic package specification.

Figure 2.37 shows part of a generic package specification derived from our record definition for Bin_Tree_Type in Section 2.2.2. The private part is copied straight from there. The public part contains the type Bin_Tree_Type only, plus specifications of three routines whose function is obvious. The Item_Type, between the keywords generic and package, is the (only) generic parameter, weird notation notwithstanding.

The generic package name Bin_Tree can be used in one way only, to instantiate an actual package while supplying a type name for the generic parameter. The instantiation package Date_Tree is new Bin_Tree(Date_Type);

declares an actual package Date_Tree for handling trees with items of the data type Date_Type from Figure 2.30 in it. After this declaration, we can use the public routine names of the package in a statement like

Print_Bin_Tree(Add_Item(New_Bin_Tree, Date));

provided a use clause use Date_Tree; has also been given. A procedure which uses the generic package is shown in Figure 2.38.

```
with Date;       -- import Date package
use Date;        -- make the names in it visible
with Bin_Tree;   -- import Bin_Tree generic package

procedure Test_Bin_Tree is
  Dt: Date_Type;
  package Date_Tree is new Bin_Tree(Date_Type);
  use Date_Tree;
begin
  Dt := Create_Date(1992, 2, 29);
  Print_Bin_Tree(Add_Item(New_Bin_Tree, Dt));
end Test_Bin_Tree;
```

Figure 2.38 A procedure using the generic package Bin_Tree.

2.5.5 Programs

A program is composed of modules; in more technical terms, an executable binary program is composed of object files resulting from the translation of implementation parts of modules. Some languages allow smaller units than modules to be compiled separately, for example subprograms and data declarations, but for the present discussion we can equate these to modules. Also, in many systems an object file resulting from a routine is indistinguishable from one resulting from a module containing only that routine.

Although the object files result from independent compilations, they are not themselves independent: they use common interfaces or they could not work together. As we have seen, the interfaces are represented by the specification parts of the modules used. When a module B uses the specification part of module A, we say that B is **dependent on** A. This means that information from A may be, and probably is, incorporated in the object file for B.

A complication is that module A may be under development and may exist in different versions. Therefore, when we are about to combine the output file B, dependent on A, with another object file C, also dependent on A, we have to ensure that both were compiled using the same version of A: we have to ensure the **consistency** of the executable binary program. (Actually, the situation is even more complicated than that: both B and C may exist in several versions, some of which are and some of which are not dependent on A. We shall not go into the details of this here.)

The main issues in program composition from object files are how to indicate which objects are part of the desired program, and how to ensure that no dependency conflicts occur. Surprisingly, even modern languages are very uncooperative on both issues. Whereas linguistic support for blocks and routines is strong in almost all languages, and support for modules is often reasonable, linguistic support for program composition is non-existent in most languages. As a result of historical development, the assembly of modules into a complete program is almost universally considered a task of the operating system rather than of the language processor. The final result of processing a module is an object file, and there the responsibility of the language processor ends. The operating system has a special facility, called a **linker**, which blindly connects the various object files it is offered into a program file, and a second facility, called the **loader**, which loads the contents of the program file into memory and starts its execution. In some operating systems, these facilities are not well separated.

The reasons behind this lamentable situation are as follows. When the first linkers/loaders were designed in the late 1950s, the only object files they had to handle resulted from assembly language, FORTRAN and later COBOL. None of these languages had any form of interface description, so naturally linkers had no provisions for them. Also, disks (or drums!) in those days were not large enough to store executable binaries permanently, and it was usual for every run of a program to first link together all object files, preferably in main memory to facilitate the subsequent load operation. This approach favoured very fast linkers combined with loaders. In these highly tuned programs there was no room for such luxuries as object file consistency checking. Times have changed, but unfortunately linkers have not.

Specifying program composition

The simplest way to specify the composition of a program is just to list its component modules. Neither C nor Ada (nor any other mainstream language) has a language construct for this. C assumes that the programmer will specify all necessary user object files in a specialized invocation of the system linker. This invocation searches the object files for a routine with the fixed external name main and constructs an executable binary program that, when called, will execute this routine main. Ada assumes that there exists a method outside the language which allows the programmer to specify the name of a procedure and which will then construct an executable binary program for that procedure containing all necessary modules.

Specifying a complete list of component modules is an error-prone affair. Such a list might easily contain too many or too few names. As a reasonable alternative, one can insert all *possibly* necessary object files in a library, as explained in Section 1.7.1. When offered the name of the main routine of a program, the linker can then retrieve from the library the necessary object files by following unsatisfied references. This is in fact what most present-day Ada systems do. The method can also be used for C, but is less suitable in that case, for reasons described at the end of the next subsection.

Dependency conflicts

The consistency problem is easy to solve if one can record, with each object file, information about the versions of the modules that played a role in its generation. A system consisting of a cooperating compiler and linker can then record in each object file F information about the identities of all files used in the creation of F, as well as all such information already included in those files. File names, time stamps and version numbers can be used to identify precise versions of files. When the linker is about to combine F with another file G, it can compare the information about the identities of all files involved in the creation of both F and G. Any discrepancies will necessitate recompilation of F, G or both, and possibly of other files as well.

Again no mainstream language has facilities for this in the language, and the standard system linkers do not support it. Some older languages, for example Pascal, Algol 60 and Algol 68, 'solved' the consistency problem by not having modules at all. A Pascal program had to be recompiled in its entirety after one line in one procedure had been changed. Needless to say, this so-called solution does not scale, and unofficial modularization proposals exist for Pascal and Algol 68, reintroducing the problem. Ada compilers are usually integrated in program managing systems, which do version control and consistency checking.

With most other languages, it is the programmer who is responsible for consistency checking. To this end, the programmer can enlist the help of the (UNIX) program Make, or any of its relatives on other systems. To use Make, the programmer prepares a list of dependencies, called a **Makefile**. The dependencies must be determined essentially by hand, although there is some heuristic software that may be of assistance. For each dependency, the programmer supplies a command that must be executed whenever the sources of a dependency are more recent than its result. When set up properly, a single invocation of the program Make will result in all necessary compilations and linker invocations to obtain a dependency-consistent executable binary program.

To determine if one file is more recent than another, Make compares the system time stamps on the files, but this method has its weaknesses. On some systems, the grain of the time stamps is too coarse. On other systems, copying or otherwise manipulating the files will change their time stamps. And time stamps may be difficult or impossible to retrieve for object files in libraries, making the library method described in the previous subsection less convenient. All in all, Make is an excellent makeshift tool.

2.5.6 Orthogonality of program composition

Although blocks, subprograms, modules and programs form a hierarchy, to which orthogonality need not apply, most languages that have blocks, sub-programs and modules allow them to be combined freely one inside the other. Programs, being the top of the hierarchy, are not allowed inside other structures.

2.6 Examples of imperative languages

C, Ada, Algol 68, Pascal and Modula-2 have already been mentioned in this chapter, and it is not difficult to extend this list with names like Algol 60, PL/I, Simula, Turing and Oberon. Because these languages have their roots in Algol 60, they are called **Algol-like**. Algol 68 deserves special mention, since it has had a great influence on language designers, if not always on language design. Many programming language concepts (coercions, dere-ferencing and void, to name a few) were formulated clearly and concisely for the first time in Algol 68. Examples of non-Algol-like imperative languages are COBOL, FORTRAN and BASIC. More modern, very different examples are ABC, Icon and SETL.

Since the reader is already acquainted with at least one or two imperative languages, we take the opportunity to introduce here two less common imperative languages, Icon and PostScript. We shall not examine these languages in detail, but concentrate on some of their more striking features instead.

2.6.1 Icon

Icon programs look deceptively like simple Pascal programs, but more goes on in them than meets the eye. Icon recognizes that many computations yield more than one answer. An example is the well-known expression for the roots of the quadratic equation ax^2+bx+c,

$$x_{1,2}=\frac{-b\pm\sqrt{b^2-4ac}}{2a}$$

which normally yields two answers. Another area in which multiple answers abound is string manipulation, a main application area of Icon. One of the many string manipulation operations Icon features is the function find(p, s), which finds positions in the string s in which p occurs as a substring (positions are counted starting at 1). The expression

write(find("m", "Amsterdam"))

will print 2 (and returns the value 2, which is then discarded), but the expression

every write(find("m", "Amsterdam"))

prints a 2 and then a 9. The reason is that the find function call yields in principle a sequence of two answers, (2|9). Although in a set-based language like SETL this would be regarded as a set, Icon's approach is subtly but fundamentally different: the sequence of answers is a genuine sequence and only as much of it is produced as is needed. The write function asks for only one answer, so the find function is run only until one answer has been obtained. The reserved word every, however, asks for all values the expression will produce, so the find function is reactivated ('resumed') until it is finally exhausted. Likewise, if the result of an expression must fulfil certain conditions, and if the first result fails to fulfil the condition, further results will be tried automatically. For example,

write(5 < find("m", "Amsterdam"))

will print 9, which is indeed the first result from find("m", "Amsterdam")) that fulfils the condition. For explanatory purposes, one could imagine that the following happens. The call of find yields the sequence (2|9), the comparison 5 < selects from the sequence those values which fulfil the condition that they are larger than 5, and write prints (and yields) the first member of the result. In practice, however, this is not what happens, and the sequence (2|9) is never actually constructed. The first call of find actually yields two entities, the value 2 and a **suspended expression**, the find frozen in mid-search. The comparison operation rejects the 2 (since 5<2 is false) and resumes the suspended expression to obtain the next candidate, which then does fulfil the condition and is duly passed on to write. Suspendable expressions are called **generators** in Icon.

The above shows that the comparison operators act as filters on their right-hand operands: a < b yields b if the comparison succeeds, and the empty sequence if it fails. This feature has the remarkable and important property of giving the correct semantics to multiple comparisons. In

a < b < c < d

a < b yields b if a < b, subsequently b < c yields c if b < c and finally, c < d yields d if c < d. If any of the comparisons fails, the empty sequence results. This is then propagated and causes the entire expression to fail.

Icon features a number of constructs and operators to manipulate

```
procedure qroots(a, b, c)
   local det
   det := b*b - 4*a*c
   if det < 0 then fail
   else {
      suspend (-b + sqrt(det)) / (2*a)
      suspend (-b - sqrt(det)) / (2*a)
   }
end
```

Figure 2.39 A generator yielding the roots of a quadratic equation.

generators implicitly and explicitly. For example, Figure 2.39 shows how
the user can write a function to generate both roots of the quadratic equation
ax^2+bx+c. If the determinant is negative, the function fails (by yielding an
empty result sequence), otherwise the function yields the value of the first
root and suspends itself. If the second root is also required, the function is
resumed by whoever is interested, yields the second root of the equation and
again suspends itself; a third resumption will fail. If the determinant is zero,
the same (single) root will be delivered twice by the code of Figure 2.39,
which may or may not be what we want.

The ability to manipulate generators, combined with the tenacity of
many operators to resume generators until an acceptable result is obtained,
makes Icon a very suitable language for both search and combinatorial problems.

2.6.2 PostScript

PostScript is primarily intended as a control language for sophisticated
printing devices. Rather than sending a text file to a printer and relying on
the printer to perform the actions needed to get it printed, a PostScript program is sent to the printer, which instructs the printer in detail. This allows
a great deal of control over the printing process and abstracts from the
actual printer instruction set: a PostScript program is generally printer-
independent. The language consists of two parts, the language proper and a
set of graphical operators for bitmap composition.

PostScript programs a stack machine: the default action is that any
operand is pushed anonymously on a stack, the operand stack, and that any
operator works on the top N elements ($N{\geq}0$) of the operand stack, removes
them and replaces them by M results ($M{\geq}0$). For example, execution of the
program fragment

40 20 add

will push the values 40 and 20 onto the operand stack, where the **add** finds them, removes them and replaces them by the value 60. The operands and operator are in postfix notation; such code is sometimes easier to understand when one reads it as 'stack 40; stack 20; do add'.

There are no variables, but name-value pairs can be created and can serve as a kind of variable. Name-value pairs are stored in dictionaries, which reside on a second stack, the dictionary stack. A new name-value pair is added in the topmost ('current') dictionary, and the value of a name is retrieved by searching the dictionary stack in a top to bottom fashion. For example,

/#copies 3 def

stacks the name **#copies**, stacks a **3** and enters the pair into the current dictionary. The value can be retrieved by just writing its name: **#copies**: the form /**#copies** pushes the name, **#copies** pushes the value.

Commands can be grouped together into procedures by enclosing them in curly brackets: { **add 2 div** } is a procedure that will replace the top two operands by their average. A procedure is a normal value and is therefore pushed on the operand stack:

/average { add 2 div } def

stacks the name **average**, stacks the procedure (as is) and enters the pair into the current dictionary. When, however, the value of the name **average** is retrieved (by using the name), the procedure is not put on the operand stack but on the execution stack. If the execution stack is not empty, commands are taken from there rather than from the program:

40 20 average

will push the values 20 and 40 onto the stack and then perform the procedure { **add 2 div** } on them.

Flow of control is done through built-in operators that work on procedures: the program fragment

a b gt {P} {Q} ifelse

stacks the Boolean value of a > b, stacks two procedures and executes the built-in **ifelse** operator. The latter unstacks three items and pushes either {P} or {Q} onto the execution stack, thus effecting what in a more traditional language would be written as if a > b then P else Q endif.

There are about 250 built-in operators, of which about 100 are concerned with processing the graphics. The latter manipulate bitmaps or fonts to compose a single bitmap, the page to be printed. The operator **showpage** then effects the actual printing.

Summary

- Imperative languages are based on the fully specified and fully controlled manipulation of named data in a step-wise fashion.
- A data declaration binds a name to a type and possibly to a value.
- Typical basic types are integers, characters and real numbers. New types can be made using type constructors. Examples of type constructors are enumerations, arrays and records.
- Types are name-equivalent if they have the same names, and structure-equivalent if they have the same values and allow the same operations. Coercions and casts allow minor evasions of the type system.
- Two features in a language are orthogonal if they can be combined freely without restricting each other in any way.
- Internal state is modified through assignment statements, external state through output statements. The values used derive from expressions.
- The main flow-control mechanisms are sequencing, selection, repetition and routine invocation.
- Run-time errors can be caught by using signals and exceptions. They turn the error into a flow-of-control issue. Both methods have their problems.
- In program construction, four levels of hierarchy can be distinguished: blocks, routines, modules/packages and programs.
- Scope rules determine which declaration or declarations define a given name. If more than one declaration is identified, contextual scope rules are needed to disambiguate.
- Procedures do not yield a value, functions do, and operators are a different notation for functions. The main parameter passing mechanisms are call by value and call by reference.
- A module defines an interface, represented by its specification part. The implementation part is separate and hidden from the interface user. In principle, a separate representation part is needed, but this is generally included in the specification part.
- An abstract data type (ADT) is a named data type defined solely through routines for creating, manipulating and deleting values of that data type; all internal structure is hidden from the user. It differs from a module in that a module *contains* a type definition from which items can be declared, whereas an ADT *is* a type that is used directly to declare items.
- A generic X-unit is a template to derive X-units from. The derivation process is called instantiation. Generic units can be parametrized.
- Final program composition is generally done using the system linker. The main problem is ensuring the consistency of the object files linked. The help of some sort of program management system is indispensable here.

Bibliographical notes

Since the imperative paradigm was for many years the only paradigm in existence and was thus not recognized as a paradigm at all, not much has been written explicitly on it. Much of the paradigm was and still is taught in books and courses on general programming and on data structures. A book that deals with imperative languages explicitly is Ghezzi and Jazayeri (1987), which gives descriptions of operational semantics of most imperative constructs, including co-routines and several parameter passing mechanisms. *The* classical paper in imperative languages is Dijkstra's 'Go To statement considered harmful' (Dijkstra, 1968b). An impression of the work that goes into the design of a large language can be obtained from the 'Rationale for the design of the Ada programming language' (Ichbiah *et al.*, 1979). Material on the rationale of Ada 9X will no doubt be published shortly. Main literature references for particular languages are given in Appendix A.

Exercises

2.1   Algol 60 had no records and no pointers. The programmer who wanted to implement a linked list of real numbers declared two arrays, **real** value[100] and **integer** next[100] and an integer **integer** nrecs. The n-th record corresponds to value[n], which holds the value, and next[n], which holds the index of the next record in the linked list. The integer **nrecs** counts how many records have already been handed out.

   Criticize the above technique on other than aesthetic grounds to somebody who claims that this works just fine, and that records and pointers are semantic sugar real programmers don't need.

2.2   Suppose type T contains N different values.
   a. How many different values does the type **set of** T contain? What are the values for when T is Boolean?
   b. Same question for bags (multi-sets).

2.3   In a language you know, find out how well-separated output and formatting are, and which tricks, if any, are involved.

2.4   Try to find the answers to the questions about selection statements listed in Section 2.4.2 for an imperative language you are not too familiar with (use Modula-2, if applicable).

2.5   For C or another language, consult the documentation and draw up the list of the expression precedence levels, with their associations. Hint: look under 'parenthesized expression' or such to find the name of the top level expression and work down from there.

2.6 In a language that traps integer overflow (for example, Ada or Modula-2), write a test that protects the addition of two integers x and y. Assume the positive and negative extreme integer values given, for example as max_int and min_int. Test your test with all combinations of max_int, max_int–1, max_int/2, 1, 0, –1, min_int/2, min_int–1, min_int for x and y.

2.7 True to the dictum that domains should be represented accurately by types, your local adherent of the Purity of Essence movement proposes to have a new basic data type divisor, which is the required type of the divisor (right-hand operand) of division, and which is identical to the type integer except that it does not include the value 0. This will effectively prevent division by zero and thus eliminate a source of exceptions. Explore the consequences of this idea.

2.8 Fill in the proper exception handling code for the Ada block in Figure 2.40. Assume that Grab_Magtape_Unit(M) makes the program the sole owner of magnetic tape unit number M; Release_Magtape_Unit(M) relinquishes ownership of the magtape unit; each call of Random returns a random number between 0.0 and 1.0; and raise Constraint_Error causes a Constraint_Error exception. So an exception may occur when between 0 and 2 magtape units have been obtained, or not at all. This models program failure at arbitrary points. Make sure that in all situations your code releases all magtape units. Make equally sure that you do not release magtape units that you do not own.

2.9 Why would the scope of a name start at the *end* of its declaration rather than at the point where the name appears?

2.10 Compare the effect of the Algol 68 declaration

```
proc(int)void pr sq =
   if debug
   then (int n): begin print(n); print(n*n) end
   else (int n): begin print(n*n) end
   fi;
```

to that of

```
proc(int)void pr sq = (int n):
   begin
      if debug then print(n); print(n*n)
      else print(n*n)
   fi;
```

```
declare
  Magtape_1, Magtape_2: Magtape_Type;
begin
  if Random > 0.5 then raise Numeric_Error; end if;

  Magtape_1 := Grab_Magtape_Unit(1);
  if Random > 0.5 then raise Numeric_Error; end if;

  Magtape_2 := Grab_Magtape_Unit(2);
  if Random > 0.5 then raise Numeric_Error; end if;


  Release_Magtape_Unit(Magtape_2);
  if Random > 0.5 then raise Numeric_Error; end if;

  Release_Magtape_Unit(Magtape_1);
  if Random > 0.5 then raise Numeric_Error; end if;

exception
  when Numeric_Error =>
    null;   -- (dummy statement for syntactic correctness)
    -- insert code here to release all magtape units grabbed
end;
```

Figure 2.40 Incomplete code for obtaining and releasing access to magnetic tape units.

2.11 Show how the Ada renaming declaration can be used to simulate the pseudo-Ada declaration

from Text_IO import Put(S: String);

3

Object-oriented Languages

Unlike the other paradigms we discuss, the object-oriented paradigm is not just a programming style but also a design method for building systems. **Object-oriented design** typically deals with the problem of building large, complex systems that are subject to change. In building such a system, programming the individual modules is often the least difficult problem. It is much harder to integrate the modules, make the system manageable and understandable and facilitate changes. Object-oriented design tries to present a solution to these problems.

3.1 Principles

The main idea in the object-oriented paradigm is to encapsulate the state of the program in objects, which can be accessed only through operations defined on them. To fully appreciate this programming paradigm, some familiarity with the object-oriented design method is required. We will therefore first look at this design method, although the focus of this chapter (and the book) is of course on programming languages rather than on design methods.

3.1.1 The object-oriented design methodology

Most present-day software systems are built using the classical **waterfall model**, which distinguishes phases such as specification, design and implementation (Boehm, 1976). The design phase uses a **top-down** functional approach. First the functions to be performed by the system are identified. These functions are subsequently divided into subtasks, each of which is analysed and refined. The result is a hierarchical description of the structure of the system, which is the basis for the actual implementation.

Although this top-down design method is certainly better than a more *ad hoc* bottom-up design, it has serious problems. Foremost, it often results in systems that are inflexible and cannot be adapted to changes easily. Experience has shown that the costs of constructing a software system may be significantly smaller than the costs of maintaining the system, and that a significant part of these maintenance costs are due to changes in the requirements of its users. Therefore, it is important that the software system is easy to change.

Most systems built using top-down design lack this property. Each layer in the hierarchy supplies exactly the functionality required by the next highest layer. Any change in the next highest level will invalidate large parts of this tight fit. For example, consider a data entry system initially designed for operation by a single user on a single machine. Now assume it evolves into a distributed (multiple-CPU) system with many users. The initial functional design of the system probably consisted of a 'get command; execute command' loop. With the new system, multiple users can enter commands simultaneously. The initial functional design must therefore be changed drastically, thus having a major effect on the implementation.

A second disadvantage of top-down design is that it does not take into account the potentially large base of software that already exists. In contrast, hardware designers frequently start out by examining a catalogue of components, such as chip sets, backplanes and power supplies. They design their systems based on what useful devices are already available and avoid developing new components as much as possible. Software designers generally put much less emphasis on reusing existing components. The top-down design method makes **software reuse** difficult, because existing software components (routines or packages) seldom do exactly what is required by a new system. The chances are high that existing software uses different data representations or behaves slightly differently from what is needed, or even that it is not clear exactly what the software does. Software reuse is typically limited to certain well-documented library routines, for example for numerical functions.

A third problem with the classical method for building software is that the different phases do not integrate neatly. Different models and notations (languages) are used for the specification, design and implementation of the system, making the transition between phases difficult and restricting the possibilities for automatic checking and program generation.

The object-oriented design methodology is intended to be a major improvement over this classical model. A key idea in object-oriented design is to focus on data objects rather than on functions. The designer does not start out by identifying the different functions of the system, but looks for the objects used in the system. One motivation for this approach is that changes in requirement specifications tend to affect the system's objects less than its functions, so the software becomes less vulnerable. Also, components of an object-oriented system are easier to reuse because, as we will see, they hide the data representation and implementation. The object-oriented design also leads to better integration of the different phases, because each phase now deals with the same kinds of entities: objects.

3.1.2 The principles of object-oriented languages

In an object-oriented language, the state of a program is encapsulated in *objects*. An object contains data and provides operations for accessing these data. The data in an object are not visible directly, but can only be accessed through the operations. The operations are the *interface* to the object for users of the object.

This principle of **data encapsulation** is essential to the object-oriented paradigm. It establishes a firewall between the user of an object and the code implementing it, thus achieving information hiding. In particular, the user does not know or care how the data of an object are represented. As an example, consider a stack object with operations for pushing and popping elements. The stack could be represented as an array, a list or whatever. Since the representation of the stack object is unknown outside the object, it can be changed without affecting the users.

Of course, data encapsulation is also provided by abstract data types (see Chapter 2). A distinguishing feature of object-oriented languages, however, is *inheritance*. Inheritance will be explained in detail in Section 3.3, but roughly speaking, it allows different kinds (or categories) of objects to be built hierarchically, with the most general one at the top and more specific ones at the bottom of the hierarchy. Each kind of object now inherits the operations from the higher levels of the hierarchy. So, an object does not have to implement all the operations itself; rather, it can reuse some operations from object kinds higher up in the hierarchy.

Besides inheritance, another key difference between imperative and object-oriented languages that we will discuss in this chapter is the binding time of operations. In Pascal, if a user calls a named procedure, it is determined during compile time which code will be invoked. In contrast, in an object-oriented language, procedures (operations) are executed by the object they are applied to and it is this object that decides which code will be executed. Since, in general, the object executing the operation is determined at run-time, the choice of which code to execute is made dynamically. This approach is called *dynamic binding*. As we will see, dynamic binding is more flexible than static binding and can ease software maintenance.

Unlike the data structures, the control structures used in most object-oriented languages are conventional and similar to those of imperative languages. An exception is the Smalltalk-80 language, as we will see. In this language control structures are fully integrated in the object-oriented paradigm and consist of operations on special (block) objects.

Below, we will look at the most important concepts used in object-oriented languages. We discuss classes, inheritance, class hierarchies, types, polymorphism, dynamic binding and reference semantics. Finally, we discuss how these concepts together help in solving the problems of flexibility and reuse.

Many object-oriented languages exist, such as Smalltalk-80, Eiffel and C++. We will use C++ for the examples in this chapter, because it is an extension to the ANSI C language discussed in Chapter 2. Different object-oriented languages use different terminologies. We will mainly (but not strictly) use the C++ terminology.

3.2 Classes

A **class** is a description of a kind (category) of object. A class contains:

- A description of the **internal variables** of objects of the class.
- The **operations** that can be applied to objects of the class.

Together, the internal variables and operations constitute the **class members**.

As a simple example, consider the declaration of a class **stack** in C++, shown in Figure 3.1. Although it is possible to write a stack class in C++ supporting generic element types, our example uses a stack of only integer values, to simplify the discussion. The class declaration defines two variables, invisible to users of the class, and declares two functions, **push** and **pop**, that can be applied to stacks.

```
class stack {
  protected:
    int buffer[100];      // variables; invisible to users
    int top;
  public:
    void push(int v);     // operations; visible to users
    int  pop(void);
};
```

Figure 3.1 Declaration of class **stack** in C++.

A class has some properties of both modules and types. It is like a module in that it groups together data and operations on these data. A class resembles a type in that it can be used for creating new variables. A class is essentially an abstract data type (discussed in Section 2.5.3). Unlike abstract data types, however, classes support inheritance, as will be discussed shortly.

In C++, a variable of the class **stack** can be **created** using the allocator **new**, which returns a pointer to the new variable:

```
stack *s;        // declare a pointer to a stack object

s = new stack;   // allocate the stack object itself
```

Such a variable of an abstract data type (class type) is called an **object**. Each object thus created contains new instances of the items declared by the class, so each new stack has its own buffer, top, push and pop. This is a difference from a package in Ada, of which there is only one instance. The storage for a package is allocated only once, whereas storage for object variables is created for each new instance.

The difference between a regular variable and an object is that regular variables can be manipulated directly, whereas objects are manipulated by applying operations to them. Such operation invocations have the following form in C++:

```
s->push(25);     // apply operation push(25) to s
x = s->pop();    // apply operation pop() to s
```

where s is as defined above.

Conceptually, the operation is executed by the receiving object itself, since only the object can access its variables. The statement

```
s->top++;        // increment (protected) top
```

is not allowed, since it directly accesses the object's internal data.

In C++, object creation can also be done directly through a data declaration, as in

```
stack s;
```

Operations on declared objects use the following syntax:

```
s.push(25);      // note the use of '.' instead of '->'
```

Now the variable s contains the stack itself, whereas in our earlier declaration s contained a *pointer* to a stack. For reasons to be discussed later (in Section 3.8), many object-oriented languages do not allow objects to be created in a declaration. A variable in these languages is always a *pointer* to an object, and objects can be created only by explicit dynamic allocation. If all variables are pointers, the syntax of variable declarations does not have to make this explicit, as C++ does with the '*' and '->' symbols. We will come back to this issue in Section 3.8.

The actual code implementing the operations specified in the class declaration is usually separated textually from the class declaration itself. Figure 3.2, for example, gives the C++ code implementing the operations of the class stack specified above. Each operation is preceded by a **scope resolution operator** of the form stack::, giving the name of the operation's class.

C++ also allows operations to be given inside the class declaration. This feature should be used sparingly, however, since it confuses the

```
// Implementation of the operation pop for class stack
int stack::pop(void)
{
    return buffer[--top];
}

// Implementation of the operation push for class stack
void stack::push(int v)
{
    buffer[top++] = v;
}
```

Figure 3.2 Implementation of class stack.

specification part and the implementation part of the class and impairs readability. In our examples we will only use this style for very short operations. Putting an operation inside a class declaration sometimes has a performance advantage, because the compiler inlines the code for such operations, which saves some procedure calling overhead. Whether or not operations are implemented inside or outside the class declaration, they can always directly access the internal variables of their class.

A final important issue is how objects are **initialized** and **deleted**. For these purposes, C++ uses two special kinds of member functions: constructors and destructors. A **constructor** initializes objects of its class; a **destructor** cleans up the object if it is to be deleted. As an example, we can extend the stack class given above by letting users specify the size of the stack (see Figure 3.3).

The constructor function **stack** initializes new objects. Its name is the same as that of the class. It allocates memory for the buffer, using the C++ operator **new**. The destructor function ~**stack** deallocates this memory. When an object is created through a data declaration, these two functions are invoked automatically, as illustrated in Figure 3.4. This has the advantage that the implementer of an object can count on the object always being initialized and destroyed properly. It is possible to have many different constructor functions, with different numbers or types of parameters. The compiler automatically selects the right one, based on the parameters used when creating new objects.

3.3 Inheritance

Inheritance allows us to define new classes by extending existing classes. In this way, we do not have to build each new class from scratch, but we can reuse operations and variables that already exist in other classes.

```
// Declaration of class stack
class stack {
  protected:
    int *buffer;
        // space for buffer allocated dynamically
    int top;
    int stack_size;
        // number of elements the stack can contain
  public:
    // constructor:
    stack(int n)
       {stack_size = n;
        top = 0;
        buffer = new int[stack_size];}

    // destructor:
    ~stack(void)
       {delete buffer;}
    void push(int v);
    int  pop(void);
};
```

Figure 3.3 A declaration of class stack with constructor and destructor operators.

```
main(void)
{
   stack myStack(500);
   // Create stack object with stack size 500. The operation
   // 'myStack.stack(500)' is invoked automatically.

   myStack.push(23);   // use the stack
   ....
   // End of function main(); 'myStack.~stack()' is
   // invoked here automatically.
}
```

Figure 3.4 A procedure using the class stack.

In C++, a class can inherit from an existing class using the following notation:

```
class NewClass : ExistingClass {
   ...  // new member declarations
};
```

The new class is called the **derived class** and the existing class is called the base class.

In general, the derived class inherits all class members (variables as well as operations) from its base class. If the base class itself is derived from yet another class, the members of this class are also inherited. As explained in the next section, classes are frequently organized in a hierarchy (a tree structure) and a class inherits from all its ancestors in this hierarchy.

We will explain inheritance in C++ in more detail by describing a class CalculatorStack that extends the class stack of Figure 3.3. A calculator stack can be used to simulate an electronic calculator. It not only supports push and pop operations, but also arithmetic operations working on the top elements of the stack. For example, to add two numbers, we would first push them, add them and then pop the result, in a manner similar to that described for PostScript.

```
// Declaration of class CalculatorStack
class CalculatorStack : public stack {
  public:
    void add(void);
      // Add two top elements, leave result on the stack
    CalculatorStack(int n): stack(n) {};
      // Constructor just calls stack(n)
};

// Implementation of operation add
void CalculatorStack::add(void)
{
  buffer[top-2] += buffer[top-1];
          // Add top element to second element
  top--;   // Adjust top
}
```

Figure 3.5 A class CalculatorStack.

The declaration and implementation of the new class CalculatorStack are shown in Figure 3.5. For simplicity, we have implemented only one arithmetic operation (addition). The derived class implements the new operation and fully reuses the existing operations and variables. The constructor function for this class first invokes the constructor for the class stack, using a special syntactical form (called a **base class argument** in C++). The body of the constructor is empty, since all variables are initialized in the constructor for class stack. If an object of class CalculatorStack is created, it will contain all variables declared in its own class and in the class stack. Since the declaration of CalculatorStack does not introduce any new variables, objects of this class have the variables top and buffer, declared in the class stack. These variables can be accessed just as if they were declared in the class CalculatorStack itself.

The new class can be used as shown in Figure 3.6. Operations can be applied to the CalculatorStack object just as if they were defined in its own class instead of its base class. Only the operation add is actually defined in its own class.

```
CalculatorStack c(500);        // Create object

c.push(2);                     // Push the two numbers
c.push(3);                     // to be added,
c.add();                       // add them,
x = c.pop();                   // pop result, yields 5
```

Figure 3.6 Using the class CalculatorStack.

3.4 Inheritance and class hierarchies

Inheritance is particularly useful if we need to define many related classes. Suppose, for example, we want to define different classes for several kinds of publications, such as books, newspapers, magazines, technical reports, PhD theses, and so on. Objects of these classes each contain information for one particular publication, such as the *New York Times* of 29 February 1992 or the *Hitchhiker's Guide to the Galaxy*.

We could of course define one class for each kind of publication, but we would soon discover that there is a significant overlap between these classes. For example, for all publications we might want to have operations that keep track of the number of copies printed. Likewise, for both technical reports and PhD theses, we want to store the institute at which they were issued. On the other hand, some operations will be unique to certain classes. Only books have ISBN numbers and only PhD theses have supervisors.

Using inheritance, we can organize the classes in a **hierarchy** or *tree*, as shown in Figure 3.7. The idea now is that each class only defines those operations and variables that are specific to its class (such as ISBN numbers for books), and *inherits* members defined higher up in the hierarchy. At the top of this hierarchy we have the new class Publication, supporting operations that are useful for all publications, so they can be invoked by objects from all classes.

Likewise, we have introduced a class Periodical. The operations of this class (SubscriptionRate and Date) can also be invoked by objects of the classes Newspaper and Magazine. Finally, we have defined a class Report with three subclasses.

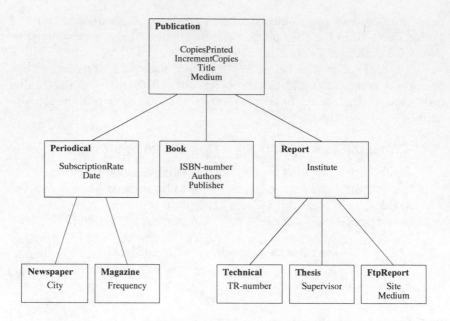

Figure 3.7 A hierarchy of classes, each defining one or more operations.

A frequent problem with such hierarchies is that operations implemented high up in the hierarchy may not be correct or optimal for all derived classes. Our publications hierarchy shows one clear example of this phenomenon. We want to have an operation **Medium** that returns the medium used for the publication. Since virtually all publications are printed on paper, it makes sense to implement the operation in the root of the hierarchy (in the class **Publication**) and have it return, say, the string "**paper**". This operation is then inherited by all subclasses. Not all publications are printed on paper, however, so subclasses should be able to **override** the implementation. In our example, an FTP report is stored on a computer and can be accessed over a network (FTP stands for File Transfer Protocol, which is a widely used protocol for transferring files between machines). The subclass **FtpReport** therefore overrides the operation **Medium**. The operation as defined in the class **FtpReport** will return a different string, say "**computer**". In general, higher levels of the hierarchy define the default operations, and lower levels can override them with specializations.

Overriding can be desirable for other reasons as well. For example, the subclass may be able to implement the operation more efficiently. The new operation will produce the same result, but it will be faster. Also, it is sometimes useful to extend the behaviour of an operation. For example, the new operation will execute some code of its own and also invoke the original operation that it overrides.

3.5 Inheritance and types

We will now take a closer look at the resemblances and differences between classes and types. In some languages, classes *are* types, but other languages treat them differently.

In C++ a class is essentially a user-defined type. A class derived from a base class supports at least the same operations as the base class. In this view, we can regard the derived class as a *subtype* of the base class. Therefore, we can assign variables of the derived class to variables of the base class.

To illustrate this idea, reconsider the hierarchy of publications shown in Figure 3.7. In Figure 3.8, we create two objects, of classes Report and Thesis, and have two variables r and t point to these objects. (The initialization of these objects is not shown here.)

It is now legal to have r point to the object of class Thesis, since any operation applied to a report can also be applied to a thesis. So, the assignment r = t; is legal. It is important to note that this assignment does not truncate t, since only a pointer is copied; t still has its Supervisor field, but r does not allow access to it.

```
Report *r;              // r points to object of type Report
Thesis *t;              // t points to object of type Thesis

r = new Report;         // allocate r
t = new Thesis;         // allocate t
sv = t->Supervisor();   // legal operation invocation
r = t;                  // legal assignment
inst = r->Institute();  // legal operation invocation
sv = r->Supervisor();   // illegal, rejected by compiler
```

Figure 3.8 C++ code illustrating subclassing and subtyping.

The operation invocation r–>Supervisor() is illegal, because r is declared as a reference to Report and the operation Supervisor is not defined for class Report. The fact that, at run time, the object currently pointed to by r happens to support Supervisor does not change this. The operation invocation is simply rejected by the compiler, just as a C compiler would reject the modulo operator on a floating point variable even though the variable's current value might happen to be an integral number:

```
float x = 3;            // a floating point variable,
                        // initialized to an integral value
int n;                  // an integer variable

n = 8 % x;              // illegal, rejected by compiler
```

Not every object-oriented language considers classes to be types. The reason is that operations can be overridden in subclasses, making it possible for subclasses to behave entirely differently from their base class. In the example given earlier, the class FtpReport overrides the operation Medium and lets it return a string indicating the right medium for FTP reports. In general, however, the redefined operation can do something else. For example, a subclass of the standard integer type can redefine the plus operator and have it return the product of its operands. In this case, the new subclass cannot really be considered as a subtype of integers.

Smalltalk-80 is an example of a language that does not treat classes as types. Instead, it considers a class to be an object. The operations defined by the class-object include at least one to create new instances of the class.

3.6 Inheritance and polymorphism

In imperative languages, the declaration of a procedure specifies the type of each formal parameter. For a **polymorphic** procedure, on the other hand, the type of the parameters is not fixed, so a formal parameter can correspond to actual parameters of different types in different calls.

Suppose we write a program that needs several different kinds of lists, such as a list of integers, a list of reals, and so on. In a language such as Ada, we could write a generic list type, as explained in Section 2.5.4. With generics, we need a separate instantiation for each element type. Also, with generic units we cannot declare a single list containing elements of different types, which would perhaps also be useful.

With inheritance, we can solve the problem in a different way. Inheritance allows polymorphic procedures and data structures that are statically type-checked. In Section 3.4 we described how inheritance results in a hierarchy of types. Because of this hierarchy, it is possible to implement polymorphic functions that accept parameters of a set of classes related through inheritance.

As an example, any procedure that has a formal parameter of type reference to Publication can also be called with references to type Book as an actual parameter. Likewise, it is possible to build lists containing references to different kinds of publications. As discussed in the previous section, such data structures are legal, because all elements support all required operations, even though they are of different classes.

In C++, we can implement a list of publications as follows:

```
struct PublListItem {
    struct PublListItem *next;  // pointer to next list element
    Publication *item;          // pointer to item itself
};
```

which allows us to store any kind of object from the Publication hierarchy in the list.

Some languages (for example Eiffel and Smalltalk-80) organize all classes in the system as one big hierarchy, with one class (the root) at the top. Operations that are common to all classes are put in the root class. With such a hierarchy, it is even possible to write polymorphic procedures that work for any type of parameter. If a parameter is declared as a reference to the root class, any object reference can be passed as the actual parameter. Of course, this also means that only operations defined for the root class may be used in the implementation of this procedure.

3.7 Dynamic binding

Now that we have looked at inheritance and polymorphism, we can explain the principle of dynamic binding in more detail. As an introductory example, we will use the linear list of publications described above. Assume we want to print the title and medium of all items on the list of publications MyPublList. The C++ code to do this is:

```
struct PublListItem *ip;

for (ip = MyPublList; ip != 0; ip = ip->next) {
    Publication *pub = ip->item;
    printf("%s %s", pub->Title(), pub->Medium());
}
```

This code traverses the list and, for each publication on the list, the operations Title and Medium are invoked and their results are printed.

As we have explained above, it is perfectly legal for the list to contain objects from different subclasses of Publication, since each of these objects supports the operations defined by Publication.

Now assume one of the elements on our list is of class FtpReport. This class redefines the operation Medium. The crucial question is: which operation Medium should we invoke for this element, the one in class Publication or the one in class FtpReport? The answer depends on the *binding* regime used by the language.

If the language uses **static binding**, the static type of pub determines the class from which the operation is taken. In our example, this class is Publication, since pub is declared as a pointer to Publication.

With **dynamic binding** (or **late binding**), on the other hand, the decision is made dynamically, by the run-time system. The system looks at the class of the object to which pub currently points. Since this is class FtpReport, the system decides to invoke the operation Medium defined in FtpReport.

Although the differences between the two binding regimes may appear subtle at first sight, they are very important. In fact, Meyer (the designer of Eiffel) calls static binding in an object-oriented language the 'gravest possible crime in object-oriented technology' (Meyer, 1992b), because it may cause the wrong version of an operation to be invoked. Indeed, in the example above, invoking **Publication**'s operation **Medium** would give the wrong result, since an FTP report is not distributed on paper.

Implementing the above example correctly using only static binding would be more complicated. We could let each publication keep track of its own class, give the operation in **FtpReport** a different name (for example **FtpMedium**) and put explicit tests in our code for selecting the right operation, as shown in Figure 3.9.

```
for (ip = head; ip != 0; ip = ip->next) {
    Publication *pub = ip->item;
    FtpReport *ftp;

    switch (pub->MyClass()) {
      case FTP_REPORT:
        ftp = (FtpReport *) pub;    // cast pub to right type
        printf("%s %s", ftp->Title(), ftp->FtpMedium());
        break;
      default:
        printf("%s %s", pub->Title(), pub->Medium());
        break;
    }
}
```

Figure 3.9 Printing a list of publication items using static binding.

If we add new kinds of publications that use other media, however, we would have to modify the switch statement of Figure 3.9 and add more cases. For example, to add a CD-ROM medium, we would have to write an operation **CDMedium**, add the declaration

```
cdRom *cd;
```

and add the following case to the switch statement:

```
case CD_ROM:
    cd = (cdRom *) pub;        // cast pub to right type
    printf("%s %s", cd->Title(), cd->CDMedium());
    break;
```

All in all, this simple extension requires many changes to existing code. With dynamic binding, on the other hand, all the testing and selecting is done automatically by the run-time system. The only modification to the code would be to add a new class cdRom. Thus, dynamic binding used in this way makes it easier to maintain programs.

Dynamic binding in object-oriented languages should not be confused with the form of dynamic binding discussed in Section 2.5.1 for imperative languages. Dynamic binding of operations looks at the class of the object to which the operation is applied (and possibly at ancestors of this class); it does not look at *scopes*, as dynamic binding in imperative languages does.

A major advantage of dynamic binding as used in C++ is that it still allows static type checking. If an operation is applied to an object, the compiler cannot always determine *which* operation will be executed, but it can make sure that the operation *exists* and that the invocation is thus legal.

Unfortunately, dynamic binding also has its price: there is some execution time overhead, since the run-time system must decide dynamically which operation to invoke. Object-oriented languages all support dynamic binding, but because of the execution time costs, they do not all enforce it.

The hybrid approach is best illustrated by C++. By default, C++ uses static binding, because it is less expensive. However, C++ also allows dynamic binding. To obtain dynamic binding the declaration of the base class Publication must be changed as follows:

```
class Publication {
  virtual char *Medium(void);
  ....
};
```

The operation Medium is now called a **virtual function**. It can be invoked as any normal operation, but if it is redefined in a derived class, the selection of which operation to invoke is made dynamically instead of statically. The overhead of virtual functions in C++ is small and it is only paid in those cases in which dynamic binding is actually needed, since the compiler knows in advance which functions are virtual. (In practice, the overhead is that of table indexing.) For member functions that are not declared as virtual, C++ uses static binding.

Smalltalk-80, on the other hand, uses a purely dynamic approach, but without static type checking. In Smalltalk-80, each class is represented at run time by a table of the operations it implements together with the names of these operations. If an operation is applied to an object, the object looks in the table of its class to see if an operation with the right name is defined there. If so, it executes the operation and returns the result. If not, it will look at the description of its base class to see if the operation is implemented there. If so, it will execute that operation, else it will examine the base class of its base class. This search continues until either the operation is found or the top of the hierarchy is reached. In the latter case, the object does not know how to perform the operation, so it gives an error message, probably causing the program to abort.

This highly dynamic approach makes Smalltalk-80 very flexible, but it also renders compile-time applicability checking impossible. If a wrong operation is applied to an object, the user will be told at run time that the object does not know what to do with the operation. In C++, on the other hand, if the user applies an illegal operation to an object, the compiler will say that *it* does not know what to do with the operation. So with Smalltalk-80 one loses the benefit of an early warning. In the worst case, this can even mean that such an error is not detected until the program is in use.

3.8 Reference semantics

Our C++ examples illustrating subtyping and polymorphism use pointers to objects instead of plain objects. The difference between the two is rather subtle, and is even hidden from the user in some languages (but not in C++). We will address this important semantic issue here.

In imperative languages, data are usually accessed through named variables. A variable R, for example, may be declared as a record with two integers in it. Although, strictly speaking, R in some sense 'refers to' or 'gives access to' the record, one often says that R *is* the record. And indeed, in most imperative languages, if R is copied the record gets copied, and if R is passed as a value parameter, it is actually the record that is passed.

In most object-oriented languages, however, there is often a clear distinction between a variable and the object it names. Objects contain data, whereas variables contain references to objects. This difference is illustrated in Figure 3.10.

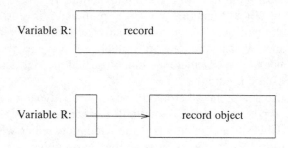

Figure 3.10 Difference between a variable naming a record (used in imperative languages) and a variable containing a reference to a record object (used in object-oriented languages).

The difference between these two models is best seen in procedure calls. In an imperative language, if R is passed as an actual value parameter to a procedure, as in

```
f(R);
```

then the *value* of R, consisting of a record with two integers, is copied and passed to f. This is called *call by value* semantics. In most object-oriented languages, on the other hand, when R is passed as a parameter, a reference to the record object will be passed automatically, since R contains this reference and not the data themselves. The called procedure can access the object in the usual way, by applying operations to it. This is called **reference semantics**.

So, in most object-oriented languages, variables are just names that contain references (pointers) to objects; they do not contain data themselves. Not all languages take this pure view, because pointers introduce some overhead. As an example, let us look at C++. As we discussed in Section 3.2, objects in C++ can be created through a declaration or with the new construct. For example, the following code

```
Report r;          // object r is allocated statically
Report *rp1, *rp2;  // two pointer variables

rp1 = &r;          // rp1 now points to object r
rp2 = new Report;  // allocate object dynamically
```

declares a new variable r containing an object of class Report and two variables, rp1 and rp2, that are pointers to report objects. The variable rp1 is set to point to object r, while rp2 will contain a reference to a newly created Report object.

The reason for having two ways of creating objects in C++ has everything to do with efficiency. The memory for objects such as r can be allocated on the language run-time stack, and is deallocated automatically at the end of the block in which it is declared, just as normal local variables in imperative languages. Dynamically created objects, on the other hand, cannot be allocated on the stack, making allocation and deallocation more expensive. In general, dynamic creation is more flexible but also has a higher overhead.

So in C++ the usage of pointers to objects is always explicit, unlike in Smalltalk-80. One subtle point is that dynamic binding (through virtual functions) and polymorphism only work for *pointers* to objects. Consider the following example:

```
Report r;
FtpReport f;

r.Medium();   // invokes Medium in class Report
r = f;        // copies part of f into r and coerces it
r.Medium();   // also invokes Medium in class Report
```

During the assignment r = f, the type of the right-hand side is coerced to that of the left-hand side (which is Report), because the memory allocated for object r is fixed and is probably less than that of object f (since FtpReport inherits from class Report). In effect, static binding is used in this case. In Figure 3.8 we showed a remarkably similar example, except that we used a pointer assignment there, which resulted in dynamic binding. Most other object-oriented languages do not have this confusing problem, since they support dynamic object allocation only.

Shared references

If objects are referred to by pointers, different objects can contain pointers to the same object x; in this case, the objects are said to **share** object x. The possibility of object sharing is one of the main reasons why reference semantics are often used in object-oriented languages.

As an example, consider the objects shown in Figure 3.11-a. Object A contains variables (class members) that are references to objects B and C. Objects B, C and F all share a reference to object E. This form of sharing is important for modelling real systems. For example, it makes a difference whether two objects share a reference to an object or references to private copies of it, as is the case in Figure 3.11-b. If, say, object B in Figure 3.11-a applies an operation to object E, the other objects sharing E will observe the effects of this operation. In Figure 3.11-b, on the other hand, object E_1 would be changed by the operation, but objects E_2 and E_3 remain unaffected, so objects C and F do not see any changes. Which of the two forms is desirable depends on the application. (See the exercises for a real-world example.)

The possibility of shared references presents problems to the language implementation. In particular, it is difficult to determine when the memory occupied by an object may be deallocated, because several objects may contain references to this object. In general, an object can be destroyed if no variable or other object contains a reference to it. In Figure 3.11, there are no references to object F, so this object might be deleted. As for imperative languages, the task of deallocating memory may either lie with the programmer or with the system. In Smalltalk-80 and Eiffel, the system takes care of this task, using **automatic garbage collection**. C++ leaves garbage collection up to the programmer, except that objects allocated on the stack are deallocated automatically at the end of the block in which they are declared.

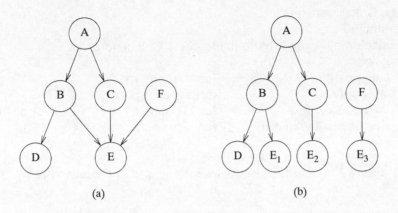

Figure 3.11 Objects containing references to each other. (a) Object E is shared by three other objects; (b) three objects each contain a private copy of E.

3.9 When to use inheritance?

We have now looked at the most important concepts in object-oriented languages. An important issue we have not addressed yet is how to use the new concepts, in particular inheritance. In this section, we will look briefly at this issue.

Inheritance is usually used for defining a class that is a specialization of an existing class. For example, the calculator stack of Figure 3.5 is a specialization of the normal stack class of Figure 3.3. It has all the properties of a normal stack, but it adds some new ones of its own. In object-oriented jargon, the class and its base class have an **is-a** relationship: a calculator stack *is a* stack.

Another form of relationship between classes is also possible, in which the classes do not inherit from each other, but one of them is used as a member in the other one. To illustrate, we could also have implemented the calculator stack as shown in Figure 3.12. (For brevity, we implemented the operations inside the class declaration, which is allowed in C++.)

The class CalculatorStack now contains an internal variable cs pointing to an object of the class stack, which holds the values of the calculator stack. The CalculatorStack is a normal user of the class stack, so it cannot access the internal variables of object cs and neither does it inherit the push and pop operations. Instead, it implements all operations itself, using the push and pop operations defined in the class stack. Both classes have operations named push and pop, but there can be no confusion, since they are applied to objects of different classes.

In the second implementation, the class and the member class have a so-called **has** relationship: a calculator stack *has* a stack. This relationship is fundamentally different from inheritance. It can also appear in imperative

```
class CalculatorStack {
  protected:
    stack *cs;    // invisible outside class CalculatorStack
  public:
    void push(int v)           {cs->push(v);}
    int  pop(void)             {return cs->pop();}
    void add(void)             {cs->push(cs->pop() + cs->pop());}
    CalculatorStack(int n)     {cs = new stack(n);}
};
```

Figure 3.12 An alternative implementation of class CalculatorStack.

languages. Records in Ada, for example, can have fields that are other records, and packages can contain other packages.

Choosing the right relationships between classes is an important issue in the design of an object-oriented program. In the example above, both approaches are feasible, but frequently only one approach is right. For example, defining a car as a specialization of a tyre is an obvious mistake, since a car has tyres but it is not a tyre.

There are also other, less common ways of using inheritance (Budd, 1991). One example is a new class that inherits members from several base classes, thus allowing more flexible classification schemes. This feature is called **multiple inheritance**. In C++, for example, the notation

```
class PublishedThesis : public Book, public Thesis {
  ...
};
```

can be used to define a new class, PublishedThesis, which inherits variables and operations from two base classes, Book and Thesis.

A problem with multiple inheritance is the possibility of name conflicts. If two or more base classes have an operation with the same name, we have an ambiguity. In C++, this problem can be solved using the scope resolution operator (::) as prefix for every occurrence of an otherwise ambiguous name (so the programmer must name the class from which the operator is inherited). In Eiffel, the programmer can rename some of the inherited operations in the derived class.

3.10 Discussion

Object-oriented languages try to provide a solution to the problems of flexibility and software reuse. We will discuss these two problems in somewhat more detail below.

Flexibility is obtained by using data access rather than functions for modularization. Classes are used to hide the internal data representation of objects from users, much as with abstract data types. If the format of the data has to be changed owing to external factors, only the class containing the data has to be updated, but not the code using the class. Unlike abstract data types, classes support inheritance, which can be used to structure classes in a hierarchy, as shown by Figure 3.7.

Another feature that makes object-oriented programs easier to change is dynamic binding. Programs written in imperative languages often use records with variants for storing data with similar types. Such programs typically contain many explicit tests to check the variant and determine which procedure is the right one for it. If a new variant is added, all these statements have to be located and modified. With dynamic binding, the changes are localized, thus easing maintenance.

The second problem object-oriented languages try to address is the reuse of code. The primary language mechanisms supporting reuse are classes and inheritance. Still, an important obstacle remains that makes reuse difficult. If a programmer is to reuse a module, he or she should know exactly what the module does. But now consider the declaration of a class in C++. The declaration of the class merely gives the names of the operations and the number and types of their parameters. It does not even say which values the input parameters may have, let alone what the operations do with these values. This information can of course be obtained by carefully studying the implementation of the class, but this is obviously not how business should be done. The last resort is documentation, but this is all too often absent or out of date.

The Eiffel language addresses this problem to some extent, by allowing classes and their operations to contain conditions that must be satisfied when an operation is entered or exited. Such conditions are called **preconditions** and **postconditions**, respectively.

A precondition forces the user of a class to obey certain rules. For example, the precondition in a square root function could be that the parameter supplied must be non-negative. Eiffel in fact supports a theory called **programming by contract** based on preconditions and postconditions, which can be used for building libraries. This theory also takes inheritance into account. For example, if an operation is redefined in a derived class, then the precondition of the redefined operation must at least be as strong as that of the original operation.

3.11 Example languages

Often a particular language (for example, Ada) is claimed to be object-oriented. What is usually meant by this is that the language can be used in combination with the object-oriented design method. We think an object-oriented language should at least support data encapsulation, inheritance and dynamic binding.

Some definitions also require that the language regards *all* entities in the system as objects. In some object-oriented languages, an expression such as '5 – 3' is interpreted as applying the operation 'subtract 3 and return result' to the integer object '5'. The computational model then consists of objects that invoke each other's operations. Other languages do not take this uniform approach and treat objects and normal variables differently. In C++, programmers can use regular variables as well as user-defined objects.

A useful distinction is that between a **pure** and a **hybrid** object-oriented language. A pure language enforces programming in an object-oriented style. A hybrid language allows but does not enforce object-oriented programming. In C++, for example, it is still possible to program in the traditional style, since the language is a superset of C.

Although the original Ada 83 standard has few facilities for object-oriented programming, the revised language, known as Ada 9X (Barnes, 1994), has remedied this situation. It provides a special kind of record, called a **tagged record**, from which new types may be derived. A type R derived from a tagged record type T contains the fields of T and supports the operations (functions and procedures) provided by T. In addition, it is possible to add new fields and operations to R. Tagged records can be seen as an extension of **derived types**, which allow the addition of new operations only. With any tagged record type T, a new **class wide** type T'Class is associated, consisting of the union of T and all types derived from it. If a variable of type T'Class is passed as a parameter to an operation, dynamic binding is used to determine which operation is invoked. All in all, the Ada 9X features for object-oriented programming resemble those of Eiffel and C++, using tagged records and derived types for implementing objects and inheritance.

Other examples of object-oriented languages are Smalltalk-80, C++, Objective C, Eiffel and Self. Simula was the first language to use a class concept. CLU uses abstract data types, but not inheritance. Below, we will look at C++, Eiffel and Smalltalk-80.

3.11.1 C++

C++ was designed by Stroustrup at AT&T Bell Labs. The language is almost compatible with ANSI C, but in addition supports object-oriented features such as classes, multiple inheritance and dynamic binding. An important goal in its design was keeping the language efficient to implement. We have already shown many small fragments of C++ code. Below, we will fill in some missing details.

Classes in C++ are similar to structures in C, except that the visibility of the class members can be specified explicitly, as described below. Class members can be variables and functions (operations).

C++'s inheritance model supports dynamic binding (through *virtual* functions) and multiple inheritance. Also, C++ has complicated but flexible mechanisms for controlling the visibility of class members. Members can be declared as either public, protected or private. In the stack example of Figures 3.1 and 3.3, the operations are all made available to users by prefixing them with the keyword public; the data are prefixed by the keyword protected and are not available to users. If another class inherits items from the class stack, however, the protected items can be used by the derived class, as shown by the CalculatorStack example of Figure 3.5. A class member can also be prefixed by the keyword private, in which case it is invisible in derived classes.

   Note that the stack example obeys the principle of data encapsulation, which prescribes that the object's data should be hidden. Since C++ programmers have explicit control over visibility, however, they can also ignore the principle and let class users manipulate the variables directly.

3.11.2 Eiffel

Unlike C++, Eiffel is not an extension to an existing language. Instead, it is a language especially designed for object-oriented programming, using a new syntax. The language described below is Eiffel version 3, the current and official version. Eiffel is designed by Meyer and managed by the Nonprofit International Consortium for Eiffel (NICE), which consists of users and developers.

   Eiffel has a fully static type system, without type checking loopholes. Eiffel provides five basic types: integer, real, double, Boolean and character. These basic types are so-called **expanded classes**. Variables of such a class contain the objects themselves (data) rather than pointers to objects. The distinction between normal and expanded classes is important, because reference semantics is used for normal classes and call by value semantics for expanded classes. Also, an assignment statement x := y will copy the *value* of y into x if they are of an expanded class type. For normal class types, on the other hand, a *pointer* will be copied.

   For variables of expanded classes the assignment x := y essentially is only allowed if x and y have the same type. If the class of y is derived from that of x, the assignment is not allowed, since the memory allocated for x might be smaller than that for y. In comparison, C++ allows such assignments but, as a consequence, has to resort to static binding for declared objects (see Section 3.8).

   The Eiffel type system also supports generics. The array type, for example, is actually a generic class type that takes a type parameter indicating the type of the array elements. Polymorphic procedures can also be defined, using inheritance, as described in Section 3.5.

   Unlike C++, the semantics of operation invocations in Eiffel are based on dynamic binding only. However, if the Eiffel compiler can determine statically which operation will be invoked, it may optimize away the overhead of dynamic binding. In C++, this optimization is essentially done by the programmer, not the compiler. The C++ programmer declares operations as being either *virtual* (resulting in dynamic binding) or *normal* (resulting in static binding).

The module structure of Eiffel also is different from that of C++. All Eiffel code appears inside classes; there is no other module concept (such as a file in C++). The programmer has control over the visibility of class members. For each variable or operation, the programmer can indicate whether it is to be visible only inside the class, visible to all users of the class, or visible only to certain users of the class.

An example Eiffel class is given in Figure 3.13. The class implements a generic stack type. The type of the elements is denoted by the generic parameter G. The example also illustrates other features of Eiffel, such as preconditions and postconditions. A stack that can contain 500 integers is created as follows:

```
s: STACK[INTEGER] -- declare a variable of type 'stack of integers'
!!s.make(500)         -- create a stack object, have s point to it
```

This code creates an object (the two exclamation marks are Eiffel syntax for object creation) and invokes the user-defined creation procedure make.

An important difference between Eiffel and C++ is that Eiffel supports automatic garbage collection of objects that are no longer accessible. The Eiffel statement

```
obj := Void
```

merely indicates that variable obj no longer points to any object. If there are other variables pointing to the object, however, the object will *not* be deleted. In contrast, the C++ delete command immediately throws away the object, even if there are other references to it. Clearly, the Eiffel approach is much safer.

3.11.3 Smalltalk-80

Smalltalk-80 was developed at Xerox PARC. Most Smalltalk-80 implementations include a programming environment that integrates many tools. For example, the editor and the command line interpreter use syntax similar to that of the language itself. The Smalltalk-80 environment also promotes the use of bitmap graphics, windows and pointing devices (for example, a mouse). The environment is open to the user; users have all Smalltalk-80 source code on-line and can change everything.

All variables in Smalltalk-80 are references to objects. The language is untyped, so the same variable can point to different classes of objects at different times, making it trivial to implement polymorphic classes and operations. An object is created dynamically, using a **new** construct, which specifies its class. For example

```
class STACK [G] creation make
feature
  push (v: G) is                        -- Push 'v' onto top.
    require                             -- A precondition
      not full
    do
      representation.put (v, last);
      last := last + 1
    ensure                             -- Postconditions
      not empty; last = old last + 1;
      top = v
    end;
  pop is                               -- Remove top element.
    require
      not empty
    do
      last := last -1
    end;
  top: G is                            -- Top element.
    require
      not empty
    do
      Result := representation.item (last);
    end;
  empty: BOOLEAN is                    -- Is the stack without elements?
    do
      Result := (last = 0)
    end;
  full: BOOLEAN is                     -- Is the stack full?
    do
      Result := (last = capacity)
    end
feature                                -- Initialization
  make (n: INTEGER) is                 -- Create a stack with 'n' elements.
    do
      last := 0; capacity := n;
      !! representation.make (0, n)     -- Create an array
    end
feature {NONE}                         -- Internal variables
  last, capacity: INTEGER;
  representation: ARRAY [G];
end -- class STACK
```

Figure 3.13 A class stack in Eiffel.

```
myStack <- new stack
```

creates a new stack object and stores a reference to the object in the variable myStack. The **new** construct allocates space for the internal variables of the object. Objects are deallocated automatically, using garbage collection.

The Smalltalk-80 terminology and syntax are unusual. An operation is called a **method**. When an object's method is invoked, conceptually a **message** is sent to the object. The receiving object will accept the message, execute the method, and return a result. The syntax of method invocations is illustrated below:

```
myStack push:25      % send push message to myStack,
                     % passing 25 as parameter
x <- myStack pop     % send pop message to myStack,
                     % store result in x
```

A message in Smalltalk-80 can be either a *unary* or a *keyword* message. A unary message does not have parameters; it merely specifies the message name. For example, pop used above is a unary message. A keyword message contains one or more keywords, one for each parameter. The push message uses one keyword. Keywords and parameters are separated by a colon. As another example,

```
flightReservations reserveOnFlight:'KL641'
         date:'25dec93' seats:2 inClass:'E'
```

sends a message with four parameters to the object flightReservations.

Keyword messages are also used for implementing **control structures**. For example, the predefined class Boolean implements a message ifTrue that takes a piece of code as a parameter, and only executes it if the Boolean object to which the message is sent contains the value True. The following code illustrates this idea.

```
flightReservations isEmpty:'KL641'
   (ifTrue: [flightReservations cancelFlight:'KL641'])
```

This code first sends an isEmpty message to the object flightReservations, passing a flight number as a parameter. The result returned by this object will be a Boolean object. This Boolean object is sent the message ifTrue, with a so-called **block** of code as a parameter. It is essential here that the block of code is not yet evaluated, but is passed literally to the Boolean object. Only if this object is the object True will it execute the code block, so sending a cancelFlight message to the object flightReservations. The advantage of the Smalltalk-80 approach is that programmers can create their own control structures.

Unlike C++, the visibility of class members is fixed in Smalltalk-80: all operations defined in the class are available to users, and all variables are inaccessible. If the class designer wants to make the value of a variable available to its users, an extra operation must be written that returns the value.

In conclusion, Smalltalk-80 is a pure object-oriented language. It treats all entities as objects and supports classes and inheritance. Even control structures are expressed through message passing between objects.

Summary

- The object-oriented paradigm not only deals with programming, it is also a paradigm for designing systems, in particular large and complex ones. Object-oriented design tries to make software systems easier to maintain and change. In addition, it eases the reuse of existing software.
- The key idea in object-oriented design is to focus on the objects in the system, rather than on the system's functions. Objects are less vulnerable than functions to changes in the system specification.
- The most important concepts in object-oriented languages are objects, classes, inheritance, polymorphism and dynamic binding.
- A class describes a category of objects. It contains a description of the internal variables of the objects and the operations that can be applied to the objects.
- If a new class is defined, it can inherit variables and operations from an existing base class. Inheritance leads to a hierarchy of classes, where each class inherits from its ancestors in the hierarchy tree. With multiple inheritance, a class can inherit directly from multiple base classes.
- Some languages treat classes as types. They apply type-checking rules similar to those for subtypes. Since a class can redefine the behaviour of an operation inherited from one of its ancestors, viewing classes as types may not always be appropriate. Other languages regard classes as objects.
- The class hierarchy makes it easy to support polymorphic procedures, which take the parameters of different types. The normal static type-checking rules (if any) can be used for polymorphic procedures.
- With dynamic binding, if an object executes an operation, the run-time class of the object determines which code will be executed. With static binding, the choice is made at compile time. For object-oriented languages, dynamic binding is to be preferred: if a class has redefined an operation, it is often an error to execute the original operation defined in an ancestor class.
- In most object-oriented languages, variables always contain pointers to objects. Other languages are less pure, and also store scalar data in variables or let the programmer decide.

- An important issue in object-oriented programming is when to use inheritance. Inheritance is usually appropriate if the 'is-a' relation holds between two classes, but not if the 'has' relation applies.

Bibliographical notes

Many books about object-oriented programming exist. Cox (1986) presents a strong case for dynamic binding; the book uses Objective C as an example language. The book by Budd (1991) is another good introductory text, which uses four different languages (C++, Smalltalk-80, Objective C and Object Pascal). The book by Blair *et al.* (1991) contains papers on several issues in object-oriented languages, systems and applications. A useful overview paper on the object-oriented paradigm is Korson and McGregor (1990).

The C++ language is described in Stroustrup (1991). The rationale behind its design is described in Ellis and Stroustrup (1991). C programmers who want to learn C++ can use the much simpler book by Pohl (1989), which is a good introduction to the features that C++ adds to C. The Smalltalk-80 language is described in full detail in Goldberg and Robson (1983). Meyer (1988) discusses object-oriented design and contains a description of the Eiffel language. A more recent book on Eiffel version 3 is Meyer (1992b). A research paper by Meyer (1990) describes the experiences in using the Eiffel language for implementing a collection of libraries. Another paper describes design by contract (Meyer, 1992a).

Other relevant sources are: the proceedings of the annual ACM SIG-PLAN Conference on Object-Oriented Programming Systems, Languages and Applications (OOPSLA), the proceedings of the European Conference on Object-Oriented Programming (ECOOP), and the *Journal of Object-Oriented Programming*.

Exercises

3.1 Suppose you want to define a class describing properties of personal computers, such as the type and speed of the CPU and hard disk, amount of memory, capacity of the power supply, and so on. A colleague of yours has already implemented classes for several of these components. How would you reuse these classes for your new class? Would you use (multiple) inheritance?

3.2 The Smalltalk-80 language uses inheritance for its **predefined classes** (similar to predefined types in imperative languages). Classes exist for integers, reals, numerical data, scalar data, arrays, lists, trees, and so on. Think of how you would organize these classes (and any others you can think of) in a class hierarchy, using inheritance.

3.3 Make a comparison between abstract data types (discussed in Chapter 2) and classes.

3.4 In Ada one can write a generic function that accepts parameters of different types. Compare this approach with polymorphic operations in object-oriented languages.

3.5 Three objects, A, B and C, in a larger program each use an object R that supplies random numbers. Should A, B and C each use a different copy of R or should they share one object R? Discuss the consequences of both choices.

3.6 Consider the following C++ declarations:

```
class T {
   public:
      virtual void f(void);
};

class S: public T {
   public:
      virtual void f(void);
};

T x;
S y;
T *p;
```

and the following operation invocations:

```
p = &x;
p->f();      // 1
p = &y;
p->f();      // 2
x.f();       // 3
y.f();       // 4
x = y;
x.f();       // 5
```

For each of the invocations of **f**, determine whether the function in class **T** or class **S** will be executed.

3.7 C++ and Eiffel use different mechanisms for deallocating objects that are no longer used. C++ has automatic deallocation of declared objects, but dynamically created objects must be deallocated by the programmer. Eiffel uses automatic garbage collection. Compare these two approaches.

3.8   C++ and Ada 9X are both designed to be backwards compatible with an existing non object-oriented language (C and Ada 83, respectively). Eiffel, on the other hand, is designed from scratch as an object-oriented language, with a new syntax. How are these decisions reflected in the language designs?

3.9   C++, Eiffel and Smalltalk-80 have different rules concerning access to the internal variables of a class from outside the class. In Smalltalk-80, the variables are invisible outside the class and thus cannot be accessed. In Eiffel, a variable can be made visible outside its class, but the variable can only be read and not written. Finally, C++ allows variables to be read and written by putting their declarations in the public part. Compare these three approaches. What are their advantages and disadvantages?

4

Functional Languages

Imperative languages allow programmers to express algorithms, which are accurate descriptions of *how* to solve given problems. The underlying computational model uses a state, consisting of the variables manipulated by the program. The state is repeatedly modified through assignment statements. This model can be implemented by storing the state in the main memory and by translating the operations on the state into machine instructions. The model resembles the underlying computer fairly closely.

This resemblance is a weakness as well as a strength. On the one hand, imperative languages can be implemented efficiently, just because the mapping to the hardware is so straightforward. On the other hand, the imperative paradigm tends to restrict the mental model of the programmer to fit the structure of the machine. It tempts the programmer to think in terms of named machine locations whose contents are in perpetual need of being changed. And even if a well-educated programmer with a sound mathematical background formulates his or her thoughts on a more abstract level, a lot of work lies ahead in implementing the abstract concepts in terms of the machine.

The latter observation has motivated researchers to develop alternative models which do not reflect the hardware, and which are easier for programmers to use. The ideal is to have the programmer merely specify *what* has to be computed, rather than *how* the computation is to be performed. Languages that try to meet this goal are called declarative languages. The primary representatives of declarative languages are functional languages (discussed here) and logic languages (discussed in the next chapter).

Of course, the difference between 'how' and 'what' is not always crystal clear, and neither is the difference between imperative and declarative languages. A point at issue that is less vague is performance. Declarative languages are usually much harder to implement efficiently. Naive implementations may easily be orders of magnitude slower than those for imperative languages. More advanced implementations get closer to the speed of imperative languages. Even without an efficient implementation, however, declarative languages can still be useful. As an example, for rapid prototyping the high level of abstraction of a language is more important than its efficiency.

4.1 Principles

Functional languages are designed as a higher-level, more abstract notation than imperative languages. Ada or C programmers are primarily concerned with low-level assignment and control-flow statements. Programming in a functional language is closer to defining mathematical functions, which are easier to reason about, since they can be understood without having to know the implementation details of other functions.

To appreciate the principles of functional languages, one first has to understand the objections that advocates of this paradigm have against imperative languages. As said before, imperative languages use a state that is repeatedly modified. The statements in the language are typically executed for their side-effects on the state. Procedure calls, for example, may change global variables. Of course, a programmer is not forced to use global variables, but nearly all programmers using imperative languages do.

The defenders of functional languages think that this model of statements modifying the global state has major disadvantages. Since different parts (for example, procedures) of a program interact indirectly through variables, programs become hard to understand. The effects of a procedure call are hard to determine without considering how the variables changed by the procedure are used in other parts of the program. In addition, the presence of side-effects is a major obstacle for correctness proofs, optimizations and automatic parallelization of programs.

A **functional** (or **applicative**) language is based on the evaluation of expressions built out of function calls (applications). A function is like a pure mathematical function: it maps values taken from one domain onto values of another (co)domain. Put in other words, a function computes a certain value, based on its input parameters (also called **arguments**) and nothing else. An infix expression like '2 + 3' is also treated as a function application: it applies the function '+' to the arguments 2 and 3.

The key issue here is that functions cannot have side-effects on the state of the program, unless this state is carried around in the arguments of the functions. This lack of side-effects results in a property called **referential transparency**, which is the most important term in functional programming. It means that the result of a function application does not depend on *when* the function is called but only on how it is called (with which arguments). In an imperative language, the result of f(x) + f(x)

need not be the same as that of

2 * f(x)

because the first call to f may change x or any other variable accessed by f. In a functional language, the two expressions are always equal.

Since the behaviour of functions no longer depends on global variables, functional programs will, in that respect, be easier to understand than programs written in an imperative language. This statement applies to a human reader as well as a machine. For example, suppose a compiler considers optimizing f(x) + f(x) into 2 * f(x). A compiler for a functional language is always allowed to do this transformation, because of the referential transparency. A compiler for, say, Ada, on the other hand, would first have to prove that the result of the second call does not depend on variables that are changed during the first call. A parallelizing compiler will encounter a similar problem if it wants to run function calls in parallel.

After discussing the advantages of functional programming, let us now also look at potential disadvantages: the lack of assignment statements and global variables, difficulties in modifying data structures and how to do I/O.

First, one may wonder whether the lack of assignment statements and global variables is not overly restrictive and makes programming awkward. This issue is, at least partly, a matter of taste. If needed, assignment to variables can be simulated using the parameter mechanism of functions.

Consider a function P that uses a local variable x. In an imperative language, P can modify x by assigning a new value to it. In a functional language, P can simulate the modification by passing the new value of x as an argument to an auxiliary function, which executes the remaining code of P. As a simple example, the modification in the program

```
function P(n: integer) -> SomeType;
   x: integer := n+7;
begin
   x := x*3+1;
   return 5 * g(x);
end;
```

can be eliminated as follows:

```
function P(n: integer) -> SomeType;
   x: integer := n+7;
begin
   return Q(3*x+1)                    % simulate x := 3*x+1
end;
```

where the new function Q is defined as:

```
function Q(x: integer) -> SomeType;
begin
  return 5 * g(x);
end;
```

A similar technique can be used for global variables. Of course, simulating imperative programming in a functional language is not the preferred style, but it can be done.

A well-known problem with functional languages is modifying a data structure. Changing, say, an element of an array is simple in imperative languages. In a functional language, the array cannot be modified. Instead, code must be written to copy the array, except for the element to be changed, and substitute a new value for this element. This approach is potentially far less efficient than assigning to the element.

Another problem with functional programming is how to model interactions with the outside world, for example the operating system or the user. Consider a function that asks the user for input from a terminal or that writes output to a printer. Clearly, this function has side-effects and is a threat to referential transparency. Solutions to this problem do exist, however, as will be discussed later on.

In summary, functional languages are based on the evaluation of expressions, which consist of function applications. Global state variables and assignment are eliminated, so the value computed by a function application depends only on the arguments. State information is passed explicitly, through function arguments and results.

In the following sections we will look at the most important concepts used in functional languages: functions, lists, types and polymorphism, higher-order functions, currying, lazy evaluation, equations and pattern matching. Recursive functions are one of the main concepts in functional languages. Higher-order functions and lazy evaluation give functional programming its power and are also important for building modular functional programs (Hughes, 1989). Polymorphism adds significant flexibility to the typing system.

For our examples, we will use the Miranda language, which is a functional language with an easy-to-read syntax.

4.2 Functions

The basic language concept in functional languages is the function. A function takes zero or more input parameters (arguments) and computes a result, which depends only on the arguments. An example function in Miranda is

```
celsius :: num -> num          || Type declaration
celsius f = (f – 32) * 5 / 9    || Convert Fahrenheit to Celsius
```

The first line declares celsius as a function taking one numeric argument and returning a numeric value. The second line implements this function and converts temperatures from Fahrenheit to Celsius. The function can be invoked as in:

```
celsius 68              ⇒ 20
celsius (–40)           ⇒ –40
```

(Throughout this chapter, we will use the notation '⇒ ...' to denote the result of an expression.) Miranda has a terse syntax and does not even use parentheses for the arguments of a function call.

Recursive functions play an important role in functional languages. They can be used, for example, instead of iteration. The classical example, used in most introductory texts, is computing the factorial of a (non-negative) number. We will comply with this tradition and show how a factorial can be computed in Miranda (and in imperative languages allowing recursion):

```
fac :: num -> num
fac x = 1, if x = 0                  || fac 0 = 1
fac x = x * fac (x–1), otherwise     || recursive call
```

The definition of fac consists of two separate equations, each containing a condition (if $x = 0$ and otherwise, respectively). The system will use the textually first equation whose condition is true, just as in an if-statement. We will explain this syntax in more detail later.

For comparison, Figure 4.1 shows how the factorial of n can be computed in an imperative language, without using recursion. This algorithm

```
function fac(n: integer): integer;
    var i, r: integer;  % r will eventually contain the result
begin
    r := 1;
    % compute n * (n–1) * (n–2) * ... * 1:
    for i := n downto 1 do
        r := r * i;
    return r;
end;
```

Figure 4.1 Computing a factorial without using recursion.

uses a state variable (r) that is modified repeatedly inside the for loop. The Miranda program does not use a for loop; instead, it contains a recursive function call. Each recursive call to **fac** corresponds to one iteration of the for loop. Thus the factorial example illustrates how functional languages can use recursion instead of iteration. Viewing Figure 4.1, it is easy to understand why many users of the functional paradigm consider iteration to be a clumsy way in which to express simple recursion.

4.3 Lists

In most functional languages, the list is the most important data structure. In Miranda, a list contains zero or more elements of the same type, for example

```
[1, 4, 9, 16]           || A list of four integers
[1..10]                 || A list with 10 integers (1–10)
['u', 'f', 'o']         || A list of three characters
[]                      || An empty list
[[2, 4, 6], [0, 3, 6, 9]] || A list containing two lists of integers
```

Lists can also be nested, as shown by the last example.

A powerful feature of Miranda and some other functional languages is **list comprehension**, which is a notation for defining lists, syntactically similar to the way sets are denoted in mathematics. As an example, the notation

$$[x \mid x <- [1..10] ; x \bmod 2 = 1]   \Rightarrow [1,3,5,7,9]$$

denotes the ordered list of all odd numbers between 1 and 10. The symbol '<–' represents the $\in$ (set-element) symbol, and the list comprehension is read as 'the list of all elements x between 1 and 10 for which x **mod** 2 equals 1'.

Many different operations on lists are conceivable. Each functional language has certain operations built in, and other operations can be defined by the programmer. The most elementary operations are those for constructing and decomposing lists. The **head** operation selects the first element of a list and **tail** returns the rest of the list:

```
hd [10, 20, 30]         ⇒ 10
tl [10, 20, 30]         ⇒ [20, 30]
```

The **hd** operation returns a single item and **tl** returns a list of items, even if the tail consists of a single item.

The **cons** operation ':' inserts an element in the front of a list:

```
5:[]                    ⇒ [5]
3:[4, 5, 6]             ⇒ [3, 4, 5, 6]
```

Many other operations on lists are usually provided, for example to get the length of a list, to reverse or concatenate lists or to select certain elements. Most of these can be built out of the elementary operations using functions, but most languages have them built in as standard functions or operators. For example, the number of elements in a list can be computed with the following recursive function **length**:

length x = 0, if x = []
length x = 1 + length (tl x), otherwise

Likewise, **list concatenation** can be implemented as follows:

concatenate x y = y, if x=[]
concatenate x y = (hd x) : concatenate (tl x) y, otherwise

These operations are typical of the recursive programming style of functional languages. The first line provides the escape hatch (see Section 1.6.1), describing the trivial case: concatenating an empty list and another list gives the latter list as the result. The second line is the general case: it partly solves the problem and solves the rest of the (now smaller) problem using recursion. The general problem of list concatenation is solved by building a new list, using the *cons* operation. The head of this new list is the head of the first list (hd x); the tail is the concatenation of the tail of the first list (tl x) and the entire second list.

Miranda has length and concatenation operations built in:

[3..7]   ⇒ 5 || length of a list
[1, 2, 3] ++ [4, 5] ⇒ [1, 2, 3, 4, 5] || concatenate lists

In imperative languages, lists can be built by the programmer. It is instructive to compare these with lists in Miranda. A list in an imperative language is built out of dynamically allocated chunks of memory which are tied together through pointers (see Section 2.2.2). The operations on such lists are implemented through low-level pointer manipulations. Allocation and deallocation of memory blocks is the responsibility of the programmer. As a result, programmers tend to use destructive updates on data structures. For example, an Ada programmer implementing list concatenation would typically write a procedure that hooks together two lists through a single pointer assignment, and not by building a new (third) list. The Ada approach would have the side-effect of modifying the first list.

In functional languages, programmers do not even have to be aware of the existence of such things as pointers and memory allocation. These exist in the actual implementation, but are effectively hidden from the programmer, thus providing a convenient level of abstraction and eliminating an important source of programming errors.

Management of the memory for list cells is done by the language's run-time system (RTS), which allocates memory whenever needed. The

RTS automatically detects if a certain block of memory is no longer in use and then deallocates it. This technique is called automatic garbage collection, as discussed in Section 3.8. Whenever the amount of free memory gets too low, a garbage collector scans the memory and looks for cells that can no longer be accessed.

4.4 Types and polymorphism

Functional languages often have a type system completely different from imperative languages. Recall that in Ada the programmer has to declare the type of every variable, because Ada uses static strong typing with explicit declarations. Most functional languages either use no (or weak) typing, dynamic typing or implicit strong typing. Also, they frequently provide the flexibility of polymorphic functions, which can be called with different types of arguments. These issues will be discussed below.

The first functional language, Lisp, did not use typing at all. A single list in Lisp can contain different kinds of elements. Although this approach is flexible and allows polymorphism, it is a mixed blessing, since it is impossible for a Lisp implementation to give early (compile-time) warnings about type errors in the program. Also, the lack of a typing system makes it hard to execute Lisp programs efficiently.

Miranda and several other functional languages use **implicit** static strong typing. All variables have a type, which is determined statically. Unlike Ada, however, the type can be inferred automatically by a **type checker**, and in most cases need not be given by the user. For example, given the definition of a function triple:

    triple x = 3 * x

the type checker will deduce that x must be a number, since it is used in a multiplication. It also concludes that the result of triple x is a number as well, so the type of this function is

    triple :: num -> num

Programmers may give this declaration explicitly for documentation purposes. Even more importantly, adding declarations gives the type checker the opportunity to detect incorrect uses of the function and generate an error message.

A very important feature supported by many functional languages is *polymorphism*. A polymorphic function accepts actual parameters of different types for a single formal parameter. Unlike overloaded procedures in Ada, a polymorphic function is a *single* function, not multiple functions with the same name. As a trivial example, consider the polymorphic function pair, which builds a list from two arguments:

```
pair x y = [x, y]
```

This function can be used as follows:

```
pair 1 2              ⇒ [1, 2]
pair True False       ⇒ [True, False]
pair [] [2]           ⇒ [ [], [2] ]
```

There is a single definition of the function **pair**, but the function can be invoked with different types of arguments, such as numbers, Booleans and lists of numbers, as long as both arguments have the same type.

In most imperative languages, on the other hand, different functions would have to be written and called, since a formal parameter of a function can have only a single type. If overloading is allowed, these functions can be given the same name, otherwise different names must be used. Either way, multiple functions are needed.

An interesting issue is the exact type of a polymorphic function. Clearly, the type of the function **pair** cannot be expressed in the same way as the function **triple** defined above, because the types of its arguments are not fixed. The solution is to introduce **type variables**. Within a type declaration, a type variable may denote any type, but the same variable denotes the same type throughout the declaration. The function **pair** then has the following type:

$$\text{pair} :: \alpha \rightarrow (\alpha \rightarrow [\,\alpha\,])$$

where α is a type variable. (Miranda actually uses rather strange names for type variables, consisting of one or more '$*$' symbols.) The above declaration means that **pair** is a function with two arguments of type α that returns a list of α values. (The reason for writing $\alpha \rightarrow (\alpha \rightarrow [\,\alpha\,])$ instead of $(\alpha\ \alpha) \rightarrow [\,\alpha\,]$ will become clear after the discussion of currying in Section 4.6.) This type definition rules out illegal usages of the function, such as

```
pair 1 True       || Arguments must be of the same type
5 + (pair 1 2)    || Result type is a list, not a number
```

In the second example, the system determines that the type of (pair 1 2) is a list of numbers, which cannot be used as an operand of the add operator.

Even though functions accept parameters of different types and explicit type declarations need not be given, the typing system described above is both static and strong. Violations of the typing rules result in compile-time error messages.

4.5 Higher-order functions

Many imperative languages treat variables and functions differently. Variables can be manipulated (read, written, passed around) while functions can only be invoked. Functional languages usually treat functions as first-class objects, which can be passed as arguments, returned as function results, and stored in data structures. A function that takes another function as an argument is called a **higher-order function**. Besides their conceptual elegance, higher-order functions also offer many practical advantages and are a cornerstone of functional programming.

An important higher-order function is **map**, which takes a function and a list as input, and returns a new list by applying the function to all elements of the original list. For example:

> map triple [1, 2, 3, 4] $\Rightarrow$
> [triple 1, triple 2, triple 3, triple 4] $\Rightarrow$
> [3, 6, 9, 12]

The function triple (given earlier) is passed as an argument to the higher-order function map, together with the list of integers from one to four. The map function applies triple to all elements of the list, resulting in the list [3, 6, 9, 12].

In languages that do not allow higher-order functions, it would not be possible to write a map function, since it requires an argument that is itself a function. We could, of course, write a specialized procedure map_triple that triples a list, but not a general procedure that can apply any function to a list.

Many other higher-order functions are predefined in most functional languages. The **foldr** ('fold right') operator is used to compute a single result (for example, the sum or product) from all elements of a given list. For example,

> foldr (+) 0 [2, 4, 7]

is equal to

> (2 + (4 + (7 + 0))) $\Rightarrow$ 13

(In Miranda, if an infix operator like '+' is passed as an argument, it must be enclosed by brackets.) Likewise,

> foldr (*) 1 x

computes the product of all elements in the list x, and

> foldr (&) True x

takes the logical 'and' of all list elements. In other words, it returns True if all elements are True and False otherwise. Clearly, foldr is a very general and powerful higher-order function. Functional languages have many higher-order functions predefined, and programmers can also define such functions themselves. These functions are fully type-checked, just as plain first-order functions.

4.6 Currying

Another important feature of most functional languages is **currying** (after the logician H. B. Curry), which is also called **partial parametrization**. Consider, for example, the function mult, defined as

mult a b = a ∗ b

If mult is applied to two arguments, it will compute their product, as expected, but in Miranda mult can also be applied to one argument. In this case, the result will be another function, with one argument, so

triple = mult 3

is an alternative implementation of the function triple given earlier. Similarly, we can define a function that sums all elements of a list by

sumlist = foldr (+) 0

The function sumlist provides two arguments to the 3-argument function foldr. The result is a function with one argument, a list, that can be invoked as:

sumlist [5, 9, 20] ⇒ 34

In Miranda, any function with multiple arguments can be curried. This fact is reflected in the type that is assigned to such functions. For example, the type of the function mult is:

mult :: num–> (num–>num)

which means mult is regarded as a function with one argument that returns another function of type num–>num.

4.7 Lazy evaluation

The simplest way of evaluating a function call is to first evaluate the arguments and then invoke the function. For example, in

mult (fac 3) (fac 4)

the function applications (fac 3) and (fac 4) would be done first, in arbitrary order, reducing the expression to

mult 6 24

Next, the function mult is applied to the arguments 6 and 24, giving the final result 144. This way of reducing the original expression to its simplest form is called **applicative order reduction**. Note that it starts with the innermost expressions.

An alternative way for reducing expressions is to start with the outermost expression and not to evaluate subexpressions until their results are needed. Using this approach, called **normal order reduction**, the expression

mult (fac 3) (fac 4)

is first reduced to

(fac 3) * (fac 4)

and next to

6 * 24

which also yields 144.

Programmers with a background in imperative languages may think that applicative order reduction is the most obvious, but it does have disadvantages. Suppose we want to implement a function cond that takes a Boolean value B as the first argument and returns its second argument if B is True or its third if B is False:

cond b x y = x, if b
cond b x y = y, otherwise

If all three arguments of cond are evaluated before the function is executed, there are two problems:

- One of the arguments of cond will be evaluated needlessly, thus wasting compute cycles.
- If the argument expression that is evaluated needlessly does not terminate, the whole expression will loop for ever.

As an example of the latter case, suppose we use this function for an alternative implementation of fac:

fac n = cond (n = 0) 1 (n * fac (n–1))

If the third argument of cond is always evaluated, the function fac will never terminate. The invocation fac 1 will invoke fac 0, which will invoke fac (−1), and so on.

These problems have led to the concept of **lazy evaluation**, which uses normal order reduction. The idea of lazy evaluation is to evaluate the arguments of a function only when their values are needed. In contrast, applicative order reduction always evaluates its arguments, and it is therefore also known as **eager evaluation**. If the value of a certain expression is never needed, lazy evaluation will not evaluate the expression, but eager evaluation will.

Using lazy evaluation, the application fac 1 is reduced as shown in Figure 4.2. The evaluation terminates and produces the correct answer. (The if-expression is a pseudo-notation we introduced.) The third argument of cond will not be evaluated if n equals zero, since in this case the argument is not needed.

```
fac 1 ⇒
cond (1 = 0) 1 (1*fac (1-1)) ⇒                    || Apply fac
if (1 = 0) then 1 else(1*fac (1-1)) ⇒            || Apply cond
if False then 1 else(1*fac (1-1)) ⇒             || Eval 1=0
1*fac (1-1) ⇒
1*(cond (1-1 = 0) 1 ((1-1) * fac ((1-1)-1))) ⇒  || Apply fac
1*((if 1-1 = 0) then 1 else ((1-1) * fac ((1-1)-1)))  || Apply cond
1*((if True then 1 else ((1-1) * fac ((1-1)-1))))   || Eval 1-1=0
1*1 ⇒
1                                                || Eval 1*1
```

Figure 4.2 Lazy evaluation of (fac 1).

A language based on eager evaluation is said to have **strict semantics**, because it always evaluates the arguments of functions. A language using lazy evaluation is **non-strict**. The semantics of Miranda are non-strict, so the function fac as defined above works correctly in Miranda.

Lazy evaluation has another important advantage: it allows one to define data structures that are conceptually **infinite**. For example, in Miranda the list of all positive integers is denoted as:

[1..]

This list can be manipulated just as any other list, for example:

```
hd [1..]                 ⇒ 1 || 1st element
hd (tl [1..])            ⇒ 2 || 2nd element
hd (tl (map triple [1..]))⇒ 6 || 2nd element of tripled list
```

The implementation of Miranda will only build the finite part of the list that is actually needed. Only when the whole list is requested, as in

sumlist [1..] || add all positive integers

or

[1..] || the length of an infinite list

will the system get into an infinite loop (or run out of memory).

Lazy evaluation can also be used to solve the problem with **I/O in functional languages**. The idea is to model I/O as communication with the Operating System (OS) (Hudak, 1989). A functional program takes a list of *responses* from the OS as input. It produces a list of *requests* to the OS, where the nth response answers the nth request. To read (part of) a file, for example, the program sends a *read* request to the OS by adding a special predefined element to the end of its request stream. The OS replies by adding an element containing the requested data to the end of the response stream. Likewise, writing a file can be modelled by sending the data to the OS and getting back a confirmation. With lazy semantics, the program can look at the responses from the OS when it wants to. The request and response lists are essentially **streams** of messages between the OS and the application.

Lazy evaluation thus has important advantages, but unfortunately it is also costly to implement. One problem is that the normal order reduction strategy may evaluate the same expression more than once, while applicative order reduction evaluates expressions exactly once. For example, consider the function:

double x = x + x

Normal order reduction evaluates the application double 23*45 as follows:

double 23*45 $\Rightarrow$ 23*45 + 23*45 $\Rightarrow$ 1035+23*45 $\Rightarrow$
1035 + 1035 $\Rightarrow$ 2070

whereas applicative order reduction would do only the following computations:

double 23*45 $\Rightarrow$ double 1035 $\Rightarrow$ 1035 + 1035 $\Rightarrow$ 2070

which clearly is more efficient. This problem can be solved using a technique called **graph-reduction**, which evaluates expressions zero or one times, but not multiple times (Peyton Jones, 1987).

Another problem is that evaluating the arguments before the call is easier than postponing their execution, causing a nontrivial overhead in lazy evaluation. Recently, optimizations have been developed for decreasing this overhead.

Not all functional languages provide lazy evaluation. Languages that do not support this feature for user-defined functions typically have some functions with lazy semantics (for example, cond) built in. Imperative languages also have features with lazy semantics built in, in particular the if-statement. C and Ada also support special short-cut AND and OR operators that evaluate their second argument only when needed, as explained in Section 2.3.2.

4.8 Equations and pattern matching

The final issues we will consider are equations and pattern matching, which are used in some modern functional languages, for example Miranda and Haskell. As we have seen, a function in Miranda can be defined using different alternative expressions followed by conditions like if x>0 or otherwise. The actual syntax is far more general and allows a choice between alternatives based on **patterns**. A function definition consists of one or more **equations** of the form

<pattern> = <expression> , <condition>

where the condition-part is optional. The pattern can use formal parameters, constants and a few other constructs. If a function is invoked, the system will try to find an alternative for this function whose pattern matches the invocation and whose condition (if present) evaluates to True. In Miranda, the first alternative (in textual order) that succeeds is chosen.

Pattern matching is best explained through some simple examples. The function cond given earlier can be implemented using equations as follows:

```
cond True x y = x
cond False x y = y
```

As another example, consider how the fac function is implemented with equations:

```
fac 0 = 1
fac (n+1) = (n+1) * fac n
```

The first pattern matches if the argument is equal to 0. More subtly, the second pattern matches only if the argument is greater than or equal to 1. The value of n is then set to the value of the argument minus 1. In general, a numerical expression appearing in a pattern may have the form v+c, where v is a variable and c is a literal constant. The pattern only matches if v can be set to a non-negative value.

More general numerical expressions are not allowed in patterns, to prevent ambiguities. For example, the pattern

```
f (n+m) = n * m
```

is ambiguous and thus illegal; a call like f 9 could result in 1*8 or 2*7, or other combinations.

A pattern may also contain a list. For example, the function that computes the length of a list (given earlier) can be reimplemented using equations as follows:

```
length [] = 0
length (a: b) = 1 + (length b)
```

The pattern in the first equation specifies an empty list, so it will only match if the argument is the empty list. The second equation will only match if the argument is a non-empty list, in which case it will make a recursive call, passing the tail of the list as the new argument.

As another example using lists, consider the function uniq that accepts a sorted list of items and eliminates all but the first occurrence of each item:

```
uniq [] = []              || escape hatch: empty list
uniq (a:(a:x)) = uniq (a:x)  || matches eg [3,3,...]
uniq (a: x) = a : uniq x     || matches all other lists
```

The second equation uses an advanced feature: the ability to specify the same variable (a) twice in the same pattern. This pattern will therefore match a list like [3,3,4], but not a list whose first two elements differ, such as [3,4,5]. If the second equation succeeds, a recursive call is made with the same list as the argument except that the head element is omitted. If the first two equations fail, the third one is selected, which also does a recursive call but keeps the head element in its output.

In the above code, the textual order of the equations is relevant, since the second and third equations can succeed simultaneously. An alternative solution is to add a condition to the third pattern requiring its first two elements to be different, but this would complicate the code. As a final point of interest, the function uniq is polymorphic. The function can be called with different types of actual parameters, as shown by the following function applications:

```
uniq [3, 3, 4, 6, 6, 6, 6, 7]   ⇒ [3, 4, 6, 7]
uniq ['a', 'b', 'b', 'c']       ⇒ ['a', 'b', 'c']
```

4.9 Example programs

We will discuss some example applications to illustrate the advantages of functional programming.

Quicksort

Quicksort is an efficient algorithm for sorting a list of items (for example, numbers). To sort a given list, quicksort first determines the value of the first element in the list, say x. Next, it creates two sublists, one with values less than or equal to x and one with values greater than x. Each of these two lists is sorted recursively (using quicksort). Finally, the resulting lists and the value x are put together and the result is returned. In Miranda, this algorithm can be coded concisely:

```
quicksort [] = []                        || Empty list is sorted
quicksort (x:tail)                       || General case:
    = quicksort [a| a<-tail; a <= x]     || first sublist
    ++ [x]                               || head
    ++ quicksort [a| a<-tail; a > x]     || second sublist
```

As usual for recursive functions, the first equation is the trivial case (the empty list). The second equation is the general case. It builds the two sublists using list comprehension. For example, [a| a<-tail; a <= x] is the list of all elements a of list tail that are less than or equal to x. Next, quicksort is invoked recursively for both lists. The results and the list [x], which contains only x, are put together using the list concatenation operator ++.

The quicksort algorithm illustrates the general style of recursive programming in Miranda, and it shows the power of list comprehension. Also, the quicksort function is polymorphic. The type of this function is:

quicksort :: [α] -> [α]

which means it takes a list with any type of elements and returns a list with the same type of elements. The function can be invoked, for example, in the following ways:

quicksort [5, 2, 9, 1] $\Rightarrow$ [1,2,5,9]
quicksort ['d', 'a', 'b', 'c'] $\Rightarrow$ ['a', 'b', 'c', 'd']

Hamming problem

The advantages of lazy evaluation can be illustrated nicely using the well-known **Hamming problem**. This problem requires to generate, in increasing order, all numbers that can be written as

$$2^i \times 3^j \times 5^k$$

Such Hamming numbers contain only the factors 2, 3 and 5. The output of our program will thus start with: 1,2,3,4,5,6,8,9,10,12,15,16 and the program will not finish until it is stopped by the user.

Intuitively, one might think that the problem can be solved trivially using three nested for loops that iterate over i, j and k. A moment's thought will reveal that the problem is much harder, because the sequence must be sorted and duplicates may not appear in the output. The Hamming problem can be solved in an elegant way using a model of parallel processes, as shown in Figure 4.3. The model uses three multiplier processes, each taking the same stream of input values and each producing a separate output stream. The first process multiplies all numbers in its input by 2 and puts the resulting numbers in its output stream. Likewise, the second process multiplies the numbers by 3 and the third one multiplies them by 5. Each of the three output streams is already sorted. A fourth process, the merger, takes these three streams and merges them in increasing order, eliminating any duplicates on the fly. The output of the merger is fed back as the input stream to the multipliers. Initially, the value 1 is inserted into this stream.

The input stream will contain exactly the Hamming numbers, in sequence and without duplicates. The initial value 1 is a Hamming number; furthermore, a Hamming number multiplied by 2, 3 or 5 is also a Hamming number, and numbers that cannot be obtained in this way are not Hamming numbers.

Although Miranda does not provide parallel processes, the above model is easy to implement in this language, using lazy evaluation. The Miranda program is:

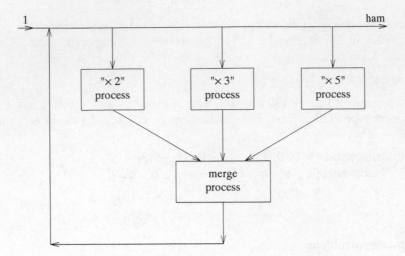

Figure 4.3 Solving the Hamming problem with pseudo-parallel processes.

```
mul :: num -> [num] -> [num]      || Multiply elements in
mul f s = [f*x| x<-s]             || list by given factor

ham :: [num]                              || Generate Hamming numbers
ham = 1 : merge3 (mul 2 ham) (mul 3 ham) (mul 5 ham)
```

A multiplier is obtained through the function mul, which multiplies all values on list s by a given factor f (2, 3 or 5). The function ham builds a list containing the value 1 and the result of a 3-way merge of the three multiplier processes. This function does not have any arguments, so the program is started by just invoking 'ham'. The 3-way merge can be implemented as two 2-way merges:

```
merge3 x y z = merge2 x (merge2 y z)

merge2 (x:xs) (y:ys)                    || Merge 2 sorted lists
  = (x:merge2 xs (y:ys)), if x<y
  = (x:merge2 xs ys), if x=y             || Eliminate duplicates
  = (y:merge2 (x:xs) ys), if x>y
```

The 2-way merge function eliminates duplicates (unlike the standard merge function defined in Miranda).

The above program relies heavily on lazy evaluation and would not work without it. With strict semantics, the first multiplier, started by (mul 2 ham), would get into an infinite loop. With lazy evaluation, however, the system first tries to reduce merge3 and only evaluates the arguments when they are needed.

4.10 Example language

We will look at one example language: Lisp. Other functional languages include ISWIM, FP, Scheme, Common Lisp, Hope, Standard ML, Miranda, Haskell and Lucid.

4.10.1 Lisp

Many concepts of functional programming were introduced in McCarthy's language Lisp, which was designed in 1958. Modern Lisp is not a pure functional language: it supports variables and assignment statements and thus is not referentially transparent. However, it was the first language to support the functional programming style. Lisp supports recursion and higher-order functions. Lists are the primary data structure. Memory allocation and deallocation are done automatically, using garbage collection.

Lisp was mainly designed for symbolic applications, such as artificial intelligence programs. For numerical computations, the early Lisp implementations were much too slow. Another often heard criticism of the language is that its programs are hard to read, because the syntax is dominated by parentheses. As an example, the code for the factorial function looks as follows in Lisp:

```
(define (fac x)
    (cond ((= x 0) 1) (t (* x (fac (– x 1))))))
```

which is much harder to read than the factorial function in Miranda, given in Section 4.2. The syntax is very uniform, however, making it easy to store and manipulate Lisp programs as normal data. This feature is useful for writing debuggers and other tools in the language itself.

Another problem with Lisp is its lack of a type system. A list, for example, can contain elements of different types. Although this freedom can be used to advantage in some cases, it also makes it impossible to detect type-system errors at compile time. Lisp uses dynamic binding, which can also be confusing, as discussed briefly in Chapter 2.

Lisp is the direct ancestor of many other languages, for example Scheme, and has influenced the design of all other functional languages. The successors of Lisp do usually have a type system, and frequently support features such as lazy evaluation and pattern matching.

Summary

- Functional programs consist of functions that map input values from one domain onto output values of another (co)domain, much as in mathematics. Pure functional languages lack imperative features such as assignment and repetition statements. Also, unlike most imperative languages, functions cannot have side-effects.

- Pure functional languages are referentially transparent, which means that the result of a function application does not depend on when the function is called but only on the arguments of the call.
- Referential transparency can make programs easier to read, transform, parallelize and prove correct.
- Problems with the functional paradigm are expressing I/O and obtaining an efficient implementation. Efficient updating of data structures poses an important implementation problem.
- The most important concepts in functional languages are recursive functions, lists, polymorphism, higher-order functions, currying and equations.
- Recursion can be used to express repetition.
- Lists are the main data structures in functional languages. Many operations on lists are predefined.
- The management of memory for data structures is done automatically. Programmers are not aware of the existence of machine addresses (there are no pointers). Deallocation of memory that is no longer used is also done automatically, using garbage collection.
- Modern functional languages support polymorphic functions, which can take arguments of different types. Many languages use strong typing, but the types are often inferred by a type checker and need not be given by the programmer.
- A higher-order function takes a function as argument. Higher-order functions contribute significantly to the flexibility of functional languages.
- Applicative order reduction first evaluates the arguments of a function and then applies the function. Normal order reduction applies the function to the unevaluated arguments, and only evaluates the arguments when needed.
- Normal order reduction is the basis of lazy evaluation. Lazy evaluation makes it possible to deal with infinite data structures. It is conceptually more elegant than eager evaluation, but it is also harder to implement efficiently.
- Modern functional languages allow functions to be defined as a set of equations. They use pattern matching to select the appropriate equation.
- Impure functional languages such as Lisp support some properties of functional languages, but are not referentially transparent.

Bibliographical notes

A good survey paper on functional programming languages is Hudak (1989), which contains a historical overview, a description of many novel language features and a discussion of several functional languages (including Haskell). Books about functional programming are Field and Harrison (1988), MacLennan (1990) and Bird and Wadler (1988). The arguments against imperative languages are perhaps best described in Backus's classical Turing award paper (Backus, 1978).

Miranda is described in Turner (1986). Several books on Lisp exist, for example Winston and Horn (1989).

The most important conferences on functional programming are the ACM Conference on Lisp and Functional Programming and the Functional Programming Languages and Computer Architecture Conference. A journal in this area is the *Journal of Functional Programming*.

Exercises

4.1   (a) What would happen if a pure functional language were extended with global (program-wide) variables? Such variables could be very useful, for example for recording a trace of the program execution. (b) What if the program could update these variables but not read them, nor base any decisions on them? Such restricted global variables would still be useful if their values were automatically appended to the program result.

4.2   Why do you think lists are the primary data structure in most functional languages? In contrast, arrays are the primary data structures in imperative languages, in particular in early languages like FORTRAN and Algol 60.

4.3   What is the main difference between polymorphic functions and overloaded functions (as used, for example, in Ada)?

4.4   A higher-order function can take other functions as arguments. In Ada, it is also possible to write a generic function that takes another function as generic argument. Discuss the differences between such generic functions and true higher-order functions.

4.5   Write down part of the normal order and applicative order reductions for the Hamming problem. Note that with applicative order reduction no real progress is made.

4.6   A programmer wants to represent a binary tree as a list with three elements: the data of the root node, the left subtree of the root and the right subtree of the root. Each subtree is again represented as a tree. An empty tree or subtree is represented as an empty list. For example, the tree in Figure 4.4 is represented as:

   [1, [2, [], []], [3, [4, [], []], []]]

Explain why this approach will not work in Miranda, while it will work in Lisp.

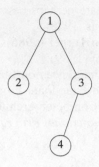

Figure 4.4 Example tree.

4.7   Write a Miranda program for the well-known problem of the **towers of Hanoi**. The goal of this program is to move *N* disks of different sizes from one peg to another, using a third peg to store disks during the move. Disks can only be moved one at a time, and putting a disk on top of a smaller one is not allowed. Initially, all disks are on the first peg, satisfying the above constraint (so the largest one is at the bottom).

4.8   Write a Miranda program for generating prime numbers, using the sieve of Eratosthenes. The program should not terminate. Try to exploit lazy evaluation to come up with a simple and efficient solution.

4.9   The parallel language Orca, discussed in Chapter 6, has some properties of functional languages, although it is an imperative language. Orca does not support pointers or global variables, so functions cannot have side-effects. A function in Orca can only modify its environment through parameters. Orca supports input parameters (call-by-value), output (result) parameters and call-by-reference parameters. A function can thus change variables that are passed as output or reference parameters, but no other variables. Within a function, normal local variables and assignment statements can be used.

Compare Orca's model with the pure functional programming model. In particular, what are the advantages and disadvantages of allowing call-by-reference parameters?

4.10 Functional languages are often claimed to be more suitable for parallel execution than imperative languages. Think of a way to automatically speed up functional programs by executing them on multiple processors.

5

Logic Languages

The paradigms discussed in the book so far show a trend from computer-oriented towards problem-oriented. With the imperative paradigm the programmer instructs the machine how to solve a problem. The object-oriented paradigm is similar, but the emphasis is more on data than on control. In the functional paradigm a problem is described through a collection of functions. The programmer can focus on the problem instead of on instructing the computer.

The idea of letting the programmer specify what the problem is rather than how the computer is supposed to solve it is taken one step further by **logic languages**. A logic program consists of facts and properties about a problem, but it is up to the system to find the solution to the problem. Although this idea sounds simple, realizing it is hard. As every programmer knows, computers are bad at inventing solutions on their own. They work best when told explicitly what to do, as in the imperative paradigm.

5.1 Principles

The success of logic programming is due to a formalism called **Horn logic** that can specify problems and can also be executed automatically. Horn logic does not achieve the ultimate goal of declarative languages: getting rid of programming altogether. For example, to achieve a reasonable efficiency, the programmer usually still has to be aware of the way the machine executes the program. Nevertheless, a significant advantage of logic programming is the ability to assign a declarative meaning to a program.

Horn logic is the basis of *Prolog*, which is by far the most important logic programming language. None the less, one should not take 'logic programming' and 'Prolog programming' to mean the same thing. Prolog also contains many non-logical features and thus is no more a pure logic programming language than Lisp is a pure functional language.

Below we will look at the most important concepts in logic languages: Horn clauses, logical variables, relations, data structures and the search order. Next, we will give some example applications and look at one language, Prolog, in more detail.

5.2 Horn clauses

A logic program consists of rules called **Horn clauses**. A Horn clause expresses that a certain condition is true if zero or more other conditions are true. For example, Horn clauses can express the following statements:

- **if** a person is old and wise **then** that person is happy.
- **if** X is the father of Y and Y is the father of Z **then** X is the grandfather of Z.

There can be zero or more conditions in the if-part and exactly one *conclusion* in the then-part. A Horn clause with no conditions expresses a *fact*.

The idea of logic programming is that the programmer just gives a list of *if-then* rules and the system will **infer** automatically whether or not a given condition is true. The system does so by starting with the given condition and working its way back to the facts. If it can derive the condition using the facts and rules it knows about, it can 'prove' the condition.

This model is very different from if-statements in imperative languages. An if-statement starts by evaluating a given Boolean expression, and then decides according to this value which other statements to execute. It does not try to 'prove' anything. Also, an if-statement is executed when the programmer directs the flow of control through it. In logic programming, there is no such notion as flow of control. The if-then rules are consulted as determined by the logic programming system, as described below.

We will now describe Horn clauses in more detail and also provide the necessary terminology. A Horn clause is a rule of the following form:

$$G_0 \leftarrow G_1, G_2, ..., G_n .$$

The **declarative meaning** of the Horn clause is: if G_1 until G_n are all true, then G_0 is true. The left-hand side of the rule is called the **head**; the right-hand side is called the **body**. G_0 until G_n are called **goals**; goals in the body are also referred to as **subgoals**.

The commas in the body should be read as logical **and** symbols. Beware that the '$\leftarrow$' symbol means *if* and not *if-and-only-if*; there may be other rules for G_0. A special case is where n is zero, so the body is empty. In this case, G_0 is always true; such a rule is called a **fact**.

Each goal consists of a **predicate** name and zero or more arguments. The exact meaning of the arguments will be explained later, but for the time being just assume that they are either variables or constants. To distinguish between the two, variables always begin with an upper-case letter. Predicates begin with a lower-case letter. As an example, the predicate

lucky(jim)

contains the constant jim and is probably intended to express that Jim is lucky.

With this information, we can write down our first Horn clauses:

old(confucius).   *(1)*
wise(confucius).   *(2)*
happy(X) ← old(X), wise(X).   *(3)*

The fragment contains two facts: confucius is old (Clause 1) and confucius is wise (Clause 2). These clauses are facts because their bodies are empty; the '←' symbol is omitted in facts.

The third line is a more general Horn clause. It uses a variable X, which begins with a capital letter. The clause expresses the statement about old and wise people given at the beginning of this section.

The first two rules are statements about a specific person (constant), while the third is a more general statement about any person. The third rule thus holds for *all* X. In the terminology of logic, variables in facts and rules are **universally quantified**.

Once the Horn clauses have been made known to the system, the user can enter questions that use them. Such a question is called a **query** and it contains one or more goal statements, also called initial goals. By entering a query, the user asks the system whether it can prove the goals from the information it currently has. For example, with the query

?– happy(charlie).

the user asks whether charlie is happy. The system will answer with either 'yes' or 'no'. (We use the Prolog convention here of putting a '?–' before the initial goal.)

The initial goals may also contain variables, as in

?– happy(X).

Variables used in an initial goal are **existentially quantified**. The user essentially asks whether there exists *any* person who is happy. If the system finds one, it will assign this person to the variable X. The variable can be retrieved or printed by the user, thus getting actual information out of the system.

5.3 Executing Horn clauses

Above, we claimed that Horn clauses can be executed automatically. To understand logic programming, one must have some idea of how this is done. We will describe the general idea here, omitting implementation details. We use the happy relation as an example. This example is very simple, because it contains only predicates with a single argument. In the next section we will look at a more complicated example, where the matching of variables comes into play.

Let us first consider the initial goals entered by the user as a query. Assume the user entered a single goal, say

    ?- happy(charlie).

In general, there may be several rules for solving the initial goal. We already gave one such rule above, but suppose we in fact have the following three rules:

    happy(X) ← rich(X), famous(X).
    happy(X) ← young(X), in_love(X).
    happy(X) ← old(X), wise(X).

This means that three possible ways of being happy are to be rich and famous, or young and in love, or old and wise, an admittedly naive view of the world. Each of these three rules is sufficient for proving the initial goal. The key idea is that the system tries all possibilities, in whatever order it wants, until one of them succeeds. Assume the system begins with the first alternative. It tries to prove rich(charlie) and famous(charlie), again using the order it prefers. If it succeeds in proving both subgoals, it has succeeded in proving that charlie is happy. If not, it continues with another clause, for example the second one, and tries to prove both young(charlie) and in_love(charlie). If either of these subgoals fails, the last clause is tried, which implies proving both old(charlie) and wise(charlie). If all clauses fail, the whole query fails and the system answers 'no'.

During this search, the system has to prove several subgoals. To prove a subgoal it applies the search strategy recursively. Assume we have the following rules for famous:

    famous(X) ← moviestar(X).
    famous(X) ← popstar(X).

To prove the subgoal famous(charlie), we have to prove either moviestar(charlie) or popstar(charlie). Eventually, we will get to subgoals that are facts, causing the search process to terminate. For example, if we had the facts

    moviestar(charlie).
    rich(charlie).

we could prove that charlie is happy. As we will see later, however, it is also quite possible to write clauses that cause infinite loops and do not terminate.

The pure logic programming model allows the system much freedom regarding the search order. We have seen two different cases above:

- the order in which alternative clauses for a goal are tried;
- the order in which the subgoals in a body are tried.

In both cases the search order is **nondeterministic**, which means it is not fixed in advance. (The word 'nondeterministic' is also used in slightly different meanings; a nondeterministic parallel program, for example, is one whose outcome may change between runs, even if the same input is being used.) Unlike this pure model, the Prolog language does use a fixed search order. The implications of this decision will be discussed shortly.

In summary, the system tries to prove the initial goal by considering all possible proofs in turn, in some nondeterministic order. Whenever it fails to prove a subgoal, it will simply try another one. This is called **backtracking**.

We can illustrate the search strategy with the tree in Figure 5.1. The root of this tree is the initial goal. Below the root are the three alternatives for solving the initial goal. At the next level we have the subgoals. All subgoals under the same node must be solved for the alternative to succeed. This is shown in the figure by a curved arc. Nodes at even levels of the tree are called OR nodes, while the nodes at odd levels are AND nodes. The root node at level zero is an OR node.

Because the system searches all possible solutions to the initial goal, it will always find a solution if one exists. This property is called **completeness of search**. If the system fails to find a proof, it will return the answer 'no', which means that, as far as the system can tell, the given goal is not true. This assumes that goals that can be proven are true and goals that cannot be proven are false (just like the **closed-world assumption** used in databases). For many applications, the programmer can provide the right facts and rules to make this assumption true. If this is not feasible, the programmer and users should be aware that a 'no' answer to a query just means that the initial goal cannot be inferred from the facts and rules, not that it is false. For example, there can be other reasons for being happy, besides the ones we listed above.

The actual implementation of Horn clauses is much more complicated than shown above, in particular if the goals have arguments. None the less, the same basic search strategy can be applied.

Horn clauses are in fact a subset of **predicate logic**, which allows multiple conclusions and thus is more general. The restriction to Horn logic

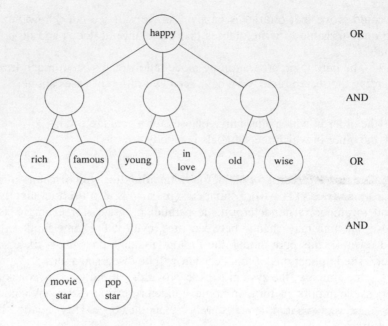

Figure 5.1 An AND/OR search tree.

makes it possible to execute clauses automatically, however, and is therefore important to its success.

Executing Horn clauses is somewhat similar to procedure calling in
conventional languages. There are two important differences, however. The
first difference is the backtracking behaviour of the system: if it chooses the
wrong alternative, it will automatically try another one. A second difference is the way in which arguments are passed, discussed in the next section.

5.4 Logical variables

Logical variables are used for storing state information and for passing
arguments between goals. We have used logical variables before, for example in the clause:

happy(X) ← old(X), wise(X).

which contains a logical variable X.

Initially, a logical variable does not contain a value; it is said to be
unbound. The variable may be assigned a value and become **bound** if it is
matched against a value or another variable, as described below. From then
on, the value cannot be changed again (except during backtracking, which
will be discussed later).

The reason for all of this is easy to understand intuitively. A clause like the one above is a general rule about any unspecified object X. Within the rule, however, X consistently denotes the same object, so the X in happy(X) should be the same as the X in old(X) and wise(X). While executing the clause, we can thus make a decision for X exactly once. So, logical variables can be bound only once and cannot be changed thereafter. Because of this property, logical variables are closer to variables in mathematics than to variables in imperative programming languages.

Another difference from variables in imperative languages is that logical variables are not declared and do not have a static type. Most logic languages are typeless, just as Lisp is.

Let us now consider how to execute a query involving predicates that contain logical variables or other arguments. In the previous section we described the search strategy for simple predicates containing a single argument. To solve a goal containing such a predicate it is sufficient to find a rule for the predicate and solve the subgoals in its body. In the more general case, both the goal and the head contain several arguments, which can be variables or constants. As an example, consider the following rules for the predicate coauthor:

coauthor(X,Y) ← author(X,Book), author(Y,Book).

author(ullman, database_book).

author(aho, awk_book).
author(kernighan, awk_book).

author(aho, compiler_book).
author(sethi, compiler_book).
author(ullman, compiler_book).

The first rule means that any two people are coauthors if there exists a book of which both are an author. Next, some facts are given about three well-known books (*Principles of database systems*, *The awk programming language* and *Principles of compiler design*).

In order to answer the query

?- coauthor(ullman, aho).

we need to find a clause for coauthor whose head **matches** the query and whose subgoals can be solved. The matching rule can be stated concisely as follows:

a head and a goal match if they are equal or if they can be made equal by binding one or more variables in the head or goal.

This is called the **unification** of the head and the goal. For the head and goal to be equal, they must have the same predicate name and the same number of arguments. In addition, each argument in the head must be equal (or made equal) to the corresponding argument in the goal. If two arguments denote the same value they are equal. If one of the two arguments is an unbound variable, the arguments can be made equal by binding the unbound variable to the other argument. If both are unbound, they are bound to each other; if one of the variables later becomes bound, the other one will thus become bound to the same value as well.

In our example only the first rule can possibly match the query coauthor(ullman, aho). The head of this rule, coauthor(X, Y), can be made equal to the initial goal by binding X to ullman and Y to aho. The query can thus be answered by solving the subgoals in the body of the clause, after replacing X and Y with the values to which they were just bound:

author(ullman,Book), author(aho,Book).

Assume that the system first tries to solve author(ullman,Book). It can do this using the fact author(ullman, database_book), so it will bind the variable Book to the constant database_book. Next, it will try to solve author(aho, database_book), to check if aho is also the author of that book. This subgoal fails, however, since it cannot be matched with any of the two facts author(aho, awk_book) or author(aho, compiler_book).

At this stage, the system will *backtrack* over its last decision, which was to use the fact author(ullman, database_book) to solve the subgoal author(ullman,Book). It will *unbind* the logical variable Book and start again, looking for another fact that also matches the subgoal. Such a fact indeed exists: author(ullman, compiler_book). So, the variable Book is now bound to the constant compiler_book. A new attempt is made to solve the second subgoal, which is now author(aho, compiler_book). This goal is given as a fact, so it succeeds, and thus the whole query succeeds.

All in all, the system uses the same general search strategy as described in the previous section, but the matching rules are complicated by the unification of variables.

5.5 Relations

The way logical variables are used may look similar to call-by-value parameter passing in imperative or functional languages. There is a very important difference, however. In matching a goal with the head of a rule, the system will make any binding necessary to make the two equal. In the previous section, we have seen examples in which a variable in the head of a goal was bound to a value passed as an argument. For example, to answer the query coauthor(ullman, aho) the variables X and Y in the head of the clause:

coauthor(X,Y) ← author(X,Book), author(Y,Book).

were bound to the values ullman and aho. This type of matching is similar to call-by-value parameter passing.

It is also possible to have binding work the other way round and pass a value from the head of the goal to a variable in the query. As an example, consider the query

?– author(X, database_book).

The query asks if an X exists that is an author of the database book. The system will try to answer this query by matching the goal with the facts about authors given earlier, in particular the fact author(ullman, database_book). To make this fact and author(X, database_book) equal, the variable X in the goal is bound to the value ullman. This type of matching is roughly similar to call-by-result parameter passing.

These examples show that logical variables can be used both as input and output arguments, without having to specify in advance which argument is input and which is output. In fact, some Prolog programs can run forwards and backwards with equal ease. In contrast, Ada requires the programmer to specify in the procedure header how each parameter is used.

In essence, the Horn clause for author does not define a procedure or function but a **relation**. A procedure maps input arguments onto output arguments, for example: compute the author of B. A Horn clause, on the other hand, specifies a relation that holds between different arguments, for example: X is an author of B. This is a fundamental difference between logic languages and functional or imperative languages.

5.6 Data structures

Until now we have assumed that arguments in a goal are either variables or constants. In practice, logic languages also support data structures. Two important type constructors are used: structures and lists (although in Prolog a list is actually a special case of a structure).

A **structure**, which is also called a **compound term**, consists of a **functor** and zero or more components. For example, the structure

person(john, 35, mary)

has the functor **person** and three components. It may contain information about a person, such as name, age and spouse's name.

The data structure that is most frequently used in logic languages is the list, which is denoted as in

[1, 4, 9, 16, 25]

Much of the power of logic languages comes from the fact that the matching rules described earlier also work for data structures. In matching a head and a goal, the system will bind whatever is needed to make the two equal, including parts of data structures. Consider the following clause:

international_access_code([44, X]) ← in_UnitedKingdom(X).

and the query

?– international_access_code([Code, london]).

The predicate international_access_code has a single argument, which is a list. The list in the head of the goal contains two elements: the constant 44 and the logical variable X, which is also used in the body of the clause. The list in the initial goal also contains two elements, a variable and a constant. To solve the initial goal, the system will try to make the arguments in the head and in the initial goal equal. To this end, it will bind X (in the head of the clause) to the value london, and Code (in the initial goal) to the value 44. Subsequently, it will try to prove in_UnitedKingdom(london). As a net result, information is passed in both directions (from the head of the clause to the goal and vice versa) through a single structured argument.

As in Lisp, a list in Prolog is actually a structure containing two elements: a head and a tail, denoted as [Head | Tail]. As an example, the list [1, 4, 9, 16, 25] is equivalent to [1 | [4, 9, 16, 25]]. This notation can also be used for splitting a list. If a list [Head | Tail] is matched against another list, the variable Head is bound to the first element of the list and Tail is bound to the rest of the list.

We can use this notation to write a **member** relation, which checks if a given element appears in a list:

member(X, [X | Tail]).
member(X, [Y | Tail]) ← member(X, Tail).

The declarative meaning of the clauses is that X is a member of a list if it is the first element or if it is a member of the tail of the list. A query such as

?– member(4, [1,2,3,4,5,6]).

results in four recursive invocations of **member** before it succeeds.

Another important operation on lists is **appending** (concatenating) two lists. A relation to append two lists to form a third list is shown below:

append([], L, L).
append([X|L1], L2, [X|R]) ← append(L1, L2, R).

The first clause is the escape hatch for the recursion. Its declarative meaning is that the result of concatenating an empty list and another list is the latter list.

The second clause is much more complicated. Its declarative meaning is that the concatenation of [X|L1] and L2 yields [X|R] if the concatenation of L1 and L2 yields R.

To see how this relation works, let us consider in some detail how the query

> ?– append([1,2], [3,4], Result).

is executed. The first clause for **append** obviously fails, so the query will use the second clause and match

> append([1,2], [3,4], Result)

with

> append([X|L1], L2, [X|R])

causing the following bindings:

> X = 1
> L1 = [2]
> L2 = [3,4]
> Result = [1 | R]

Next, a recursive invocation

> append([2], [3,4], R)

is done. This goal is again matched against the head of the second clause, causing variables in this head to be bound. These variables have the same static names as in the first invocation of the same clause, but of course each recursive invocation of **append** generates new variables. To distinguish all these variables, we will use names like R' during our explanation.

The recursive call makes the following bindings:

> X'= 2
> L1' = []
> L2'= [3,4]
> R = [2 | R']

and causes another recursive call:

> append([], [3,4], R')

Now the recursion stops, since this goal matches the head of the first clause, append([], L, L), making the binding:

> R' = L = [3,4]

The first recursive call is now completed, resulting in

> R = [2 | R'] = [2,3,4]

Finally, the original query completes, setting

> Result = [1 | R] = [1,2,3,4]

so the final result of the query is the list [1,2,3,4].

These examples have shown the general principles of logical variables and of their binding rules. The exact unification rules were proposed by Robinson (1965).

5.7 Controlling the search order

A logic programming system providing completeness of search will always find a solution to a query if one exists. It does so by considering all possible solutions to the problem. Unfortunately, this systematic search can be prohibitively expensive. In many cases, parts of the search space can and must be pruned. Also, with a clever search order a solution may be found much quicker than with a random search order.

Prolog provides a simple mechanism for controlling the order. It ensures that:

- alternatives for a given clause are always tried one at a time, in textual order, and
- within the body of a clause, the subgoals are tried one at a time, from left to right.

This allows programmers to order the alternatives and subgoals to reduce the total search time. Prolog's search order results in a **depth-first** traversal of the AND/OR tree.

Unfortunately, the strict depth-first order also implies that Prolog will not always guarantee to find a solution if one exists. The following clauses:

$$x(1) \leftarrow x(1).$$
$$x(2).$$

will loop for ever on the initial goal

$$?- x(N).$$

The system will infinitely often try the first clause, so the second clause will never be tried. It immediately follows that Prolog does not have the completeness of search property.

Another mechanism for improving efficiency is the **cut operator**. This operator tells the system not to backtrack in certain cases. Consider the following clause:

$$g_0 \leftarrow g_1, g_2, g_3, !, g_4, g_5.$$

The cut operator '!' appears between the third and fourth subgoals in the body. A Prolog system will try all subgoals one at a time, from left to right. During this process, the cut operator is initially ignored. If the goals to the right of the '!' fail and cause backtracking, however, the system will *not* backtrack over the cut operator. If g_5 fails, the system will try another alternative for g_4. If g_4 fails, the current goal (g_0) will immediately be given up. Therefore, g_0 will fail in this case, even if alternative clauses for g_0, g_1, g_2 or g_3 exist.

The idea is that success of g_1, g_2 and g_3 is sufficient for g_0 to succeed, so g_4 and g_5 should now also succeed. If they don't, something is wrong and other solutions to g_1, g_2 and g_3 will not help, and neither will it help to try other solutions to g_0.

The cut operator is useful in many cases. Sometimes the programmer knows that only one of several alternatives for a certain goal (such as g_3) can possibly succeed. Hence, if a successful alternative for this subgoal is found, the program can essentially *commit* itself to this choice. A common example is a set of mutually exclusive cases, such as

    fee(Age, Fee) ← Age < 18, !, childrens_fee(Fee).
    fee(Age, Fee) ← Age >= 18, Age < 65, !, adults_fee(Fee).
    fee(Age, Fee) ← Age >= 65, seniors_fee(Fee).

The first argument fully determines the alternative, so there is no need for backtracking.

Although the cut operator is useful, it is a controversial language construct. It not only gives up completeness of search, but can also destroy the declarative meaning of logic programs. It should be used with care.

Even with all this extra machinery, it may still be hard to obtain efficient programs. For example, if the optimal search order depends on dynamic conditions, such as the values of arguments, this cannot be expressed with Prolog's static mechanisms. A notorious example is that of the **grandfather** relation. One of the clauses for this relation is:

    grandfather(X,Y) ← father(X,Z), father(Z,Y).

expressing that X is a grandfather of Y. If the first argument is bound, as in

    ?– grandfather(richard, S).

it is most efficient to solve the leftmost **father** goal first. Its argument X is bound, so the system can easily look up the children of X and the children of these children. If the rightmost **father** goal is tried first, however, neither of its arguments are bound. The system will then enumerate all possible fathers Z it knows about and check if **richard** happens to be their father. If the database is large, this is clearly much less efficient.

Interestingly, if the second argument is bound, as in

    ?– grandfather(G, johnny).

the inverse reasoning holds and it becomes more efficient to solve the rightmost subgoal first. Unfortunately, in Prolog the search order is fixed statically, so it is difficult to write an optimal **grandfather** relation in Prolog. (The relation can be written efficiently in Prolog using a special metalogical predicate; see the exercises.)

A more fundamental problem with logic programming in general is that merely formulating a problem specification using Horn clauses is often not enough to obtain an efficient program. An application illustrating this point is sorting. The problem of sorting a list can be specified with Horn logic as follows:

sort(List, SortedList) ←
        permutation(List, SortedList), ordered(SortedList).

which says that SortedList is the result of sorting List if SortedList is a permutation of List and the elements of SortedList are ordered. Of course, we would also have to write clauses for the **permutation** and **ordered** clauses. The resulting program would correctly sort the initial list, but it would also be extremely slow. The reason is that the number of permutations of a list grows extremely fast with the length of the list. As the program generates permutations more or less at random, it would take a long time to execute the program for long lists.

Merely changing the textual order of the clauses or adding some cut operators does not help here. The problem is more fundamental than that. What is needed is a way of telling the system how to generate the permutations more efficiently. In comparison, a sorting program written in an imperative language does not generate permutations randomly. It typically reorders the initial list in such a way that it gets closer and closer to the final sorted list, using one of many algorithms. The same can be done with logic programming, but it requires a formulation of the clauses which is totally different from the one above. More efficient formulations mimic traditional sorting algorithms like quicksort, as discussed in the next section.

5.8 Example programs

Logic programming has been used successfully for implementing a wide variety of applications, in particular non-numerical ones. Among these applications are databases, knowledge-based systems, reasoning systems, heuristic search problems and compiler construction. Below we look at some example logic programs.

Summing

The first problem we look at is a rather trivial one: summing all integers from 1 to N. We have included this example to show how arithmetic can be done in logic languages. Prolog has several arithmetic operations built in. Of special importance is the **is** infix operator, which is used as in

X is 3 + 4.

It forces the evaluation of the expression on the right and matches the result with its left operand. The left operand is usually an unbound variable, so **is** binds the value to this variable. The left operand can also be a value, in which case the operator tests whether the expression on its right (when evaluated) equals the left operand. Either way, the right operand must only contain bound variables or values.

We use the relation sum(N, S) to mean that the sum of integers 1 to N equals S. The relation can be defined using two clauses:

sum(1, 1).
sum(N, S) ← N2 is N − 1, sum(N2, S0), S is S0 + N.

The first clause specifies that the sum of all integers from 1 until 1 equals 1, which is trivially true. The second one specifies that the sum from 1 to N equals the sum from 1 to N−1 plus N. The clause uses the predicate sum recursively and binds the result to S0. It uses the is operator for computing N − 1 as well as S0 + N.

If the predicate is used as follows:

?− sum(2, S).

the system will first try to match sum(1, 1) with sum(2, S). This will fail, because the first argument does not match. Next, it will try the second clause, causing N to be bound to 2 and N2 to 1, resulting in a recursive call sum(1, S0). The recursive call will match the first clause, sum(1, 1), and binds S0 to 1. Subsequently, the final result of the initial goal will be S = 1 + 2 = 3.

The above program depends on Prolog's search order. If the order of the two clauses were reversed, the program would get into an infinite loop.

Another interesting remark about the program concerns the is operator. As a disadvantage of using this operator, our predicate sum does not work in the opposite direction. If the predicate is used as

?− sum(N, 6).

one might expect it to succeed and bind N to 3, since 1+2+3 = 6. However, the subgoal N2 is N − 1 will produce an error message, because N is not bound. So, sum as implemented above is not really a true relation.

Sorting

As a second and more interesting application, we reconsider sorting lists, this time using a more efficient approach. Our program, shown in Figure 5.2, uses the quicksort algorithm discussed in Section 4.9. It contains two clauses, qsort and split.

The qsort predicate uses the first element of the list to be sorted as a *pivot*. The predicate first splits the list without the pivot into two sub-lists. The first sub-list will contain all items of the list (without the pivot) that are less than or equal to the pivot. The second sub-list will contain the remaining elements. Subsequently, the program sorts both lists, using a recursive invocation of **qsort**. Finally, the two sorted sub-lists and the pivot are put together to form the final result, using the relation **append** defined earlier.

```
qsort([], []).
qsort([Pivot| Tail], Sorted) ←
  split(Pivot, Tail, SmallerEqual, Larger),
  qsort(SmallerEqual, SE),
  qsort(Larger, L),
  append(SE, [Pivot|L], Sorted).

split(Pivot, [], [], []).
split(Pivot, [X|Xs], [X|S], L) ←
  X <= Pivot, split(Pivot, Xs, S, L).
split(Pivot, [X|Xs], S, [X|L]) ←
  X > Pivot, split(Pivot, Xs, S, L).
```

Figure 5.2 A quicksort algorithm.

The second predicate, **split**, takes the pivot and a list as input and splits the list into two parts. Again, an escape hatch is used in case the input list is empty. If the first element X of the (non-empty) input list is less than or equal to the pivot, X is included in the first output list; otherwise, it is included in the second. Either way, a recursive call is made.

The resulting program is far more efficient than our first proposal, which generated permutations of the input list in arbitrary order. The example shows that sorting can be implemented efficiently in a logic language. However, it also shows that merely specifying a problem is not always enough. Programmers often still have to think about algorithms that instruct the computer how to solve the problem efficiently.

Searching in a graph

The two examples discussed so far do not fully demonstrate the power of logic programming, as they do not exploit backtracking. For example, the **split** predicate in the quicksort example makes a choice based only on its two input arguments (the pivot and the list to be split). It will thus never backtrack over this decision. Similarly, the other relations used in our examples have no real choice between multiple alternative clauses. Such programs are therefore said to be **deterministic**.

The next problem we discuss does rely on backtracking and is non-deterministic. The problem is to find whether there exists a path between two given nodes in a directed acyclic graph. Such a graph could, for example, represent a group of lakes, connected by rivers flowing in the direction

indicated. We can represent such a graph by listing all its arcs, as shown in
Figure 5.3. The graph itself is shown in Figure 5.4.

arc(1,2).
arc(1,3).
arc(3,4).
arc(4,2).
arc(4,5).
arc(5,2).
arc(5,6).

Figure 5.3 Representation of a graph.

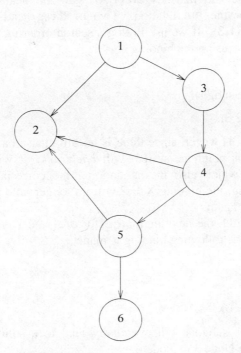

Figure 5.4 An example directed acyclic graph.

We can now easily test whether a path exists between a source and a
destination node using the following relation:

path(S, D) ← arc(S, D).
path(S, D) ← arc(S, X), path(X, D).

The first clause is the simple case, in which there is a direct arc from the
source to the destination. The second clause checks if there is a direct arc

from the source to any other node X such that a path exists from this node X to the destination.

The code for solving this problem can be kept very short, because the actual searching is done automatically by the system, using backtracking wherever necessary. If the same problem were to be solved in an imperative or functional language, the searching process would have to be programmed explicitly.

This backtracking behaviour requires more explanation. Consider the following query:

   ?- path(1,6).

asking whether there exists a path from Node 1 to Node 6. The system begins with the first clause, arc(1,6), which immediately fails. Next, it tries the second clause and matches arc(1,X) with the heads of the various clauses given for the arc relation. Two of these heads match, namely arc(1,2) and arc(1,3). If we use Prolog's search ordering, the first alternative is tried first, causing the binding

   X = 2

and leading to the subgoal

   ?- path(2,6).

The subgoal fails, however, since there is no arc clause having 2 as its first argument. At this point the system will *backtrack*. It will undo its most recent decision, which also means undoing the corresponding bindings. After backtracking, the binding X = 2 will no longer hold and X will be an unbound variable again.

Subsequently, the next alternative for arc(1,X) is selected, which is arc(1,3). Now, the following binding is made

   X = 3

and the subgoal

   ?- path(3,6).

is executed. This subgoal will eventually lead to a solution, since there exists a path from Node 3 to Node 6.

During the search, the variable X takes different values, which may seem strange since logical variables can be assigned only once. However, after a variable is bound it can only be assigned again after its binding is undone through backtracking. This form of assignment is thus quite different from destructive assignments in imperative languages.

We finally note that the above program does not work for graphs containing cycles, at least not if it is executed by Prolog. The reason is that the system may get into an infinite loop and try the same arcs over and over again, owing to the fixed search order of Prolog. So, if an arc from Node 2 to Node 3 were added to the graph of Figure 5.4, the query

```
?- path(1,6).
```

would endlessly try the following steps:

path(1,6) → arc(1,2), path(2,6) → arc(2,3), path(3,6) →
arc(3,4), path(4,6) → arc(4,2), path(2,6) → ...

Even though a path from Node 1 to Node 6 exists, the system will not find it. Owing to Prolog's lack of completeness of search, it gets stuck in the loop 2-3-4-2. To solve this search problem for cyclic graphs, the program should keep track of which nodes are on the current path and avoid visiting the same node twice (Bratko, 1990).

5.9 Example language

Below we will look at the most important logic language, Prolog, in more detail, although we have already explained its most important features.

5.9.1 Prolog

Prolog was developed by Colmerauer and colleagues at the University of Marseilles, in the mid-1970s. It was based on ideas for logic programming by the group at Marseilles and by other researchers, in particular Kowalski. The availability of reasonably efficient implementations (for example, DECsystem 10 Prolog implemented by Warren at the University of Edinburgh) contributed to its success.

Prolog is based on Horn logic, as described above. It supports structures as its main data structures and lists as a special case of structures. Prolog implementations have many predicates built in. Several of these are so-called meta-logical or extra-logical predicates.

Meta-logical predicates, for example, test the state of variables. One example is the nonvar predicate, which checks if a given variable is bound. It can be used to write an efficient grandfather relation (see Section 5.7) in Prolog by testing which argument is bound and deciding the search order based on this knowledge (see the exercises).

Extra-logical predicates do not fit into the framework of logic programming. Examples are predicates for input and output. I/O is a difficult problem, since it is not possible to backtrack over an I/O command. If output is sent to a screen or a printer, it is not possible to undo that effect.

Of particular interest are the extra-logical predicates for operations on a database, which is one of the main application areas for Prolog. We have already looked at a trivial database in this chapter, containing information about authors. Our database not only contained facts, but also rules, enabling it to generate new conclusions. For example, it did not store the fact that Ullman and Aho are coauthors, but it was able to derive that information from other data. Such a database system is called a deductive database.

With any real database, it clearly ought to be possible to add or delete data and rules dynamically. For this purpose, Prolog has the meta-logical predicates **assert** and **retract** built in. For example, new facts and rules can be added dynamically as follows:

```
assert(happy(george)).
assert((happy(X) ← married(X))).
```

Although these primitives are powerful, they also make it more difficult to analyse Prolog programs statically (for example, to compile them to machine code). Moreover, adding and deleting rules dynamically makes it possible to change the program at run time. Such programming tricks were abandoned in imperative languages long ago, because they were considered bad programming practice. Modern Prolog systems often require special declarations for relations that are changed dynamically.

Prolog uses the textual depth-first search order described earlier. If a solution to a query is found, the user can force the system to backtrack and find an alternative solution by typing a ';', as shown below:

```
?- author(X, awk_book).
X=aho
;
X=kernighan
;
no
```

The user first asks for an author X of **awk_book**. After the system has found a solution (shown in italics), the user asks for an alternative solution. The system now backtracks and finds another solution. If the user asks for yet another solution, the system replies negatively.

Summary

- Logic programming is based on Horn logic. A Horn clause is an *if-then* rule with one conclusion in the *then* part (head) and zero or more goals in the *if* part (body).
- The programmer specifies a problem by giving a set of Horn clauses describing facts and properties about the problem.
- The user can ask questions to the system by giving it goals to prove. The system automatically tries to prove the goals using the Horn clauses. If the system is unable to prove the goal from the Horn clauses it has available, it assumes that the goal is not true.
- A logic programming system that has the completeness-of-search property will always find a proof if one exists. Such systems typically use a search strategy based on backtracking.

- Horn clauses may use logical variables, denoting unspecified objects. A logical variable is initially unbound. It can be bound only once, unless its value is unbound again during backtracking. Binding occurs as a side-effect of matching a goal with the head of a clause.
- Horn clauses express relations rather than functions. The arguments of a clause are not marked in advance as being input or output, but can often be used in both ways.
- Structures and lists are the most important data structures in logic languages.
- For efficiency, the programmer may control the order in which alternative clauses for a goal are tried as well as the order in which different subgoals in one clause are tried.
- Prolog is by far the most popular logic language.

Bibliographical notes

Several textbooks on logic programming exist, for example Sterling and Shapiro (1986). Bratko's (1990) book focuses on using Prolog for Artificial Intelligence applications. Many fundamental ideas about logic programming are exposed in Kowalski's (1979) classic book. An overview paper on logic programming is Genesereth and Ginsberg (1985).

The most important conferences in this area are the International Conference on Logic Programming, the IEEE Symposium on Logic Programming and the Fifth Generation Computer Systems Conference. Journals in this area include the *Journal of Logic Programming*, *New Generation Computing* and the *Future Generation Computer Systems* journal.

Exercises

5.1 For the quicksort program given in the text, manually simulate an execution trace for a simple query, for example qsort([2,3,1], X). Use the same approach as for the **append** predicate and write down which bindings are generated and which subgoals are executed.

5.2 Write a Prolog relation that counts the number of elements in a given list.

5.3 Write a Prolog program for the towers of Hanoi problem described in Exercise 4.7.

5.4 Write a Prolog program that reverses a given list, using the **append** relation discussed in the text.

5.5 Implement a sorting algorithm other than quicksort in Prolog (for example, mergesort, bubble sort or insertion sort).

5.6 If you had a meta-logical predicate for testing whether a given variable is bound (such as **nonvar** in Prolog), how could you efficiently implement the grandfather relation of Section 5.7?

5.7 Consider the following puzzle. A set of 9 square tiles is given with a figure of half a witch on each of the four sides; either the top or bottom of a witch is shown. Each witch can have one of four colours. The goal of the puzzle is to put the 9 tiles in a 3×3 matrix, such that two adjacent tiles show the figure of one witch (the top and bottom) in one colour.

Try to write a Prolog program that efficiently solves this problem, employing Prolog's backtracking facility. Beware that the number of combinations one can try is large, so think of a good order in which to place the tiles.

To test your program, you can use the following description of the tiles. Each line enumerates the four sides of one tile in clockwise order:

[top,blue], [bottom,red], [bottom,blue], [top,green]
[top,green], [bottom,red], [bottom,blue], [top,blue]
[top,red], [bottom,blue], [bottom,purple], [top,green]
[top,red], [bottom,green], [bottom,purple], [top,green]
[top,purple], [bottom,red], [bottom,purple], [top,green]
[top,blue], [bottom,purple], [bottom,red], [top,green]
[top,purple], [bottom,blue], [bottom,red], [top,blue]
[top,red], [bottom,green], [bottom,purple], [top,blue]
[top,purple], [bottom,green], [bottom,red], [top,blue]

5.8 A logic program has much potential for parallel execution. How do you think the performance of a logic program can be improved automatically by distributing its computations over multiple computers? Hint: think about the AND/OR tree given in Figure 5.1.

5.9 As a significantly larger project, write a move generator for chess in Prolog. Make sure your program handles castling, promotion and *en passant* moves correctly.

6

Parallel and Distributed Languages

In Chapters 2 to 5 we discussed various paradigms for general-purpose languages. We will now turn our attention to languages designed for solving specific types of problems. We will look at languages for parallel and distributed programming in this chapter, and at various languages for other problems in the next chapter.

6.1 Principles

Parallel and distributed languages differ from the languages described in the previous chapters in that they contain explicit constructs for running pieces of a program in parallel. There are three different reasons why language constructs for **parallelism** are useful:

- Some problems are easier to solve using parallel constructs, because they exhibit inherent parallelism.
- Some problems are not parallel by themselves, but efficiency can be gained by implementing them on a parallel machine and dividing the work over different processors.
- The nature of some applications requires them to run on multiple processors or workstations connected by a network, the so-called *distributed* systems.

In the first case, we can regard parallel programming as a paradigm, just as functional or object-oriented programming. In the second case, getting the desired parallelism is a problem, and parallel programming is the paradigm for that. The third case requires a related distributed programming paradigm. Let us now look at each of the three cases in more detail.

We have already seen one inherently parallel application in the chapter on functional languages, where we discussed a solution to Hamming's problem based on parallel processes. As another example, consider a discrete event simulator. This program deals with multiple active entities, such as clients and servers. A convenient approach for writing a simulator might be to use one piece of code for each active entity, and have all these pieces run in parallel.

Although both programs are intended for single processors rather than multiple processors, they are just simpler to implement with parallelism than without. Since there is only one processor, the different parts of the programs do not really execute at the same time; they run in **pseudo-parallel**. They all compete for the single CPU, and are all allocated some portion of the CPU cycles.

The second reason for using parallel language constructs is to exploit the performance potential of parallel hardware systems. If the different parts of a parallel program are indeed executed by different processors, the program may take less time to finish. To sort a list of numbers, for example, the list could be partitioned over several processors. Each processor sorts its own portion of the list and all these sorted sub-lists are then merged together.

To achieve real parallelism, one needs a **parallel system**, which we define as any system with multiple CPUs. Many different parallel systems exist. We will only consider parallel machines in the so-called **MIMD** (Multiple Instruction Multiple Data) class. Each processor in a MIMD system executes its own instruction stream (program) on its own data. Each processor in a MIMD system is to a large degree independent. Therefore, processors in a MIMD system must be able to **communicate**. Communication can either be done through a shared memory or over a network, giving rise to two subclasses of MIMD machines: **multiprocessors** and **multicomputers**, as shown in Figure 6.1.

In a multiprocessor, all CPUs access a single global **shared memory**, which is used for communication between the CPUs. In a multicomputer, the memory is distributed. Each CPU can only access its own local memory, but CPUs can communicate through a **network** that connects them. We will also use the term **distributed system** for this type of machine.

The third case where parallel language constructs are needed is for the construction of programs that run on distributed systems made out of workstations connected by a local area network such as an Ethernet. The user on one workstation may want to send electronic mail to users on other workstations. The e-mail program is a distributed application that runs on multiple machines. Other example applications are banking or airline reservation systems.

We should point out that there is some confusion in the literature about what exactly parallel and distributed systems or applications are.

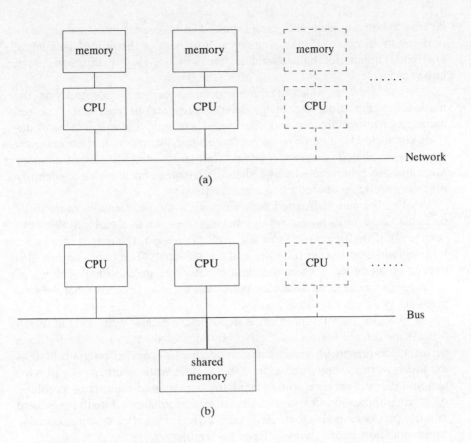

Figure 6.1 (a) Multicomputer; (b) Shared-memory multiprocessor.

Some authors use the term 'distributed system' only for collections of independent workstations. Likewise, there is confusion about the difference between parallel and distributed programming. At least part of this confusion is due to the duality described above: parallel programming can be regarded as a paradigm or as a problem.

Many authors try to solve the confusion by introducing additional terms (for example, **concurrency**), but these do not have standard meanings and may easily lead to more confusion. In this book, we use the term **parallel programming** to denote both the first and second cases above, and **distributed programming** to denote the third case. A parallel language can be used for parallel programming and a distributed language can be used for distributed programming. There is significant practical overlap between these definitions, however. For example, a distributed system can also be used for running parallel programs.

Both parallel and distributed languages support parallelism. The parallel parts will have to cooperate in solving an overall task, so they must be able to communicate with each other. The languages therefore also support communication. (Some languages, in particular distributed languages, also give support for fault tolerance; we will not look at this issue here, however.)

The way in which communication is expressed depends on the hardware being used, especially on the presence or absence of shared memory. Multicomputers and distributed systems consisting of workstations connected by a network do not have shared memory; a multiprocessor does have shared memory. Often (but not always), shared-memory machines are programmed using shared variables and non shared-memory machines are programmed using message passing.

Parallel and distributed programming are fundamentally more difficult than sequential programming, because certain kinds of problem can occur only if multiple processors are used. Foremost, the output of a parallel program need not be fully defined by its input. The outcome can also depend on the order in which the parallel activities are executed. The job of the programmer is to constrain the possible execution orders so that the program always gives consistent results.

Another potential problem is **deadlock**, which is a situation in which processors are waiting for each other, so none of them can proceed. Many performance-related problems can also occur. If a parallel program assigns too much work to some processors and too little work to others, it will have nonoptimal performance, and is said to have a **load-balancing** problem. Also, communication delays may decrease performance. Finally, it is hard to write programs that run efficiently on different parallel systems, because communication architectures differ considerably.

All in all, writing efficient, correct and portable parallel or distributed programs is difficult. Below, we discuss how language mechanisms can ease this task. We will look at various language constructs for parallelism and for communication on either shared-memory or non shared-memory machines.

We should emphasize that this area of computer science is still very much under development. Unlike the situation for sequential programming, there are very few widely used languages yet. Also, parallel programming is still often done in sequential languages, using special library routines for expressing parallelism and communication. In our examples, we will write programs using a pseudo-notation rather than an existing language, except where indicated.

6.2 Parallelism

There are several language constructs for expressing parallelism. Of these, we will discuss co-routines, parallel statements and processes.

6.2.1 Co-routines

A language construct for expressing pseudo-parallelism is the **co-routine**. Co-routines are routines that are executed in an interleaved fashion. At any point during its execution, a co-routine may **block** (also called **suspend**) and resume another co-routine. If a co-routine is resumed, its state is restored by the system, and it continues at the point where it was before it suspended.

As a trivial example, we could have two routines, one computing the squares of odd numbers and one computing the squares of even numbers, as illustrated in Figure 6.2. Each routine repeatedly prints a square and then resumes the other routine, so they execute in turn. During a resume statement, the system saves the local variables (such as i and j), so if the routine is later resumed its variables still have the right value. The example shows that co-routines can only be used for expressing pseudo-parallelism, since only one co-routine at a time is active.

```
procedure Odd:
  var i: integer;
  for i := 1 to N by 2 do
    print i*i;
    resume Even;
  done


procedure Even:
  var j: integer;
  for j := 2 to N by 2 do
    print j*j;
    resume Odd;
  done
```

Figure 6.2 Example co-routines.

6.2.2 Parallel statements

True parallelism can be expressed through parallel statements. Two examples are the **parbegin** statement, which executes a given list of statements in parallel, and the **parfor** statement, which runs multiple iterations of a loop in parallel:

```
parbegin                  parfor i := 1 to 10 do
   Statement 1                   Statements(i)
   Statement 2            done
   Statement 3
parend
```

As an example, suppose we want to add two vectors (1-dimensional arrays) and store the result in a third vector. All elements of the result vector can be computed independently, so all additions can be done in parallel, using the parfor statement:

```
A,B,C: array[1..N] of real;

parfor i := 1 to N do
   C[i] := A[i] + B[i];   -- Executed in parallel
done
```

The effect of the parallel statement is the same as that of a sequential for-statement, because the different iterations do not depend on each other in any way.

In the above example, each parallel activity only involves one addition and three array accesses, which take little time. Such a program is said to use **fine-grained parallelism**. Other applications use larger **grain sizes**. For example, we can parallelize matrix multiplication by computing all elements of the result matrix in parallel, using the program in Figure 6.3. This example uses a doubly nested **parfor** loop. To compute an element C[i,j], N floating point multiplications will be executed, so the granularity of the parallelism is higher than in the first example. The granularity can even be increased by replacing the second (inner) **parfor** by a sequential **for** loop as well. In either case, all iterations of the parallel loops are independent, so the result is the same as that of a sequential execution.

```
A,B,C: array[1..N : 1..N] of real;

parfor i := 1 to N do
   parfor j := 1 to N do
      -- multiply A[i:*] and B[*:j];
      C[i,j] := 0;
      for k := 1 to N do
         C[i,j] := C[i,j] + A[i,k] * B[k,j];
      done
   done
done
```

Figure 6.3 Parallel matrix multiplication using the **parfor** statement.

Although the parallel statements can express parallelism, they provide little support for structuring parallel programs and are not as general as other constructs. They are mainly used in languages for numeric programming, such as parallel dialects of FORTRAN. Also, much research is being done on automatically parallelizing existing FORTRAN codes by having the compiler discover loops that can be executed in parallel. We do not look at this issue of **implicit parallelism** any further in this book, however, since it concerns language implementation rather than language design.

6.2.3 Processes

By far the most common way of expressing parallelism is through **processes**. A process is an abstraction for a physical processor. It executes code sequentially and it has its own state and data. Parallelism is obtained by creating multiple processes, possibly running on different machines.

In most parallel languages, the number of processes that can be created is variable. Typically, one first defines a process type, much like a procedure, which describes the code to be executed by processes of this type. Next, any number of processes of this type can be created using a **fork** statement:

fork process-type(parameters);

Forking a new process is similar to calling a procedure. The crucial difference is that, with procedures, the calling procedure waits until the called procedure has finished. With process creation, both the invoking parent process and the newly created child process continue in parallel. This immediately raises the question of how these processes recombine, which brings us to the important issue of **synchronization**.

The simplest method for synchronizing processes is to have the parent wait explicitly until its children have terminated. As an example, suppose we want to compile a program consisting of several modules. We can compile the modules in parallel, by forking one compiler process for each module. Next, we have to wait until these processes have finished before we can link the resulting object files into one executable file. The pseudo-code to implement this scheme for the compilation of two files is given in Figure 6.4.

The example uses two primitives: **fork** and **join**. The **join** primitive blocks (suspends) the calling process until all its children have finished. In some systems, **join** blocks until one child has finished; in this case, the main process should invoke the primitive repeatedly.

Synchronizing the parent and children by waiting for termination is a rather crude method. Sometimes, the parent only wants to wait until a child has produced an intermediate result, say part of an output file. Also, the different processes involved in a computation frequently want to exchange

```
process compile(sourcefile, targetfile: string);  -- child
begin
  compile source file
  store generated object code in target file
  exit;      -- terminate process
end;

process main(void);  -- parent process
begin
  -- create two parallel processes
  fork compile("file1.c", "file1.o");
  fork compile("file2.c", "file2.o");
  join;      -- wait until all children have finished
  link file1.o and file2.o into an executable program file
end;
```

Figure 6.4 Compiling two modules file1.c and file2.c in parallel.

data, resulting in more complicated synchronization and communication patterns. In the next section, we will look at more general solutions to the problem of process communication and synchronization. As this problem is the most important issue in parallel programming, most of this chapter is devoted to it.

6.3 Communication and synchronization

Two important classes of communication primitives are shared variables and message passing. We will first discuss these classes. Next, we look at communication primitives that have some properties of shared variables and some of message passing, so they are in between these two classes.

6.3.1 Shared variables

A **shared variable** is a variable that is known by name to more than one process and can be used as a normal variable by these processes. Shared variables can be used for transferring information between processes, since data stored in the variable by one process can be read by all other processes. Shared variables are used mainly to program uniprocessors and shared-memory multiprocessors. On a multiprocessor, shared variables are stored in the shared memory.

Below, we first give an introductory example of parallel processes communicating through shared variables. Next, we will look at the important issue of synchronizing access to shared variables. Finally, we discuss several language constructs introduced for synchronization through shared variables.

Example application

Let us reconsider the compiler discussed earlier. Assume that the compiler consists of two passes, a *front-end* that generates assembly code, and an *assembler* that turns the assembly code into object code. On a multiprocessor or multicomputer, we can make our compiler more efficient by running the compiler front-end and the assembler in parallel, as shown in Figure 6.5. The two passes can be run in parallel, but clearly the assembler needs to wait for input from the front-end before it can proceed. Each time the front-end produces some output, the assembler can continue. This form of communication is called **producer/consumer communication** and it occurs frequently in parallel programs.

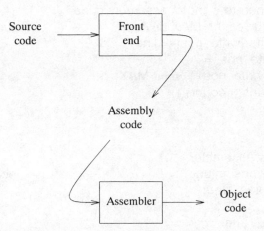

Figure 6.5 Structure of a parallel compiler.

The front-end can pass data (lines of assembly code) to the assembler through an array variable shared between these two processes. This variable is a **buffer** between the processes. The front-end stores lines into the buffer, and the assembler takes them out of it. We assume that the buffer has a finite capacity of MAX lines.

Synchronization

Clearly, the two processes must synchronize their actions. Two forms of synchronization are needed. First, the producer and consumer have to wait for each other if the buffer becomes full or empty. Second, they should prevent writing the same shared variable simultaneously. We will look at both forms of synchronization in turn.

The assembler cannot read data from the buffer before the front-end has stored them. Also, if the buffer is full the front-end should be blocked when it tries to put more data into the buffer. For this purpose, we add a second shared variable, a counter, containing the number of lines of assembly code produced by the front-end but not yet consumed by the assembler.

```
count: integer := 0;                     -- shared variable
buffer: array[0..MAX-1] of line_type;    -- shared buffer

process Front-end
   write_pos: integer := 0;              -- local variable
   line: line_type;
begin
  while ... do
    generate a line of assembly code
    while count=MAX do done;             -- busy waiting
    buffer[write_pos] := line;
    write_pos :=
      (write_pos+1) mod MAX;             -- to wrap around
    count := count+1;
  done;
end;


process Assembler
   read_pos: integer := 0;               -- local variable
   line: line_type;
begin
  while ... do
    while count=0 do done;               -- busy waiting
    line := buffer[read_pos];
    read_pos :=
      (read_pos+1) mod MAX;
    count := count-1;
    process a line of assembly code
  done;
end;
```

Figure 6.6 Code for the front-end and assembler (without mutual exclusion synchronization).

Figure 6.6 shows the code that the front-end and assembler execute to produce and consume data. The front-end first waits until the counter is less than MAX. This is expressed using a while statement with an empty body. In other words, the process continuously tests the value of the counter. This form of waiting keeps the CPU busy wasting cycles, and is therefore called **busy waiting** (or **polling**). When the counter indicates that the buffer is not full, the front-end deposits a line of assembly code into the buffer. A local variable write_pos is used to indicate the position in the buffer where the next line has to be stored. This variable and the shared counter are updated. The assembler executes the dual actions. It has a local variable read_pos, indicating the position of the next buffer element to read.

Another form of synchronization is needed to control access to shared data. This is the hardest problem in parallel programming with shared variables. Reconsider the variable count shared between the front-end and assembler. The statements incrementing and decrementing the shared integer may take multiple machine instructions to execute. Even if there is a single machine instruction for incrementing or decrementing a memory location, the hardware is going to need two memory accesses for each. Either way, incrementing or decrementing a shared integer is going to take multiple steps (machine instructions or memory accesses). If two of these multi-step actions overlap in time, the result is unpredictable, because the order in which the steps will be executed is not determined in advance.

To illustrate the problem, suppose the front-end adds a line to the buffer and, simultaneously, the assembler tries to fetch a line from it. Also assume that the current value of the counter is 5 and that MAX is larger than 5. The two processes simultaneously execute the statements:

```
count := count+1;   -- executed by front-end
count := count-1;   -- executed by assembler
```

They both read the memory location containing the current value of count, which is 5. Subsequently, they both try to update the counter by writing back the values 6 and 4, respectively, to the memory. The resulting value of the counter will depend on which write is done last, but it will be incorrect in both cases. The counter should have kept the value 5, since the number of lines in the buffer is not changed by adding and deleting one line. The correct value would have been obtained if one of the processes had executed its assignment statement entirely before the other. Such an undesirable situation, where the result of a program depends on the exact timing of process execution, is called a **race condition**. The problem is how to prevent race conditions.

To summarize, we have seen two forms of synchronization in this example. First, the assembler and front-end must wait for each other to produce or consume data. This is called **condition synchronization**. As illustrated by the while statements in Figure 6.6, it can be solved using polling, but this is undesirable since it wastes CPU cycles. Second, processes should not simultaneously access shared variables, since that may result in race conditions. This is called **mutual exclusion synchronization**. A parallel language using shared variables must address both issues.

Race conditions occur if multiple processes simultaneously execute regions of code in which they access shared variables. Such regions are called **critical sections**. Race conditions can be avoided by allowing only a single process at a time to enter a critical section. To implement this idea, many different constructs have been proposed, such as locks, semaphores and monitors. The latter two can also express condition synchronization. We look at all three language constructs below.

Primitives for shared variable synchronization

A simple construct is a **lock variable**; a lock is a shared Boolean variable with two operations:

* **lock**(L) sets (obtains) a lock on L.
* **unlock**(L) releases the lock on L.

Both operations are **indivisible**. If two or more processes simultaneously try to execute a **lock** or **unlock** operation on the same lock variable, these operations are (at least conceptually) executed one after another, so they do not interfere with each other.

At most one process at a time may have the lock of a given lock variable. If a process has the lock, other processes trying to execute **lock** will be suspended until the first process has executed **unlock**. We can eliminate race conditions from the example program by introducing a shared lock variable L and surrounding the statements (in Figure 6.6) that increment and decrement the shared counter with **lock** and **unlock** primitives. The front-end thus executes:

```
lock(L);
count := count+1;
unlock(L);
```

to increment the counter. The assembler executes:

```
lock(L);
count := count-1;
unlock(L);
```

Only one process at a time can now increment or decrement the counter.

We do not have to use locks for the local variables write_pos and read_pos, since these are not shared, or for the buffer (as explained shortly). The code for accessing the buffer and updating the positions is therefore the same as in Figure 6.6.

Although we can avoid race conditions using lock variables, this primitive is far from ideal for parallel programming. It is a low-level primitive that makes programming difficult, and should be used with care. Also, it does not solve our second synchronization problem, condition synchronization.

A better synchronization primitive is the **semaphore**, introduced by Dijkstra (1968a). A semaphore is a non-negative shared integer variable with two operations, **V** and **P**:

- **V(s)** increments the variable by one.
- **P(s)** tries to decrement the variable by one; if the variable is zero, however, it blocks until the variable becomes non-zero first.

The two operations are indivisible, so if several processes simultaneously try to execute a **P** or **V** operation on the same semaphore, the operations are conceptually executed one at a time.

Assume that a semaphore is zero and that one or more processes are blocked in a **P** operation on it. If another process executes a **V** operation, the semaphore will temporarily get the value one. One of the processes blocked in a **P** operation will succeed in decrementing the semaphore to zero, and this process may continue. Since the operations are indivisible, only one process will be able to execute a **P** operation, although many can be waiting.

The **P** operation has a similar role to the **lock** operation on lock variables. A lock variable, however, is either locked or free, while a semaphore can have many different values. We can use this property to improve the condition synchronization in our example, and get rid of the polling. The idea is to use two semaphores, one containing the number of lines in the buffer, LinesFull, and one containing the number of empty slots in the buffer, LinesEmpty:

```
LinesFull: semaphore := 0;   -- shared semaphores
LinesEmpty: semaphore := MAX;
```

These semaphores replace the variable count as well as the lock variable. The resulting code is much simpler. The front-end executes:

```
P(LinesEmpty);                -- block until there is an
                              -- empty slot; grab that slot
buffer[write_pos] := line;    -- store line in slot
write_pos :=
   (write_pos+1) mod MAX;     -- update position index
V(LinesFull);                 -- release full slot
```

and the assembler executes:

```
    P(LinesFull);                    -- block until there is a
                                     -- full slot; grab that slot
    line := buffer[read_pos];        -- get line from slot
    read_pos :=
      (read_pos+1) mod MAX;          -- update index
    V(LinesEmpty);                   -- release empty slot
```

This code does not have a race condition because, unlike operations on normal shared variables, the operations on semaphores are indivisible. The **P** and **V** operations are each guaranteed to happen in one single step. To guarantee this behaviour, the underlying implementation may have to use lock variables, but these are hidden from the user of the semaphores.

Using semaphores avoids polling. If a process is blocked in a **P** operation, the implementation can decide to run another process, until a **V** on the same semaphore is executed. In this way, no CPU cycles are wasted.

In conclusion, semaphores can be used for mutual exclusion synchronization as well as condition synchronization. Like lock variables, however, semaphores are a low-level mechanism and are difficult to program. Inserting **P** and **V** operations in the right places in the program is far from trivial, and mistakes can easily lead to subtle errors that are hard to trace.

There are two main reasons for this. One has to do with the question of exactly which shared variables should be protected with semaphores. Protecting them all is safe but inefficient, and often unnecessary. In our example, we did not protect the buffer variable because the producer and consumer will never access the same element of the buffer array at the same time. We assume that different elements can be accessed independently, so no mutual exclusion synchronization is needed for the buffer. If, for whatever reason, this were not the case, the program would be erroneous. It would have to be fixed by using additional semaphore variables for the buffer elements. The second problem with semaphores is their dynamic intractability. In a correct program, the **V**s and **P**s on a given semaphore have to pair up exactly, otherwise deadlocks or race conditions can occur. Since corresponding **V** and **P** operations occur in different places in the code, this invariant is often hard to get right. To avoid the above problems, a synchronization construct has been invented that has built-in solutions for them, the **monitor**.

A monitor is similar to an abstract data type. It encapsulates shared data and operations on these data. As with abstract data types, the data themselves are hidden from users of the monitor. The distinguishing feature of a monitor is the guarantee that at any given time only one process can be executing any of the operations in the monitor. When a process is inside a monitor, it can be certain it is the only one active there. This restriction is guaranteed by the compiler, which automatically inserts lower-level primitives (such as locks) in the operations.

Since the process's presence inside a monitor may block and impede other processes, it has an obligation to leave the monitor in a short time. This causes a problem, since the process may find that it has to wait for some data to arrive. Several approaches have been proposed. The most common is the **condition variable**, which has two operations defined on it, **wait** and **signal**:

- **wait**(v) blocks the invoking process, and
- **signal**(v) reactivates one process blocked in a **wait**(v).

While a process is blocked in a **wait** inside a monitor, other processes are allowed to enter the monitor. We can use the monitor construct to implement a buffer for our parallel compiler, as shown in Figure 6.7.

```
monitor buffer;
    -- shared variables encapsulated by the monitor
    count: integer := 0;
    buffer: array[0..MAX-1] of line;
    write_pos, read_pos: integer := 0;
    NotFull, NotEmpty: ConditionVariable;

    operation put(in line: line_type);
    begin
      if count = MAX then wait(NotFull); end if;
      buffer[write_pos] := line;
      write_pos := (write_pos+1) mod MAX;
      count := count + 1;
      if count = 1 then signal(NotEmpty); end if;
    end;

    operation get(out line: line_type);
    begin
      if count = 0 then wait(NotEmpty); end if;
      line := buffer[read_pos];
      read_pos := (read_pos+1) mod MAX;
      count := count - 1;
      if count = MAX-1 then signal(NotFull); end if;
    end;
  end;
```

Figure 6.7 A monitor implementing a shared buffer.

The monitor encapsulates all the variables we used before, including the buffer itself, the counter and the current positions for getting and putting elements. (We could omit the counter, since its value can be determined from write_pos and read_pos, but we believe the code as given is clearer.) In addition, it contains two condition variables, NotFull and NotEmpty.

The operation put blocks as long as the buffer is full. Next, it stores a line in the buffer and adjusts its current position and the counter. Finally, if it has just added to an empty buffer it signals the condition variable NotEmpty. If the assembler was suspended on this variable (see below), it will now proceed.

The operation get blocks as long as the buffer is empty. It then fetches a line from the buffer and updates its position and counter. If necessary, it signals the condition variable NotFull, allowing the front-end to proceed.

Once the monitor has been defined, it can be used by the front-end and assembler without further concern about synchronization. Except perhaps for termination, the code for these two processes is trivial. The front-end calls buf.put(line) whenever it has produced a line of assembly code. The assembler calls buf.get(line) to get a line of data. Synchronization is neatly hidden by the monitor, making this solution well-structured. Languages based on monitors include Mesa and Concurrent Pascal.

6.3.2 Message passing

The second class of communication primitives is **message passing**. With message passing, each process has its own variables, which cannot be accessed by other processes. Processes communicate by sending messages to each other. A message contains data that are transferred from the sender to the receiver.

With message passing, there is no risk of simultaneous updates of the same variable, since each variable can only be accessed by a single process. Hence, there is no need to protect variables by locks, semaphores or monitors. Another advantage of message passing over shared variables is that it is more suitable for distributed systems, in which processors do not have a common shared memory. In distributed systems, physical communication between processors takes place by sending messages over a communication network. Implementing message passing on distributed systems is easy; implementing shared variables is harder, but not impossible, as we will see.

On the down side, with message passing, processes can no longer share state information. For many applications this is a severe disadvantage. As an illustrative example, consider **clock synchronization**. With shared variables it is trivial to have all processors agree on the current time. The value of the clock can be stored in a shared variable, where it can be read by everyone. With the message passing model, this is not possible. Instead, complicated algorithms are needed to have everyone agree on the same time. There are many similar cases where state information has to be shared among different processes.

The basic message passing model

We will first describe the basic message passing model as proposed by Hoare for his Communicating Sequential Processes (CSP) language and used in the occam language. Many alternatives to the CSP model exist, some of which are discussed later in this section.

The basic message passing model consists of two blocking primitives. The sender S calls the **send** primitive

send message to R

and the receiver R invokes the **receive** primitive:

receive M from S

The message is transmitted from the sender to the receiver. If these two processes run on different machines, the transfer goes over the network. The message is stored in the receiver's variable M. If the sender executes its statement first, it waits until the receiver is ready to accept the message. If the receiver goes first, it waits for the sender. Either way, the two processes fully synchronize. This basic model is therefore called **synchronous** message passing.

The two statements together achieve the effect of a **distributed assignment statement**. The contents of **message** at the sender are assigned to the variable M at the receiver. In practice, languages differ in the kinds of data structures that can be stored in a message. Often, only certain types of message are allowed, such as scalars, records and arrays (but not pointers or complex data structures like trees and graphs).

The basic model has many variations, which we will discuss shortly. First, however, we show how the parallel compiler can be implemented using synchronous message passing. The front-end and assembler can no longer share a buffer. Instead, they must exchange data using messages. The simplest solution is to have the front-end send a message as soon as it has produced assembly output. The two processes execute the code given in Figure 6.8.

As a disadvantage of this solution, both processes have to wait for each other, so they run in lock-step. If they produce and consume assembly lines at exactly the same speed, they will not delay each other. In the more likely case that one of them is faster, the fast one will be held up by the slow one. As we will see, there are various ways to fix this problem.

Besides the CSP primitives, many forms of message passing exist. Below, we will look at the most important alternatives. We consider direct versus indirect naming, synchronous versus asynchronous message passing, explicit versus implicit message receipt and one-way versus two-way communication.

```
process Front-end
begin
  while ... do
    generate line of assembly code
    store line in message
    send message to Assembler
  done;
end;


process Assembler
begin
  while ... do
    receive M from Front-end
    get line from M
    assemble line
  done;
end;
```

Figure 6.8 Message passing code for the front-end and assembler.

Naming the sender and receiver

The first issue we consider is how the sender and receiver should address each other. In the simplest case, which we used above, both the sender and the receiver explicitly name each other. This form is called **symmetric direct naming**. It is used, for example, in CSP.

Requiring the receiver to specify the sender of the message is rather inflexible. For example, it rules out the possibility of writing a generic server (for example, a file server) that accepts requests from any client. A better solution, used in many languages, is to let the receiver accept messages sent by any process:

receive M

The **from**-part has now been omitted. This form is called **asymmetric direct naming**, since the sender specifies the receiver, but not vice versa. If the receiver needs to return an answer to the sender, the original message should contain the identity of the sender. Alternatively, two-way communication can be used, which will be described later.

Yet another option is **indirect naming**, which uses an intermediate object, called a **port**, rather than process names. In this case, both the sender and receiver specify a port, declared as:

P: port-name;

The sender executes:

send message **to** P

and the receiver executes:

receive M **from** P

Multiple processes may send messages to the same port, but usually only one process is allowed to receive messages from a given port. A port that allows multiple receivers is often called a **mailbox**. Ports and mailboxes are more flexible than direct naming, since neither the sender nor the receiver needs to know the identity of the other.

Message sending: synchronous versus asynchronous
The most controversial issue in message passing concerns synchronous and asynchronous messages. Both forms use **send** and **receive** primitives, but differ in when the sender continues. As explained above, with synchronous message passing the sender waits until the message has been delivered at the receiving processor and the receiver has finished executing the receive statement and has stored the message in its local variable. This is implemented by having the receiver return an **acknowledgement** message, but this message is invisible to the programmer.

With **asynchronous** message passing, the sender continues immediately after issuing the send statement. Processing of the message will be done in the background, while the sender continues its execution. Usually, the send statement just copies the message into a local buffer. After the sender resumes execution, this buffer is sent over the network to the receiver.

There are important differences between the two models. Synchronous message passing is simpler to use, because when the sender continues it knows the message has been processed. With asynchronous messages, this is not the case. If we use our analogy with assignment statements again, communication through asynchronous message passing is like executing an assignment whose effect will not take place immediately, but at some time in the future. Obviously, such semantics do not make programming any easier.

On the other hand, synchronous message passing is more restrictive, because the sender is forced to wait. For parallel applications, this limitation may be too severe. We have already seen the implication in our compiler example. With asynchronous message passing, the front-end can send its output to the assembler without waiting until the assembler is ready to accept it. The two processes then no longer run in lock-step. Many languages (for example, SR and Hermes) provide both synchronous and asynchronous communication. CSP, occam and Ada only provide synchronous message passing.

Message receiving: explicit versus implicit receipt

The issue of synchronous versus asynchronous message passing has to do with the way in which messages are sent. On the receiver's side, there are also some options. The most common way of receiving messages is through an **explicit receive** statement, as discussed above. This method gives the receiver control over when it wants to get a message.

A completely different way of accepting messages is through **implicit message receipt**. With this method, a new sub-process is created within the receiver every time a message arrives. This sub-process services the message, executing whatever statements are needed, and then terminates. A sub-process, usually called a **thread**, is like a normal process, except that it shares the address space with the receiving process and it runs in pseudo-parallel with that process. The processes can communicate through shared variables and synchronize using locks, semaphores or monitors.

One-way versus two-way communication

The send and receive primitives used above transfer information in one direction, from the sender to the receiver. In many cases, the receiver wants to return a reply to the sender. With send/receive, the programmer needs two messages, one in each direction. An attractive alternative is to use a single message-passing construct that transfers data in both directions.

Two-way interactions occur frequently in distributed systems that are based on the **client/server model**. The system is then structured as a collection of **servers** which provide certain services (for example, file service, directory service, printer service). The users of these services are called **clients**. Communication between clients and servers is two-way: the client sends a request (for example, to read a file) and the server returns a reply (for example, the file contents).

Two widely used message passing constructs based on this idea exist: rendezvous and Remote Procedure Call (RPC). Both use two-way synchronous communication but differ in the way in which messages are received and serviced. We will discuss both concepts below.

Rendezvous

The **rendezvous** construct is based on two-way message passing and explicit message receipt. It is used in Ada, so we use the Ada syntax and terminology during our discussion of rendezvous.

With the rendezvous construct, the receiver (server) contains procedures that other processes (clients) can ask to be executed. Such procedures are called **entries** in Ada. The declaration of an entry is similar to that of a procedure, for example:

```
entry Get(Line: out Line_Type);
```

If a client issues a request to execute an entry, it is said to do an **entry call**. The receiving process explicitly asks for the next incoming entry call, so entries are not serviced until the receiver is willing to accept them.

The client calls an entry, specifying the server and the parameters, for example:

Buffer.Get(Next_Line);

The client now blocks until the entry call has been processed by the server (Buffer) and it has received the result of the call. In this example, the result is assigned to the variable Next_Line which is passed as a parameter in the entry call.

The receiver (server) asks for entries by executing an **accept statement**, for example:

accept Get(Line: out Line_Type) do
    -- service the request
    Line := ... ;
end Get;

The accept statement blocks the server until an entry call for it is available. Next, the server executes code to service the request. When the server finishes executing this code, the result will be sent back to the client through the formal **out** parameter. The client is blocked while the server is executing its accept statement; the arrival of the result causes the client to resume execution.

Note the difference between the receive and accept statements. With the receive statement of one-way message passing, the client is blocked until the server receives the message. With the accept statement, the client is blocked until it has received the results of the entry call. In both cases, the client and server are fully synchronized, but with rendezvous the client waits until the server has finished executing its accept statement and has returned the results (if any).

In many languages, the programmer has control over the order in which entry calls are serviced. A server need not accept and service any call immediately it arrives. It may be busy working on another entry call, or it may just not want to service the call now, for whatever reason. Messages that have arrived but are not yet accepted by the server are said to be **pending**. Several entry calls may be pending for a given server, sent by many different clients. Such calls are stored away in a safe place by the run-time system, without the programmer noticing it.

Often, the server wants to choose the order in which pending entry calls are accepted. In most languages the accept statement can specify which entry to accept. For example, a server executing the accept statement shown in the example above will block until a client has called the server's entry Get. Any other entry calls to the server will not be accepted yet and will remain pending.

A powerful statement for controlling acceptance of entry calls is the **select** statement, which was introduced in Hoare's CSP (where it was called a **guarded command** statement). This statement allows selection between different incoming entry calls. For each entry a constraint can be given, which may enable or disable the entry. The select statement chooses one enabled entry for which a call is pending, or blocks if no such entry yet exists.

A select statement consists of one or more *alternatives*. Each alternative is an accept statement, possibly preceded by a constraint. In Ada, such constraints are called **guards** and they have the form 'when Boolean-expression =>'. As an example, we can extend the accept statement shown earlier with a guard that checks if input lines are available, and use the resulting statement as part of a select statement:

```
select
  when Nr_Lines > 0 =>
  accept Get(Line: out Line_Type) do .... end Get;
or
  ....
end select;
```

In general, a select statement blocks until at least one alternative exists for which an entry call has been made and for which the guard expression is true. Next, one of the successful alternatives is chosen non-deterministically and the do-part in its accept statement is executed.

To illustrate the select statement, we will discuss a **buffer process** that can be used by the front-end and assembler. Unlike our earlier solutions, the buffer is now an active process that accepts requests to store and retrieve lines of assembly code. The implementation of the buffer process in Ada is shown in Figure 6.9. Note that processes are actually called **tasks** in Ada.

The task specification lists three entries that can be called by users of a buffer task: Put stores a line in the buffer, Get retrieves a line from the buffer, and Stop asks the buffer task to terminate. The implementation of the buffer task repeatedly executes a select statement. It accepts calls to Put (unless the buffer is full) and calls to Get (unless the buffer is empty). Only if the buffer is empty does it accept calls to Stop, in which case the process exits the loop.

The front-end and assembler are now easy to implement. They use one buffer task, declared as:

```
Buffer: Buffer_Task;
```

The front-end repeatedly produces a line and executes

```
-- specification of the buffer process
task type Buffer_Task is
    entry Put(Line: Line_Type);            -- these three entries can
    entry Get(Line: out Line_Type);        -- be called by clients of
    entry Stop;                            -- the buffer task
end Buffer_Task;


-- implementation of the buffer process
task body Buffer_Task is
    Max: constant := 10;                   -- size of the buffer
    Buffer: array(Integer range 0..Max-1) of Line_Type;
                                           -- the buffer itself
    Write_Pos: Integer := 0;               -- position for writing
    Read_Pos: Integer := 0;                -- position for reading
    Nr_Lines: Integer := 0;                -- number of lines in buffer
    Finished: Boolean := False;            -- used for termination
begin
    while not Finished loop
        select
            when Nr_Lines < Max =>         -- put line in buffer
            accept Put(Line: Line_Type) do
                Nr_Lines := Nr_Lines + 1;
                Buffer(Write_Pos) := Line;
                Write_Pos := (Write_Pos + 1) mod Max;
            end Put;
        or
            when Nr_Lines > 0 =>           -- get line from buffer
            accept Get(Line: out Line_Type) do
                Nr_Lines := Nr_Lines - 1;
                Line := Buffer(Read_Pos);
                Read_Pos := (Read_Pos + 1) mod Max;
            end Get;
        or
            when Nr_Lines = 0 =>           -- terminate process
            accept Stop do
                Finished := True;
            end Stop;
        end select;
    end loop;
end Buffer_Task;
```

Figure 6.9 A buffer task in Ada.

Buffer.Put(Next_Line);

The assembler repeatedly calls

Buffer.Get(Next_Line);

and assembles the line. After receiving the last line, the assembler calls Buffer.Stop.

Several other languages have a stronger form of select statement than Ada. In Ada, the constraints (guards) cannot depend on the parameters of the entry call. This is reflected in the Ada syntax, in that the guards appear *before* the accept statement. As a small advantage of the restriction, the guard expressions need to be evaluated only once, whereas with the more general form they must be evaluated once for every incoming entry call. On the other hand, the restriction sometimes complicates programming.

Remote Procedure Call

Like rendezvous, the **Remote Procedure Call** (**RPC**) construct is based on two-way message passing. The idea behind RPC is to allow communication between clients and servers through procedure calls, even if they run on different machines. Conventional procedure calling is well understood by programmers using imperative languages, so using it for parallel and distributed programming is simpler than sending messages back and forth.

Unfortunately, calling a procedure in a remote process introduces some problems. Unlike conventional procedures, the calling and called procedures have separate address spaces. If the procedure call contains a pointer to a data structure as an actual parameter, the invoked procedure cannot access this data structure, since it is located on a different machine. Also, it is impossible to use variables that are global to both the calling and called procedures. Notwithstanding these problems, the goal of RPC is to mimic local procedure calls as much as possible.

From the caller's side (the client), a remote procedure call is similar to an entry call. The caller specifies the server and the procedure and supplies actual parameters. The caller blocks until the receiver (server) has executed the procedure and has returned any results, as shown by the following pseudo-notation:

next_line := buffer.get();
buffer.put(next_line);

The calls look deceptively simple, but much activity is going on behind the scenes. The language implementation will pack all input parameters into a message and send it to the server. On the server's machine, this message is unpacked and passed to the server like normal data. The result returned by the server is treated similarly and goes in the opposite direction. Packing and unpacking of parameters is also called **marshalling** and **unmarshalling**.

Let us now consider how remote procedures are implemented at the server side. As we have seen before, there are two ways of accepting messages: explicitly by a receive or accept statement (as used by rendezvous) or implicitly by a new thread. With conventional procedure calls, control is passed automatically from the calling to the called procedure. The latter procedure clearly does not use any form of receive statement. We therefore reserve the term RPC for implicit receipt, since it is much closer to conventional procedure calls. Other authors, however, use the term RPC for explicit as well as implicit receipt.

A server **exports** one or more procedures that can be invoked by clients. The interface to the server, often called the **service**, gives a specification of these procedures, much as with entry declarations in an Ada task specification. The server contains a definition for each remote procedure specified in the interface.

Whenever a client invokes a remote procedure, a new thread is created within the server. This thread executes the procedure, returns the result, and then terminates. Since a server can have multiple threads running in parallel, these threads must synchronize, just like processes communicating through shared variables. In contrast, an Ada task has only one thread of control, which services entry calls one at a time.

6.3.3 In between message passing and shared variables

Above, we have described the two main classes of communication primitives: shared variables (Section 6.3.1) and message passing (Section 6.3.2). The two classes differ in several ways. In general, shared variables are easier to program with, especially if the application requires processes to share global state information. With message passing, any state information that is to be shared among processes must be transferred explicitly. In addition, a shared variable can be accessed by any number of processes, whereas a message transfers data between two processes.

As we have seen, the main difficulty with shared variables is synchronizing concurrent accesses to them. Also, shared variables and their synchronization mechanisms can only be implemented efficiently if (physical) shared memory is available. Distributed systems and many large-scale multicomputers provide only local memory.

There exist communication constructs that have some of the properties of message passing and some of shared variables. They try to combine the advantages of both and supply an easy-to-use mechanism that can be implemented without shared memory. One related area is simulating physical shared memory on distributed systems, called **shared virtual memory**, which we will not look at in this book (but see the Bibliographical notes for a reference). Below, we discuss two such communication constructs: Linda's Tuple Space and Orca's shared data-objects.

The Linda Tuple Space

One interesting model is Linda's Tuple Space. Linda is a set of primitives rather than a complete language. The Linda primitives can be embedded in an existing host language, resulting in a parallel language, for example C/Linda or FORTRAN/Linda. Linda provides a communication model called **Tuple Space**. Conceptually, Tuple Space is a shared memory consisting of tuples (records) that are addressed associatively (by content). The implementation of Tuple Space, however, does not require physical shared memory. Depending on the underlying hardware, the implementation can, for example, partition the Tuple Space among the local memories, or replicate the Tuple Space on all machines.

Three indivisible operations are defined on the Tuple Space: **out** adds a new tuple, **read** reads an existing tuple and **in** reads and deletes a tuple. Tuples are addressed by specifying the values or types of the fields. For example,

x: integer;
read("abc", 3.1, ? &x);

tries to find a tuple with three fields: the string constant "abc", the real constant 3.1 and any integer. If it finds such a tuple, it assigns the contents of the third field to the variable x. If no matching tuple exists, the operation blocks until some other process adds a matching tuple using **out**, for example by executing:

out("abc", 3.1, 27);

If multiple matching tuples exist, one is chosen arbitrarily.

Tuple Space can be used to simulate other communication primitives, such as shared variables and message passing. To simulate a shared integer variable X, for example, one can use a tuple ("X", value), initialized by a statement like:

out("X", 0);   −− set initial value to zero

To read the variable, one can execute the statement:

read("X", ? &x);   −− read value into local variable

The shared variable can be changed by executing:

in("X", ? &void);   −− delete tuple; ignore current value
out("X", newvalue);   −− generate new tuple

This assignment is executed indivisibly. If two processes try to modify the variable, the second one will be blocked in the **in** until the first process has put the tuple back into Tuple Space.

The Tuple Space can also be used for building distributed data structures which can be accessed simultaneously by multiple processes, leading to novel parallel programming styles.

Shared data-objects in Orca

Distributed data structures can also be expressed through **shared data-objects**, as supported by Orca. Orca is an imperative language for writing parallel programs for systems that need not have physical shared memory.

Processes in Orca may communicate through shared variables, but only if these variables are of an *abstract data type*. Such variables are called shared data-objects. Processes can share objects even if they run on different machines. The objects can be accessed solely through the operations defined by the abstract data type. All these operations are executed indivisibly.

The following example specifies an object type *IntObject* encapsulating a single integer:

```
object specification IntObject;
    operation Value(): integer;              # return the value
    operation Assign(v: integer);            # assign a value
    operation AwaitValue(v: integer);        # wait for a value
end;
```

The implementation part (see Figure 6.10) contains the data used to represent variables of the type, the implementation code of the operations and (optionally) code for initializing variables of the type.

Objects are created and used as follows:

```
X: IntObject;      # create an object
X$Assign(3);       # apply operation "Assign" to object X
```

Orca allows processes to be created dynamically through a fork statement. If an object is passed as a *shared* parameter in a fork statement, the newly created process can access the shared object. All operations are applied to single objects, making the model efficient to implement. Since all operations are indivisible, programmers do not have to worry about mutual exclusion synchronization. This is the reason why Orca only allows variables of abstract data types to be shared, and not plain variables (such as integers or arrays).

Condition synchronization in Orca is expressed by allowing operations to block. The AwaitValue operation (see Figure 6.10) blocks until the current value of the integer x contained in the object equals the parameter v.

In comparison, Orca allows users to define their own operations, whereas Linda has a fixed number of built-in operations. Also, Orca does not use associative addressing. A practical advantage of Linda is its ease of integration with existing languages.

```
object implementation IntObject;
  x: integer;              # local data of the object
  ....
  operation Value(): integer;
  begin
    return x;              # return the current value
  end;

  operation Assign(v: integer);
  begin
    x := v;                # assign a new value
  end;

  operation AwaitValue(v: integer);
  begin
    guard x = v do od;
  end;
end;
```

Figure 6.10 Part of the implementation of object type IntObject.

It is also interesting to compare Orca's shared data-objects with monitors. A monitor can only be implemented efficiently on a shared-memory multiprocessor. Data-objects, on the other hand, can be implemented without using shared memory by replicating them in the local memories. Operations that only read the object can be executed locally, without doing any communication or synchronization with other processors.

6.4 Languages based on other paradigms

Much research is being done to try to solve the parallel and distributed programming problem by adapting paradigms other than the imperative one. As a result, many parallel object-oriented, parallel functional and parallel logic languages have been proposed, most of which are still experimental.

One motivation for this research is the belief that these paradigms may be better suited for parallelism than the imperative paradigm. By definition, a program written in an imperative language fully determines the order in which statements will be executed. Even if the ordering of two statements does not matter, the programmer has to specify an order. This problem is known as **overspecification**. If the order had not been specified, it would have been easier for a compiler to run the two statements in parallel. Overspecification thus makes automatic parallelization hard, which may explain why constructs for explicit parallelism (for example, processes) are needed.

A second and more pragmatic reason for the wide interest in parallel non-imperative languages concerns improving the performance of these languages. Unlike imperative languages, functional and logic languages are often inefficient. The use of parallelism can help in solving this problem. Below, we briefly discuss how parallelism can be exploited in object-oriented, functional and logic languages.

An object-oriented program uses many different objects, each containing executable code. This view immediately suggests how parallelism can be introduced in such languages: have many objects execute simultaneously. In other words, objects now become **active**, whereas in a sequential object-oriented language an object remains **passive** until one of its operations is invoked. Communication between active objects is naturally based on operation invocation, as in sequential object-oriented languages. A similar model is used by **actor languages**, which use a set of autonomous agents (actors) that cooperate through message passing (Agha, 1986).

In Chapter 4 we discussed the referential transparency of functional languages. Owing to this property, the results of a function application depend only on the parameters and not on when the function is called. For example, in Miranda the expression

mult (g 3) (h 5 6)

is guaranteed to give the same result, independent of which of the two operand expressions of the multiplication is computed first. As a consequence, it is also possible to evaluate the two operands in parallel. We can have one processor computing (g 3) and another evaluating (h 5 6) simultaneously. After the two results have become available, the multiplication is done by either of the two processors, or by a third processor. The main problem with this approach is efficiency. If the functions g and h do little work, the overhead of doing them in parallel far outweighs the gains.

Finally, logic programs can also be executed in parallel. We recall that a logic program consists of Horn clauses, such as:

a ← b, c.
a ← d, e, f.

There are two distinct opportunities for parallelism in such programs. First, we can try both clauses for a in parallel, until one of them succeeds. This is called **OR-parallelism**. Each of the two clauses contains a body with multiple goals that have to be solved. For the first clause, we can execute b and c in parallel; for the second clause, we can do d, e and f in parallel. This form is called **AND-parallelism**.

6.5 Example languages

Many languages for parallel and distributed programming have been proposed. For distributed programming alone, there are more than 100 languages (Bal *et al.*, 1989). Example languages are: Algol 68, Mesa,

Concurrent Pascal (imperative shared-variable languages); CSP, occam, Concurrent C, Hermes, Ada, SR (imperative message-passing languages); ConcurrentSmalltalk, ABCL/1, Emerald (object-oriented languages); Multilisp (functional language); Concurrent Prolog, Parlog, KL1 (logic languages).

Below we will look at three representative languages: the shared-variable language Mesa and the message-passing languages SR (Synchronizing Resources) and Ada.

6.5.1 Mesa

Mesa is a monitor-based language (Geschke *et al.*, 1977; Lampson and Redell, 1980) developed at Xerox PARC. It provides support for concurrent programming in the form of processes, monitors and condition variables. It was designed to be a systems programming language.

Parallelism in Mesa is expressed through processes, which are created dynamically using the **fork** call. This call accepts a procedure name as a parameter, and returns a process identifier. In a subsequent **join** call, the calling process will be delayed until the process whose identifier was given is finished (if it is not already), and the result will be returned to the caller.

Processes communicate through shared data, encapsulated in monitors. A monitor contains 'entry' procedures which processes can call to manipulate the shared data. Processes synchronize using condition variables. When a process calls **wait** with a given condition variable as a parameter, it is suspended until another process calls **notify** with the same parameter. Several processes can be blocked on the same condition variable. The **notify** is only a hint to the signalled process that the condition variable now may – but need not – be true. The signalled process is not necessarily run immediately after being notified. It must therefore test the condition variable again after its **wait**. Mesa also provides a **broadcast** primitive, which resembles the **notify**, except that all processes waiting on a given condition variable are notified, rather than just one.

6.5.2 Synchronizing Resources (SR)

SR is one of the many languages based on sequential processes and message passing (Andrews *et al.*, 1988; Andrews and Olsson, 1993). SR has been developed at the University of Arizona since 1980. The philosophy behind SR is that none of the message passing alternatives is ideally suited for all applications. Therefore, SR provides many different forms of message passing. It supports synchronous and asynchronous messages, RPC, rendezvous and more.

SR lets the programmer decide how a message is sent as well as how it is received. When sending a message, the options are synchronous (blocking) and asynchronous (nonblocking). The receiver has the choice between explicit receipt through a receive statement and implicit receipt. With explicit receipt, the receiver can order the messages based on their arrival time or contents.

These two ways of sending and receiving messages can be combined in all four ways, yielding four different communication primitives. This orthogonal design keeps the language reasonably simple.

6.5.3 Ada

Ada was designed to support applications that can use multiple processes and run on shared-memory multiprocessors. Ada 9X also has facilities for partitioning programs on distributed systems (Intermetrics, Inc., 1993). Below, we will look at Ada's language concepts for parallelism and communication.

The definition of a task (process) in Ada consists of two parts: a specification part and an implementation part (see Figure 6.9). A task can be created by declaring an entity of a task type. Tasks can also be created dynamically, using an allocator, as in

```
type Buffer_Access is access Buffer;
My_Buffer: Buffer_Access;

My_Buffer := new Buffer;
```

Tasks in Ada can communicate through three different mechanisms:

- rendezvous,
- protected objects, and
- shared variables.

Shared variables are to be used sparingly, however, and are subject to several restrictions, which we will not discuss here. The basic rendezvous model is described in Section 6.3.2, but Ada supports several extensions, as will be discussed first. Next, we will discuss protected objects, which are present in Ada 9X but not in Ada 83.

A *server* in Ada can use the select statement not only for selecting among different incoming entry calls, but also for handling time-outs and termination. For example, it is possible to express that an entry call should arrive within a certain time limit, otherwise the statement times out. A *client* can also use the select statement, for example for doing a **conditional entry call**, which tries to do an entry call but gives up if the server does not accept the entry immediately. It should be noted that the two forms of select statement as used by the server and client are very different: one *accepts* entry calls and one *does* entry calls. Both forms are called select statements, which may be confusing.

The second form of communication in Ada is through a **protected object**, which is essentially the same concept as the shared data-object introduced in Orca (see Section 6.3.3). Protected objects are included in Ada 9X to allow secure and lightweight sharing of data. In Ada 83, shared data can be encapsulated by a task, as demonstrated by the buffer example of Figure 6.9. This mechanism is heavyweight and expensive, however. Protected objects, on the other hand, are inexpensive, as they are passive constructs which do not embody a process.

In good Ada tradition, a protected type definition has a specification and an implementation part. The specification part declares operations which can be applied to variables of the type, and the local data of such variables. For example, a protected type encapsulating a shared integer may be specified as follows:

```
protected type Int_Object is
    function Value return Integer; -- return the value
    procedure Assign(V: Integer); -- assign a value
    entry Await_Zero;              -- wait for value to become zero
private
    X: Integer;                    -- local data
end;
```

The implementation part of Int_Object is given in Figure 6.11.

```
protected body Int_Object is
    function Value return Integer is
    begin
        return X;
    end;

    procedure Assign(V: Integer) is
    begin
        X := V;
    end;

    entry Await_Zero when X = 0 is
    begin
        null;
    end;
end;
```

Figure 6.11 Body of protected type Int_Object.

A variable of this type, called a protected object, can be declared and used as follows:

```
X: Int_Object;   -- create a protected object
X.Assign(3);     -- apply procedure "Assign" to X
```

As in Orca, all operations on X will be executed indivisibly. Unlike the specification of object types in Orca, Ada 9X makes a distinction between operations that read the protected object (functions) and operations that potentially modify it (procedures). Multiple function calls (such as X.Value) can be executed simultaneously in the same protected object, while procedure calls are serialized. Orca does exactly the same optimization, but this is implemented by the compiler and is transparent to the programmer. In addition, Orca replicates objects if no shared memory is present, and executes read-only operations using the local copy.

Condition synchronization for protected objects is also expressed similarly as for Orca's objects, except that Ada again uses special syntax: operations that potentially block are declared as **entries**, as shown in Figure 6.11. Unlike Orca, Ada 9X does not allow the test in the entry to depend on a parameter of the entry. We therefore implemented an operation Await_Zero (which waits for the integer to become zero) instead of the more general operation AwaitValue (which waits for any value).

Ada also supports constructs for real-time programming, as we discuss briefly in Chapter 7.

Summary

Figure 6.12 gives an overview of the language concepts and primitives discussed in this chapter.

- A parallel system contains multiple processors. In a multiprocessor, the CPUs are connected to a shared memory. In a multicomputer, they are connected through a network.
- Parallelism in a programming language is useful, because (1) some problems are easier to solve in parallel; and (2) many applications can exploit the physical parallelism of parallel machines. Parallel programming means writing a program that uses parallelism for either of these reasons. Distributed programming is writing a program that runs on a collection of machines connected by a network.
- Most parallel imperative languages use processes for expressing parallelism. Alternative constructs are co-routines and parfor and parbegin statements.
- Communication between processes is usually based on shared variables or message passing.
- With shared variables, additional primitives for mutual exclusion and condition synchronization are needed, such as locks, semaphores or monitors.

Concept	Primitives	Goal
Parallelism		
Co-routines	**resume**	pseudo-parallelism
Parallel statements	**parbegin** statement	true parallelism
Parallel loops	**parfor** statement	true parallelism
Processes	**fork**, **join**	true parallelism
Shared variables		
Polling	test variable	condition synchronization
Locks	**lock**, **unlock**	mutual exclusion
Semaphores	**P**, **V**	mutual excl., cond. synchr.
Monitors	**wait**, **signal**	mutual excl., cond. synchr.
Message passing		
Message passing	**send to**, **receive [from]**	1-way message passing
Rendezvous	entry call, **accept**	2-way message passing
RPC	call, shared var. synchr.	2-way message passing
Select statement	**select**	nondeterminism
Mixed models		
Tuple Space	**read**, **in**, **out**	general communication
Shared objects	abstract data types	general communication

Figure 6.12 Overview of language primitives for parallel and distributed
        programming.

- Issues in message passing are: how to address the sender and receiver; whether or not to block the sender; accepting messages explicitly or implicitly; controlling the order in which messages are accepted; and one-way versus two-way communication.
- Rendezvous and Remote Procedure Call are two frequently used high-level language primitives.
- Alternative communication primitives for imperative languages include Tuple Space and shared data-objects.
- To express parallelism and communication, non-imperative languages often use constructs that better fit in with their paradigm. Examples are parallel objects, parallel expressions and AND/OR parallelism.

Bibliographical notes

The issue of parallel programming is covered in depth in the book by Andrews (1991). Several survey papers on language constructs exist, for example Andrews and Schneider (1983) on parallel languages and Bal *et al.* (1989) on distributed languages.

    Hoare's (1978) paper on CSP is a classical one in the literature on message passing. The most influential paper on Remote Procedure Calls is that by Birrell and Nelson (1984). The issue of implicit versus explicit receipt of remote procedures is discussed by Scott (1983).

Bal and Tanenbaum (1991) give a more detailed comparison between shared variables and message passing.

Distributed implementations of Prolog are described in a book edited by Kacsuk and Wise (1992). Distributed logic programming is considered by Eliens (1992). Parallel logic languages are discussed in Shapiro (1989).

For a detailed discussion of parallel hardware and software, we refer to the book by Almasi and Gottlieb (1989). The basic ideas for Shared Virtual Memory are given in Li and Hudak (1989).

Linda is described in Ahuja *et al.* (1986) and in Carriero and Gelernter (1989). Orca is described in Bal (1991) and Bal *et al* (1992). Ada 9X is described in Intermetrics, Inc. (1993) and Barnes (1994). A comparison between SR, Linda, Orca and other languages is given by Bal (1992).

Many journals on parallel and distributed computing exist, such as *Parallel Computing, Parallel and Distributed Computing, IEEE Transactions on Parallel and Distributed Systems* and *Concurrency: Practice & Experience*. Important conferences in this area are: the IEEE International Conference on Distributed Computing Systems, the International Conference on Parallel Processing and the ACM Symposium on Principles and Practice of Parallel Programming.

Exercises

6.1 Incorrect programs containing race conditions are often very hard to debug. For example, adding a simple print statement for debugging purposes may drastically change the behaviour of the program and may even cause a bug to no longer manifest itself. Think of a situation where this might happen.

6.2 Some processors support a hardware **test-and-set instruction**, to be used in a multiprocessor environment. The instruction reads a memory location, tests if it is zero and stores a non-zero value into the location. It returns the previous value of the location. It is executed indivisibly, so no other processor on the same bus can read or write any memory location while the test-and-set is in progress. Why do you think such an instruction is useful?

6.3 Another shared-memory synchronization primitive is **sleep/wakeup**. The execution of sleep(x) suspends the current process. The execution of wakeup(x) wakes up all processes (if any) that are blocked in a sleep on **x**. Here, **x** can be any value, for example a memory address.

This primitive is generally considered to be harder to use than semaphores. Also, it is easier to make synchronization errors with sleep/wakeup. Why do you think this mechanism is inferior to semaphores?

6.4   An important problem with monitors is that of **nested monitor calls**. If an operation **F1** defined in monitor **M1** calls an operation **F2** defined in **M2**, the call to **F2** is said to be a nested call. What problem is caused by the possibility of nested calls? Hint: think about what happens if **F2** blocks on a **wait**.

6.5   In the text we described how the front-end and assembler of a parallel compiler communicate and synchronize through a monitor (see Figure 6.7). The implementation described there does not handle termination correctly. Try to solve this problem by slightly modifying the interface and implementation of the buffer. The producer (front-end) must be able to indicate that no more data will be generated.

6.6   Both the case statement and the select statement in Ada can make a selection between a number of alternatives. Is it possible to delete the select statement from the language and use the case statement instead? If not, what is the fundamental difference between the two statements?

6.7   Rewrite the **Buffer_Task** of Figure 6.9 as an Ada 9X protected type. Since a protected object is passive, the **Stop** entry is no longer needed.

6.8   Write a parallel program in Linda that multiplies two N by N matrices A and B by computing all elements of the result matrix in parallel. First, store $N{\times}N$ tuples in Tuple Space of the form ("compute", i, j), representing the job of multiplying row i by column j. Next, start up a number of worker processes (one per processor) that repeatedly take these jobs out of Tuple Space, do the required computation, and store the result back in Tuple Space in tuples of the form ("result",i,j,r). Finally, use one separate process that prints the elements of the result matrix in row order. You may assume that all processes have a copy of the A and B matrices and you do not have to worry about proper termination of the worker processes.

7

Other Paradigms

In the previous chapters we have discussed four general-purpose programming paradigms – imperative, object-oriented, functional and logic – and one special-purpose paradigm, parallel and distributed processing. Together, these cover almost all programming activities and research at present, but that does not mean that the programming language landscape ends there. Other paradigms have been and are being proposed, both general-purpose and special-purpose, and we will turn to these now. Most of these paradigms have not (yet) been worked out in full detail, and to avoid just listing odds and ends, we shall first give a provisional classification of programming paradigms. It will be clear that such a classification will be open-ended.

When a program is run, a process is created that will, hopefully, achieve what the program was intended for. To this end, the computer *manipulates* the *state* of the process, as specified by the program. Our classification is based on questions that can be asked about the way in which the state and its manipulation are specified in the program. Important questions are 'How is the state accessed in the program?' and 'How is state manipulation specified in the program?'. To the degree that these two questions are independent, answers to the first combine freely with answers to the second. Figure 7.1 summarizes the results of combining three general ways of accessing state with two general ways of specifying state manipulation.

State is manipulated explicitly, by commands, in the imperative and object-oriented languages; such languages have a more operational character. This contrasts with the functional and logic languages, in which the manipulation is specified more implicitly, through pattern matching (and conditions) and inference, respectively; such languages have a more declarative character.

State is accessed as named variables in the imperative languages, through operations in the object-oriented languages and exclusively as named parameters in the functional and logic languages.

| State | manipulated by ... | | |
	commands	patterns	inference
as named variables and parameters	imperative		
by operations	object-oriented		
as named parameters only		functional	logic

accessed ...

Figure 7.1 A simple classification of paradigms.

Not all languages in each paradigm conform equally strictly to the answers supplied above. The meta-logical predicates **assert** and **retract** in Prolog, for example, introduce the database as an anonymous variable and so the language does not strictly access state as named parameters only. But, as the name 'meta-logical predicate' already implies, **assert** and **retract** are not considered to be essential concepts in the logic paradigm.

This classification is open-ended in two ways. Each time somebody provides a new answer to one of the existing questions, Figure 7.1 gains a row or column, and each time somebody comes up with an independent question about state, the figure gains another dimension. Examples of new independent questions about state are: 'Is the state manipulated by one process only or possibly by several processes?', and if there can be more than one process, 'Can all processes access the state on an equal basis?' We will find new answers to old questions in the sections below.

As an illustration we shall now try to classify the language PostScript, which was discussed as an example of an imperative language in Section 2.6.3. Every step in a PostScript program is fully prescribed, so the state manipulation is definitely by commands (Figure 7.1). But when we look, for example, at the definition of **average** as **add 2 div** to find out how the state is accessed, we find no named variables or parameters. Upon closer examination we see that the state (the values to be averaged) can be found anonymously on the stack. This suggests that PostScript treats state essentially differently from the imperative languages, and that Figure 7.1 must be extended with a fourth row, labelled 'accessed as anonymous parameters'. Indeed, programs in PostScript look and feel very different from Pascal or Ada programs. We must, however, note that the PostScript dictionaries are equivalent to named variables. Like most languages, PostScript does not conform strictly to one paradigm.

The above addresses the classification of general-purpose programming paradigms. Special-purpose paradigms serve to solve programming problems with special requirements. Examples of such requirements that we have seen are the utilization of parallel hardware and the solution of problems whose data are distributed over many computers. Special-purpose paradigms include concepts and methods that assist the user in coming to grips with the special requirements. Once such methods are in place, they can sometimes contribute to the structuring and the solving of more general problems. An example of this is the Ada *task*, which is primarily intended for parallel programming, but which can also be used to express independency of program components even if there is no need to execute the components in parallel.

In the next two sections we discuss three additional general-purpose paradigms and four special-purpose paradigms. Unlike the earlier chapters, literature references will be provided at the end of each subsection.

7.1 Additional general-purpose paradigms

We will discuss here three general-purpose paradigms: constraint programming, access-oriented programming and single-datastructure languages. Constraint programming is a powerful paradigm, on which much research is being done; access-oriented programming is interesting since it is in some sense the mirror image of object-oriented programming, but much less research has been done on it; and single-datastructure languages represent interesting attempts to simplify programming.

These do not exhaust the known general-purpose paradigms. A further example is the grammatical paradigm, in which the solution to a problem is characterized by writing a phrase-structure grammar for it. Methods from formal languages are then applied to produce solutions from the grammar. Not enough research has been done on the grammatical paradigm to warrant a section on it here.

7.1.1 Constraint programming

In an ideal **constraint programming** system, the user defines the solution to a problem as a data type, the domain of the solution, and supplies constraints on the values in it that restrict them to the desired solutions. The system will then find these solutions. An example is the so-called 8-queens problem, which asks for a position on a chess board (the data structure) with the following constraints:

- there are exactly 8 queens on the board and no other pieces;
- no queen attacks any other queen.

Activating the system will then produce some solution or all 92 solutions, depending on the system and its exact activation. Constraint programming is attractive since many problems can easily be brought into a constraint form, as the above example shows. Of all known paradigms, it is the most declarative, and it comes closest to the ideal of automatic programming.

Constraint programming is not restricted to symbolic manipulation, but can also be profitably applied to numerical problems. A standard example is the conversion between degrees Celsius and degrees Fahrenheit. The domain consists of two numerical values, C and F, which are constrained by one constraint:

$$9 * C + 160 = 5 * F$$

To do a specific conversion, we add a second constraint, for example F = 68, and the system will respond with

$$(C = 20, F = 68)$$

On most systems, the constraint F = C (that is, the temperature at which the Celsius and Fahrenheit scales have the same numerical value) will result in

$$(C = -40, F = -40)$$

A constraint can generally work in more than one way. For example, a constraint can express that the value of a variable in memory and a value displayed in a certain place on the terminal screen be the same. Now, if the value of the variable in memory is changed, the displayed value will change accordingly, and if the user edits the value on the screen, the variable in memory will be modified to reflect this.

It will be clear from the above examples that constraint programming relieves the programmer of the burden of inventing an algorithm to reach the desired solution and places that burden squarely on the shoulders of the system. The problem with this is that these shoulders cannot carry it. For one thing, full constraint programming requires a general problem solver, which does not exist. And for another, it is very easy to write down a set of constraints that do have a solution, but this solution cannot be found by any reasonable automatic method. Therefore, all of the more powerful constraint programming systems compromise in one way or another. There are two directions in which systems try to find this compromise. One is restriction to a very specific domain. Examples are systems that calculate properties of electronic circuits, or draw geometric figures. The second is to require the programmer to supply code (generally in an imperative language) that will satisfy a constraint by changing the value of one of the variables in it. Normally, the implementation of a programming language is not the user's concern, but when working with a constraint programming system the user has to be aware of the underlying constraint-satisfaction mechanism.

Constraint programming systems with a specific numerical domain (for example, that used for the Celsius/Fahrenheit conversion) rewrite the constraints to algebraic equations, if necessary, and then use an equation solver to satisfy the constraints. The simplest of these scan the constraints for equations they can solve right away, and repeat this process with the newly obtained results, hoping to satisfy all constraints in this way; this process is called **local propagation**. More general equation solvers are sometimes used, but none solve the problem completely.

Constraint programming systems with a symbolic domain (such as that used for the 8-queens problem) generally do exhaustive search, essentially in a Prolog-like fashion.

Systems that require the user to supply code to satisfy constraints are often called **condition-action systems**, since such systems contain descriptions of actions to be performed when given constraints are violated. Such systems are half-way imperative, but have the methodological advantage that they clearly separate the requirements from the methods to fulfil them.

Examples of constraint programming systems are ThingLab and OPS5. The temperature conversion constraint written in ThingLab is shown in Figure 7.2. The constraint is followed by two actions (indented further) that may help to restore the constraint.

Part Descriptions
    celsius: a Real;
    fahrenheit: a Real;
Constraints
    9 * celsius + 160 = 5 * fahrenheit
        celsius ← 5 * (fahrenheit − 32) / 9
        fahrenheit ← 9 * celsius / 5 + 32

Figure 7.2 Temperature conversion in ThingLab.

There is a strong connection between constraint programming and Prolog. The relations in Prolog describe constraints on a symbolic domain and Prolog has a built-in constraint-satisfaction mechanism, depth-first search. Indeed, Prolog can be seen as a special case of constraint programming.

Constraint programming has the advantage that it makes very clear what exactly is being calculated, and it requires a minimum of algorithmic effort from the programmer. A good constraint programming system can be a good prototyping tool. The main user problem with constraint programming is that it is often not easy to formulate the constraints correctly and in such a way that they will be accepted by the system. Formulating constraints correctly is trickier that it first seems. For example, in a constraint programming system for graphical purposes, one can describe a regular hexagon as an arbitrary hexalateral polygon with the following constraints:

- all 6 sides have the same length;
- sides 1 and 4, 2 and 5, 3 and 6 are pairwise parallel.

In addition to the expected regular hexagon of Figure 7.3 (a), however, this also describes a double triangle as depicted in Figure 7.3 (b). (For clarity, the two triangles have been shifted a bit with respect to each other, without breaking the connections.)

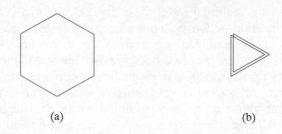

(a)   (b)

Figure 7.3 Two figures satisfying the same overly simple constraint.

Constraint programming was pioneered by Sutherland in his thesis (1963) which described Sketchpad, a system for generating and editing geometrical figures. It was far ahead of its time and required hardware and software that were next to unavailable then. Some recent systems are OPS5, which is a general-purpose condition-action system, and IDEAL, which restricts itself to the drawing of geometrical figures and uses a built-in equation solver. The Make program mentioned in Section 2.5.5 can be considered a rudimentary constraint system of the condition-action type. Make finds the conditions and actions in a 'Makefile', which specifies a number of source-result relations between files. Furthermore, there is the implicit constraint that the result should always be more recent than the source. Actions can be specified to update a result whenever such a constraint is violated.

The constraint paradigm is valuable even if there is no constraint-satisfaction system to back it up. It leads the programmer to concentrate on the essential properties of the desired solution and can thus be viewed as a specification paradigm. If a constraint programming system is available, the constraint specification may be executable, but even in the absence of a constraint programming system, it can serve as a basis for hand-coding a program.

A general book on constraint languages is by Leler (1988); it gives a broad introduction and illustrates the principles using the language Bertrand.

7.1.2 Access-oriented programming

With **access-oriented programming**, variables can be annotated with procedures such that, if the variable is accessed, the procedure is invoked automatically. Such annotations are useful in several cases. For example, a constraint can be imposed on a variable by annotating it with a procedure that verifies the constraint. The procedure will be called automatically every time the variable is changed. The annotations can also be useful during debugging of programs, since one can now set a trap on a variable, causing the debugger to be invoked when the variable is read or written.

Annotations can also be used for visualization. In a simulation program, the entities being simulated (for example, cars in a traffic system) can be monitored using annotations. Every time a car changes its position, the part of the program displaying the simulated system can be informed automatically, so it can update the display.

Invoking a procedure automatically whenever a variable is accessed is not without danger. The annotations should not make the program incorrect, and neither should annotations interfere with each other. In general, the invoked procedure should not have any side-effects that interfere with the main program or other invoked procedures.

Access-oriented programming is used in the Loops programming system developed at Xerox PARC. Loops in fact integrates several paradigms, including object-oriented and functional programming. Access-oriented programming is dual to object-oriented programming. In object-oriented programming, whenever an operation is applied to an object, the object is read or modified. In access-oriented programming, whenever an object is read or modified, an operation is invoked. Loops makes a distinction between accessing (reading) the object and changing it, so different operations can be invoked. Annotations can be installed dynamically in Loops, and annotations can also be recursively nested.

The popularity of access-oriented programming does not come near that of object-oriented programming. The paradigm has not made it into any major language, although an important application of the paradigm can be found in spreadsheet programs.

The Loops programming system is described in Stefik *et al.* (1986).

7.1.3 Single-datastructure languages

Single-datastructure languages attempt to simplify programming by casting everything into a single data structure, for which powerful operations are provided. The paradigm can be summarized as 'All the world is a ...'. Well-known examples are APL, which induces the user to formulate everything in terms of arrays and operations on them, and SETL, which does the same with sets. Icon has enough string manipulation support for it to be used in an 'All the world is a string' approach to programming. Lisp can be seen as an 'All the world is a list' language.

Once the user has become accustomed to the single-minded world view of a single-datastructure language, the language can be a great help in rapid prototyping. For many problems, a program in, for example, SETL is typically much shorter, easier to write and easier to debug than the corresponding program in C. The resulting program is much slower, though.

APL

APL was designed by Iverson (1962) more than 30 years ago to endow computers with a mathematical notation. Its basic data types are integer, character and real. It has no type constructors besides arrays, which may be multi-dimensional; one-dimensional arrays are called **vectors**, two-dimensional arrays are called **matrices**. Arrays must be homogeneous in type and there are no arrays of arrays; arrays may have zero length. APL owes its striking appearance partly to the fact that, like mathematical notation, it has no keywords and partly to the exuberance of unusual operators and separators. In addition to the letters and digits, APL has about 60 special symbols; examples are ∇ for operator definition, ϕ for rotation and reversal and $\square$ for input/output.

An APL program consists of a collection of generally very short operator definitions, each containing a number of expressions; the operators can be recursive. The notation is very concise and a typical example of an expression is

$$\wedge / T = \phi\, T$$

which yields 1 if T is a palindrome and 0 if it is not. This requires an explanation. An array is called a **palindrome** if it is its own reverse; the notion is normally restricted to strings, but the above expression works for any array. Operators in APL have no precedence and are all right-associative; this means that we have to read each expression from right to left. In the above expression, T is reversed by the operator ϕ and each element in it is compared to the corresponding element of T by the operator =; the latter works on two arrays here and yields an array of 0s and 1s. The reduction separator / inserts the logical AND operator $\wedge$ between each pair of elements of the resulting array, thus reducing it to one Boolean value, the answer. Figure 7.4 shows the process for T = 'MADAM IM ADAM'.

$$
\begin{array}{rcl}
T & \Rightarrow & \text{'M' 'A' 'D' 'A' 'M' ' ' 'I' 'M' ' ' 'A' 'D' 'A' 'M'} \\
\phi\,T & \Rightarrow & \text{'M' 'A' 'D' 'A' ' ' 'M' 'I' ' ' 'M' 'A' 'D' 'A' 'M'} \\
T = \phi\,T & \Rightarrow & \text{1 1 1 1 0 0 1 0 0 1 1 1 1} \\
\wedge / T = \phi\,T & \Rightarrow & 1 \wedge 1 \wedge 1 \wedge 1 \wedge 0 \wedge 0 \wedge 1 \wedge 0 \wedge 0 \wedge 1 \wedge 1 \wedge 1 \wedge 1 \\
& \Rightarrow & 0
\end{array}
$$

Figure 7.4 Evaluation of $\wedge / T = \phi\, T$ for T = 'MADAM IM ADAM'.

The main flow-of-control mechanism in APL is the operator activation in expressions. Repetition is often implicit in the operators, as the above example shows. Selection can often be done by expressions:

□ ← ('pos', 'neg') [1 + A < 0]

will print neg if A < 0 and pos otherwise. Again, this requires an explanation. Reading from the right, A < 0 yields a 0 or a 1, 1+ yields a 1 or a 2 and the indexing yields the character array 'pos' or 'neg', respectively. That result is then sent to (←) the output (□). If these flow-of-control substitutes do not suffice, there is an explicit goto operator, → N, which transfers control to line number N in the present function. Needless to say, N can be an arbitrary expression.

APL is an extreme language, with which only a strong love or hate relationship is possible. It seems a toy, but large real-world applications have been written in it. It will continue to amaze, confuse and delight a select group of programmers for years to come.

SETL

SETL is less strict in its adherence to a single-datastructure than APL; besides sets, it features tuples and maps. Sets correspond to mathematical sets: they contain unique values in undefined order. Tuples are like lists in that they may contain duplicate values and maintain their elements in order. Maps are like arrays that can be indexed by values of arbitrary type; they are equivalent in SETL to sets of tuples consisting of two values.

The values in a set, tuple or map need not all be of the same type, and may themselves be sets, tuples and maps. All values are finite. Sets can be created by enumerating their contents or by specifying ranges: {1..5} is the set {1, 2, 3, 4, 5}. Operations for the construction of unions, intersections, set differences and power sets are available, as are tests for membership and subset relations.

One of the most powerful set operations in SETL is the such-that set former, abbreviated to |. The | is called a *set former* rather than a set operator, since its operands are not values to be operated upon. The left-hand side of the | is a special form called a *set generator* and the right-hand side is a Boolean expression used to filter the set being generated (hence the |, used both in UNIX and MS-DOS as the filter symbol). The expression

{x: x IN {1 .. 5} | x mod 2 = 0}

results in the set {2, 4}: the original set {1, 2, 3, 4, 5} is filtered through the condition that each number be even.

As a more powerful example, the statement

print({[x, y, z]: x IN {1..10}, y IN {1..10}, z IN {1..20} | x*x + y*y = z*z}) prints all integer values x, y, z with $1 \leq x \leq 10$, $1 \leq y \leq 10$, $1 \leq z \leq 20$, such that x*x + y*y = z*z. So it prints the lengths of the sides of all right triangles with integral lengths, whose right sides are shorter than 11. Note that all sets are finite and that even z must be restricted.

The such-that operation can be combined with the Boolean EXISTS operation in expressions like

EXISTS x IN {0..a} | x*x = a

to test if a is the square of an integer.

In addition to sets, which support breadth-first search, SETL has two special constructs to support depth-first search. These are the Boolean oracle function OK and the FAIL statement. When called upon to choose between two possibilities, the OK function will always seem to choose the right alternative. To make this work, the programmer has to execute a FAIL statement whenever it becomes clear that a solution will not be found.

Suppose we have two doors; behind one is the Lost Baby, behind the other is the Evil Wizard, and we have to choose on zero information. The IF OK statement in Figure 7.5 will do just that. (The $ sign starts a comment.) The trick is that the OK will first yield one Boolean value and the program will continue with that value. If the guess was wrong, somewhere a FAIL will be done, which causes the system to backtrack to the latest OK, which then tries the other Boolean value. Continuing in this way, a solution will be found, if one exists, and the program of Figure 7.5 prints 'Lost Baby found behind right door!!'.

SETL is a Very High Level Language (VHLL) with powerful data types and operators. The OK/FAIL search mechanism allows simple formulation of complicated searches, but each additional OK in a program may potentially double its running time.

7.2 Additional special-purpose paradigms

We shall consider here four special-purpose paradigms: dataflow programming, little languages, database languages and real-time programming. Dataflow programming strives to exploit dataflow machines; little languages fill programming niches for which normal programming languages are too general; database languages give access to a complex data object, a database; and in real-time programming the timeliness of the result is part of its correctness.

7.2.1 Dataflow programming

The basic idea in dataflow programming is to have a separate processor for each operation in the program. Operations here include arithmetical and logical operations, function calls and if-else decisions. Each operation waits

```
PROGRAM Quest;
  CONST door = { ['left', 'Evil Wizard'], ['right', 'Lost Baby'] };
    $ A constant SETL map with two "door"s in it.

  IF OK THEN move('left'); ELSE move('right'); END IF;
    $ This will always choose correctly and
    $ print 'Lost Baby found behind right door!!'.

  $ Procedure declarations come at the end of a SETL program:
  PROCEDURE move(dir);          $ Move in direction "dir".
    IF door(dir) = 'Lost Baby' THEN
      print('Lost Baby found behind', dir, 'door!!');
    ELSE
      FAIL;                     $ Cause backtrack.
    END IF;
  END PROCEDURE move;

END PROGRAM Quest;
```

Figure 7.5 Demonstration program for the SETL OK/FAIL mechanism.

until the values of its operands become available and then makes the result of the operation available as quickly as possible. Since all processors are independent and do their work at the earliest possible moment, this provides optimal fine-grained parallelism without requiring explicit programmer help. The order in which the operations are performed is determined solely by the flow of the data, hence the name of the paradigm.

Suppose we have two values, a and b, and we want to calculate their average and the average of their squares. A program for this is:

```
av := (a + b) / 2;
avsq := (a * a + b * b) / 2;
```

which contains six operations:

```
1:   sum := a + b;
2:   av := sum / 2;
3:   asq := a * a;
4:   bsq := b * b;
5:   sumsq := asq + bsq;
6:   avsq := sumsq /2;
```

Sequential execution would require six steps. On a dataflow machine, operations 1, 3 and 4 can be performed immediately and in parallel (assuming a and b are available). This makes the values sum, asq and bsq available. Now operations 2 and 5 can execute, resulting in av and sumsq. The latter frees operation 6 and the calculation has been performed in three steps. The data dependencies, and thus the dataflow, are shown in Figure 7.6.

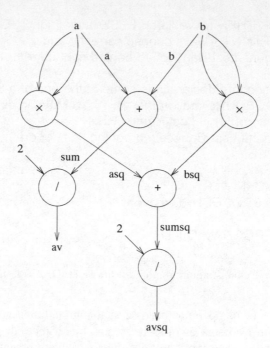

Figure 7.6 A simple dataflow graph.

The processors can be conceptual, in which case the dataflow paradigm is a general programming paradigm which allows programming without overspecification of execution order; or they can be real processors in a dataflow machine, in which case the paradigm is a special-purpose paradigm for programming such machines. Lucid is a language that allows both views. To understand what kind of language is suitable to support the dataflow paradigm, we have to make a number of observations.

- The dataflow model includes (named) values only; there are no variables.
- There cannot be side-effects: each processor sees only its own input values and can affect only its own output values.
- There is no global memory; the only memory there is exists in the interfaces (pipelines) between the processors.
- Values can be given names, but there can only be one such definition of a given name. If redefinition were possible, a processor would not know whether to wait for the original value or for its redefinition. A

dataflow language must be **single-definition** (also called **single-assignment**).
- Processors cannot just give up upon an error in their input values, since there is no central program counter to manipulate in error handling. Each processor must terminate and yield a result value. This requires an explicit error value for each data type.

Going through our inventory of programming languages, we immediately find a language type that fulfils the above requirements perfectly: functional languages. They use no variables, they do not allow side-effects, they have no global memory, they are single-definition and many of them have error values. Functional languages are ideal languages with which to program the ideal dataflow machine.

Unfortunately, this beautiful plan does not stand up in the harsh light of reality. A dataflow machine with enough processors to assign one processor to each operation in even a moderately sized program has never been built, and if it were, it would probably suffer badly from communication overhead. Also, functional languages use recursion extensively, whereas the hardware is not recursive.

To simulate many processors with few actual processors (between two and 100 is usual), a present-day dataflow machine consists of a memory, which contains the operations with their partially evaluated operands, a bank of processors, and one or more dispatchers. The dispatchers scan the memory for operations whose operands are available and dispatch them to free processors, as shown in Figure 7.7. This setup entails some communication overhead, but allows the processors to be utilized efficiently. Moreover, the memory helps to support code copying and queueing, which are discussed below.

There are two approaches to the recursion problem. The first is to ignore the problem and just do the recursive call; this requires allocating new processors for the operations in the function (so-called **code copying**) and renaming the values in it. Both the ideal and the actual machine can perform this action. In the actual machine, the operations in the function are copied to memory, and renaming is done by tagging the data with a recursion level indicator. At the expense of some increased complexity in the tagging, the code copying can often be avoided. This works, but can be very inefficient.

The second approach is to forbid recursion in the language, but this too comes at a price. Since functional languages use recursion to express iteration, we lose iteration in giving up recursion. Dataflow languages differ in the special constructions they feature to allow iteration in again, but most methods entail some restricted form of redefinition. An example is the FOR ... DO ... IF ... ITER construct of VAL. The VAL statement in Figure 7.8 calculates x^n.

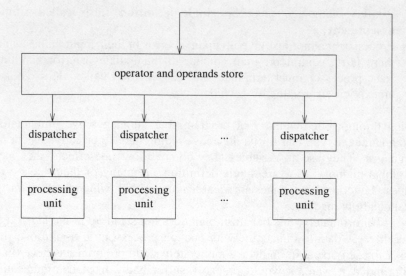

Figure 7.7 A simplified diagram of a dataflow machine.

```
power :=
  FOR
    i: REAL := n;
    res: REAL := 1;
  DO
    IF i = 0 THEN res ELSE
      ITER i := i – 1; res := res * x; ENDITER
    ENDIF
  ENDFOR
```

Figure 7.8 A VAL statement to calculate x^n.

```
i₀ := 3;
res₀ := 1;
test₀ := i₀ = 0;
power :=
  IF test₀ THEN res₀ ELSE
    ITER i₁ := i₀ – 1; res₁ := res₀ * 5; ENDITER
  ENDIF;
```

Figure 7.9 The first cycle of the **FOR** loop of Figure 7.8.

```
i₁ := i₀ – 1;
res₁ := res₀ * 5;
test₁ := i₁ = 0;
power :=
    IF test₁ THEN res₁ ELSE
        ITER i₂ := i₁ – 1; res₂ := res₁ * 5; ENDITER
    ENDIF;
```

Figure 7.10 The second cycle of the FOR loop of Figure 7.8.

It should be emphasized that, contrary to appearances, this does not describe a static repetition of the same code, but rather a dynamic unrolling of a loop. For, say, $n = 3$ and $x = 5$, the FOR loop is initially equivalent to the code shown in Figure 7.9. Once $test_0$ has been calculated (yielding false), the IF expression becomes available. It results in the activation of the ITER clause, and consequently the operations in Figure 7.10 are offered to the machine. This continues until finally i_3 is 0 and the remaining operation is

```
power := res₃;
```

The index manipulation is done by tagging the values in memory.

A very different approach to iteration is taken by Lucid. In a Lucid program, value names do not denote a single value but rather a stream of values. The definition $a = b + c$ defines a processor that reads a stream of b values and a stream of c values and produces a stream, named a, consisting of their sums. As soon as a b and a c value have arrived, a sum is appended to the stream a. Likewise, constants are considered infinite streams of values, all identical; the Lucid expression 2 is equivalent to «2, 2, 2, ...». This provides one level of iteration but requires the machine to be able to queue values occasionally. Lucid also allows recursion.

Lucid values can be defined in terms of themselves, for example by using the operator fby (an abbreviation of 'followed by'):

```
n = 0 fby (n + 1);
```

The fby operator produces a stream consisting of the first value in its left-hand stream followed by all values in its right-hand stream. Initially, only a value from the 0 stream is required by the process defined for n. This is immediately available and yields the first value of the stream n. Next, fby looks at the first value of its right-hand stream. The first value of the stream n (that is, 0) arrives at the +, which reads it, adds it to one value from the infinite stream of 1s, and puts the sum (that is, 1) on its output, where it is accepted by fby. The latter appends it to n, thus extending the stream to «0, 1, ?, ?, ...». The process will temporarily suspend itself when there are no customers for values of n.

Processes can be combined to create new streams by using a **where** clause, the Lucid equivalent of a block. The definition

```
y = x * flip
    where
        flip = 1 fby (-flip);
    end;
```

defines y as x with alternate values negated, since flip is defined as the stream «1, -1, 1, -1, ...».

Although this description suggests that the dataflow machine will have to handle very long streams, the semantics of Lucid is such that it is almost never necessary to have more than one value of a stream available at any one moment. In effect, Lucid value streams act exactly like normal variables most of the time.

Input and output are done in Lucid by attaching some of the streams to files, keyboards, screens and printers, much like the UNIX redirection feature. It has, in fact, been argued that the UNIX Shell with its pipeline mechanism is a dataflow language, but it is a very limited one in that it only allows anonymous streams.

Like the parallel programming paradigm, the dataflow paradigm has a dual nature. It can be considered as a general programming paradigm with the principle 'Programming by specifying connected processes', but it was developed mainly as a special-purpose paradigm to utilize dataflow machines. Dataflow languages are good at expressing fine-grained parallelism, but whether fine-grained parallelism is a good idea remains to be seen.

Work on dataflow programming started with a paper by Karp and Miller (1966). A recent survey of dataflow programming is given by Gaudiot and Bic (1991). The February 1982 issue of *IEEE Computer* is dedicated to dataflow principles, and contains much information. The structure of dataflow machines is described by Veen (1986).

7.2.2 Little languages

Most languages we have discussed so far are big, in the sense that they have taken many months or years to design and implement. Languages such as PL/I, Algol 68 and Ada have been designed by large teams of people over a period of years. The results are languages with many features, fat reference manuals and complicated compilers. If a language is intended to be used for a wide range of applications, this is perhaps inevitable.

Other languages were designed by one or two people, who tried to keep the language reasonably small. Good examples are Pascal and C. They do not support all features desired by all programmers, but make restrictions to keep the language simple.

A third class of languages are the so-called **little languages**. A little language is intended for a special purpose, is designed in a few days or weeks, and can hopefully also be implemented in a short period of time. A little language should often be thought of as a 'useful tool' rather than as a full-blown, general-purpose programming language.

The primary characteristic of little languages is their orientation towards a specific problem domain, such as picture drawing, job control or parsing. A good example is the UNIX Shell, which is used for executing programs. As an example, the following Shell program counts the number of words in each file constituting this book:

```
for i in chap?.n
do
        wc $i > $i.wc &
done
```

The expression chap?.n evaluates into a list of file names. For each element in this list, the UNIX program wc (Word Count) is invoked and its output is written to a file with suffix .wc. The ampersand at the end of the line causes all commands to be run in parallel.

Although the Shell has many features of algorithmic languages, such as case, if- and for-statements, it is not a general-purpose language. Most importantly, it lacks many data types found in general languages. This is typical for little languages: they often lack features that are essential in conventional languages.

Another interesting little language is PIC, which is used for drawing pictures. For example, the tree in Figure 4.4 of this book was generated by the PIC program in Figure 7.11.

```
c=0.25
R1: circle "1"
R2: circle "2" at R1 - (3*c, 6*c)
R3: circle "3" at R1 - (-3*c, 6*c)
R4: circle "4" at R3 - (2*c, 6*c)
line from R1 to R2 chop
line from R1 to R3 chop
line from R3 to R4 chop
```

Figure 7.11 PIC program drawing the tree of Figure 4.4.

The PIC language has many figures built in, such as lines, circles and boxes. The command

```
R1: circle "1"
```

draws a circle with a number in it, and gives it the name R1. The next three commands also draw circles at certain positions. The three line commands connect the circles. Without the chop attribute, each line would connect the centres of two circles; the attribute chops off part of the line to achieve the desired effect. In conclusion, PIC is an easy-to-use language for drawing pictures.

Neither the Shell nor PIC is really a small language that is easy to implement. Moreover, many little languages start out being small, and are later extended with many features. The first version of PIC was implemented in a week, but it grew significantly over the years.

Little languages are often implemented by compiling them into existing languages. PIC, for example, is translated into troff, a UNIX typesetting language. Little languages can themselves be used as the target for other, even more specialized languages. The language GRAP, for example, is a specialized tool for drawing graphs, and is translated into PIC.

Several other little languages exist. Lex and Yacc are well-known tools for writing lexical analysers and parsers. The language Awk is useful for scanning and processing text files. For example, the Awk program

prints all lines in the input file that contain more than 80 characters.

The difference between a language and a program is sometimes fuzzy. To illustrate this, let us compare PIC with an interactive drawing program. Such programs are also useful for drawing pictures, but they cannot be programmed. PIC supports repetition statements, making it easy to draw regular pictures with large numbers of items (for example a grid with 50×50 boxes, each connected to its four neighbours). With a pure interactive program, all items and lines would have to be drawn separately. Thus PIC is a (specialized) programming language, while an interactive program is not. The Shell, Lex, Yacc and Awk can be programmed, and all are languages in their own right.

Little languages are discussed in Bentley (1986), who looks at PIC and several of its preprocessors, and also gives some principles of little languages.

7.2.3 Database languages

Relational database languages are tuned fully to a single compound data type, a set of related tables with a very specific structure. The values of the entries in these tables are of the usual basic types and the columns in the tables carry names. The data type represents a relational database; since all access to the database is through commands, it is an abstract data type. Generally there is only one, anonymous variable of this type in the program, the database itself; it is a persistent variable. Although relational database languages may be seen as representing the paradigm 'All the world is a set of tables', they do not aim at general programming; they support a special-purpose paradigm.

The prime example of a database language is SQL. SQL provides a small number of powerful commands to manipulate the database. Each command starts with an identifying keyword and has a specific structure. Most commands have parts to identify a table to operate on, to specify an action and to restrict the action to certain rows only. Auxiliary tables can be created to serve as variables.

An example of an SQL command is

```
SELECT   name, street, house_nmb, zip_nmb, zip_letters, city
FROM     address_list
WHERE    house_nmb = zip_nmb
```

The FROM part determines the table, the WHERE part selects the rows that fulfil the condition and the SELECT part tells which columns to print from those rows. So this selects from the table address_list the rows in which the house number is equal to the zip code number, and prints the indicated six fields from each row. For the address list of Amsterdam this could yield: 'Vrije Universiteit, de Boelelaan, 1081, 1081, HV, Amsterdam'.

An example of a command in which an update is restricted to specified rows is

```
UPDATE   address_list
SET      telno = telno + 6000000
WHERE    telno > 99999 AND telno < 1000000
```

This command will put a 6 in front of all telephone numbers in address_list that are exactly six digits long, by restricting the SET part to those rows for which telno > 99999 AND telno < 1000000 (assuming that telephone numbers do not start with a 0).

Normally, SQL commands are embedded in programs in another language. As an independent language, SQL is only used interactively.

Although it is sometimes claimed otherwise, SQL is a fully imperative language. The user is isolated from the implementation details of the database and the operations are powerful, thus giving a sense of automatic programming, but the state of the database has to be manipulated explicitly by the user. SQL is an example of a 4GL (fourth-generation language).

A recent book about database languages is by Vossen (1991). A good textbook on SQL is the second edition of Date's book (1989); the third edition by Date and Darwen (1993) is more of an annotation to the SQL standard.

7.2.4 Real-time languages

Another important class of languages intended for a specific application area are the **real-time languages**. The differences between conventional and real-time applications will first be explained. The correctness of a conventional program is determined only by its logical results. The correctness of a real-time program, however, also depends on *when* the results are produced. In general, a real-time program is restricted in when to respond to its inputs. It should produce its outputs neither too soon nor too late. Real-time programs are frequently used as part of a larger system, such as an airplane or a missile. Such systems are called **embedded systems**.

Real-time applications need programming support in several areas. We will look at three of the most important issues: timing (performance), reliability and low-level programming. Real-time programs frequently use parallelism to increase performance or reliability, or to control multiple hardware devices simultaneously. Parallelism has been addressed in Chapter 6.

Above all, a real-time program needs to deal with *time*. At the very least, it must be able to obtain the current time. In Ada, for example, a task can read the current time by calling the function Clock in the standard package Calendar.

Probably the most important issue in real-time programming, however, is how to meet **deadlines**. The designer of a real-time system should be able to specify that a certain output must be generated in a given time interval. Unfortunately, only very few languages give programming support for deadlines, owing to lack of a sound underlying theory. The usual practice is to first write a program that is logically correct (which means it produces the right outputs, but probably not at the right times), and then tune the program if it does not meet its timing specifications. Tuning may involve rewriting parts of the program in assembly code, or running different parts of a program in parallel.

Parallel programs can be tuned by assigning priorities to computations, so the system can give more CPU cycles to time-critical computations. A priority is a number that can be assigned to a process, either statically or dynamically. The scheduler will always pick the process with the highest priority and run it. To prevent other processes from starving, the priority of the currently running process may be decreased periodically, so that eventually some other process will have the highest priority. If a computation has a tight deadline, it can be given a high priority, increasing the chance of meeting the deadline. Priorities are supported by several languages, but they do not give absolute guarantees that deadlines will be met.

The second issue to be addressed by a real-time language is **reliability**. A real-time program controlling, say, an aircraft should continue functioning no matter what happens. Ideally, it must survive malfunctionings in the devices it controls, crashes of CPUs it runs on and even errors in its own software. In general, such problems must be addressed during the design of the system. A language, however, must allow exceptional situations to be detected, so the appropriate software can be run to solve the problem.

Several language constructs exist for detecting errors during run time. The mechanism most frequently used is exception handling, which was discussed in Chapter 2. An exception is an unexpected hardware or software error, which causes an exception handler to be invoked. The idea is for the exception handler to start a software module that solves the problem causing the exception. Usually, the designer of the real-time system must have decided beforehand how to react to the problem, once it occurs.

The third issue is support for **low-level programming**. A real-time program that controls hardware devices must be able to send data to the device interface, receive data from it, and respond to interrupts generated by the device. With memory-mapped devices, for example, the program has to write bits or bytes to fixed hardware addresses. The language, therefore, must allow programmers to get around the typing mechanism and write arbitrary data to arbitrary locations.

Ada supports low-level programming in the form of **representation specifications**. Such a specification may, for example, specify the memory address of a variable. So, a device register of an interface can be treated much like a normal variable, except that its address is given by the programmer. As another example, interrupts can be associated with task entries, so a device interrupt will be treated like an entry call.

Several languages for real-time programming exist, including Ada, occam, CONIC, Pearl and Real-Time Euclid. No widely-accepted paradigm for real-time programming has emerged yet, however. Most languages use some mixture of processes, priorities, exception handling and low-level programming features.

Real-time systems and programming languages are discussed in depth in a book by Burns and Wellings (1990).

Summary

- A classification of paradigms can be based on how it suggests that state and its manipulation should be specified in a program.
- In constraint programming, the user defines the solution to a problem as a data type and a set of constraints. The system then finds values of the data type that obey the constraints.
- In access-oriented programming, variables are annotated with procedures. When a variable is accessed, a procedure is invoked automatically. This allows the monitoring of variables and the propagation of effects.
- Single-datastructure languages simplify programming by casting everything into a single data structure, for which powerful operations are then provided.
- In dataflow programming, a separate processor is, in principle, available for each operation in the program. Operations here include arithmetical and logical operations, function calls and if-else decisions. Each operation executes as soon as the values of its operands become available. This provides optimal fine-grained parallelism without requiring explicit programmer help.
- Little languages are intended for special purposes. A little language

should be thought of as a 'useful tool' rather than as a full-blown, general-purpose programming language.

• Relational database languages provide access to a compound data type, a relational database. Since all access to the database is through commands, it is an abstract data type. Typical commands are conditional data retrieval (selection) and conditional data update.

• The correctness of a real-time program depends on *when* the results are produced. Real-time programs are frequently used as part of embedded systems. Important issues are meeting deadlines, reliability and low-level programming.

Bibliographical notes

Ambler, Bunnet and Zimmerman (1992) analyse the manipulation specification axis of paradigms. Luker (1989) supplies material for thought about further developments in paradigms.

Exercises

7.1   Write down a constraint program for sorting the integer array A, in the following form:

> The desired solution is an integer array B with the following constraints:
>
> ...

   (Hint: be careful not to lose elements and not to allow spurious elements in, not even in the presence of duplicate values in A.)

7.2   APL often has the look and feel of a functional language. Name important similarities and differences.

7.3   If Lucid allows recursion anyway, why would it go to some lengths to supply several constructs to allow iteration?

7.4   What are the low-level facilities of the languages you know? In particular: How do you catch an interrupt? How do you read the byte with machine address 128 from your address space?

7.5   Write a prime number generator for primes < n in SETL, using the facilities described in this chapter plus the logical negation operator NOT.

7.6   Drawing a picture like Figure 4.4 in an imperative general-purpose language (for example, Ada) is more difficult than in the special-purpose language PIC, even if you can use convenient drawing routines like

procedure Draw_Line(Start, Stop: Point);
procedure Draw_Circle(Center: Point; Radius: Float);

Why?

7.7   Why is it not possible to implement the constraint $9*C + 160 = 5*F$ directly in Prolog?

Appendix A: References to Languages

Since there are roughly as many programming languages as there are natural languages on earth (between 2000 and 4000), with several books written about some of them, it will be clear that the list below, with its 75 entries, shows only the tip of the iceberg. For some languages, there is more than one recommendable book; rather than mentioning them all or choosing one of them arbitrarily, we have tried to list the most recent one available.

Language	Paradigm	Reference
ABC	imperative	(Geurts *et al.*, 1990)
ABCL/1	object-oriented/parallel	(Yonezawa *et al.*, 1986)
Ada 83	imperative/parallel	(US Department of Defense, 1983)
Ada 9X	imperative/obj.oriented/parallel	(Barnes, 1994)
Algol 60	imperative	(Andersen, 1964)
Algol 68	imperative/parallel	(Lindsey and van der Meulen, 1977)
Alphard	imperative	(Shaw (ed.), 1981)
APL	single-datastructure	(Katzan Jr, 1971)
Autocode	imperative	(Willey *et al.*, 1961)
Awk	little language	(Aho and Kernighan, 1988)
BASIC	imperative	(Bent and Sethares, 1990)
Bertrand	constraint	(Leler, 1988)
C	imperative	(Kernighan and Ritchie, 1988)
C++	object-oriented	(Ellis and Stroustrup, 1991)
CLU	imperative	(Liskov *et al.*, 1977)
COBOL	imperative	(Stern and Stern, 1991)
Common Lisp	functional	(Steele Jr, 1984)
Concurrent C	imperative/parallel	(Gehani and Roome, 1989)
Concurrent Pascal	imperative/parallel	(Brinch Hansen, 1975)
Concurrent Prolog	logic/parallel	(Shapiro, 1987)
ConcurrentSmalltalk	object-oriented/parallel	(Yokote and Tokoro, 1986)
CONIC	real-time	(Kramer and Magee, 1985)
CSP	imperative/parallel	(Hoare, 1978)

Eiffel	object-oriented	(Meyer, 1992b)
Emerald	object-oriented/parallel	(Black *et al.*, 1987)
Forth	imperative	(Brodie and Forth, Inc., 1987)
FORTRAN	imperative	(Brainerd *et al.*, 1990)
FP	functional	(Backus, 1978)
GRAP	little language	(Bentley and Kernighan, 1986)
Haskell	functional	(Davie, 1992)
Hermes	imperative/parallel	(Strom *et al.*, 1991)
Hope	functional	(Bailey, 1990)
Icon	imperative	(Griswold and Griswold, 1983)
IDEAL	constraint	(Van Wyk, 1982)
ISWIM	functional	(Landin, 1966)
KL1	logic/parallel	(Ueda and Chikayama, 1990)
Lex	little language	(Levine *et al.*, 1992)
Linda	imperative/parallel	(Ahuja *et al.*, 1986)
Lisp	functional	(Winston and Horn, 1989)
Loops	access-/object-oriented	(Stefik *et al.*, 1986)
Lucid	dataflow/functional	(Wadge and Ashcroft, 1985)
Make	constraint	(Oram and Talbott, 1993)
Mesa	imperative/parallel	(Geschke *et al.*, 1977)
Miranda	functional	(Turner, 1986)
Modula-2	imperative	(Wirth, 1985)
Multilisp	functional/parallel	(Halstead Jr, 1985)
Oberon	imperative	(Reiser and Wirth, 1992)
Objective C	object-oriented	(Cox, 1986)
occam	imperative/parallel	(Burns, 1988)
OPS5	constraint	(Cooper and Wogrin, 1988)
Orca	imperative/parallel	(Bal *et al.*, 1992)
Parlog	logic/parallel	(Clark and Gregory, 1986)
Pascal	imperative	(Cooper and Clancy, 1982)
Pearl	real-time	(Werum and Windauer, 1983)
PIC	little language	(Kernighan, 1982)
Plankalkül	imperative	(Zuse, 1989)
PL/I	imperative	(Hughes, 1986)
PostScript	imperative	(Adobe System Inc., 1989)
Prolog	logic	(Bratko, 1990)
Real-Time Euclid	real-time	(Kligerman and Stoyenko, 1986)
Scheme	functional	(Dybvig, 1987)
Self	object-oriented	(Ungar *et al.*, 1992)
SETL	single-datastructure	(Schwartz *et al.*, 1986)
Shell	little language	(Arthur, 1990)
Simula	imperative	(Pooley, 1987)
Sketchpad	constraint	(Sutherland, 1963)
Smalltalk-80	object-oriented	(Goldberg and Robson, 1983)
SQL	database language	(Date, 1989)
SR	imperative/parallel	(Andrews and Olsson, 1993)
Standard ML	functional	(Milner *et al.*, 1990)
ThingLab	constraint	(Borning, 1981)

troff	little language	(Emerson and Paulsell, 1987)
Turing	imperative	(Holt *et al.*, 1988)
VAL	dataflow	(McGraw, 1982)
Yacc	little language	(Levine *et al.*, 1992)

Appendix B: Answers to Exercises

Chapter 1

1.2   One sample possibility: Since Zuse emphasizes data structure very much, with the bit as the basic data type, early hardware might have been bit-addressable. Such hardware might then supply arithmetic operations like 'Add the 15-bit integer ending here to the 19-bit integer ending there and store the result in the 20-bit integer ending yonder'. Languages would have to reflect such operations.

1.3   For: 1. Elegantly recursive. 2. Allows commenting away code which already contains comments. Against: 1. Unnatural: comment contains characters, not lexical units. 2. Strings and comments do not nest mutually, so why should comments and comments? 3. Potential source of 'difficult' errors.

1.4   a. 1.3 and 1.03 will both call the dot operator with the same values of the operands, 1 and 3, making the result equal. b. with difficulty: 6e23 would be interpreted as a 6 followed by the identifier e23.

1.5   Efficiency differences only, in correct implementations.

1.6   If A is the empty string, B_2 will *not* be smaller than B, and no progress will be made.

1.7   Warnings about correct constructions annoy users no end, reduce their confidence in the heuristic tests, and thus lead them to ignore justified warnings.

1.8   Ada/Modula-2: with/IMPORT clauses allow the system to detect dependencies. C: same for the #include compiler control lines, except that these can be conditional upon #ifdefs.

249

1.9   The construct if a[i] > 100 then show(a[i]); produces if a[i] > 100 then write 'a[i] =', a[i]; writeln;. Now, the writeln will be done regardless of the condition.

Chapter 2

2.1   1. There cannot be strong type checking on the indices which fake the pointers, since they are integers and could index any (simulated) record. 2. There is no way to handle a record as a unit, for example in assignment or in parameter passing. 3. Fixed memory allocation.

2.2   a. 2^N; {}, {true}, {false}, {true, false}. b. infinitely many; {}, {true}, {false}, {true, true}, {true, false}, {false, false}, ...

2.3   In C, see sprintf. In Ada, conversion can be done independently from I/O, using the function 'Image that is a predefined attribute of any discrete type. In standard Pascal, there is no way.

2.4   For Modula-2: 1. actions can be labelled with lists of ranges; 2. case values have to be constants; 3. it is an error if a value occurs more than once; 4. the manual does not cover the case where the value of the expression does not occur as a label and there is no ELSE statement sequence; extrapolating from what is said for the if-statement, we can guess that nothing should happen.

2.5   16 top; 15 comma; 14 assignment; 13 conditional; 12 logical-or; 11 logical-and; 10 bitwise-or; 9 bitwise-xor; 8 bitwise-and; 7 equality; 6 relational; 5 shift; 4 additive; 3 multiplicative; 2 unary; 1 postfix; 0 primary.

2.6   (x >= 0 AND y <= max_int – x) OR (x < 0 AND y >= min_int – x)

2.7   No arithmetic operator produces a value of type divisor, so there has to be a built-in monadic operator convert_arith_to_divisor, which will have to cause an exception when called with the value 0. In short, it moves the exception from where the value is used to where it is produced, which is a small but decided advantage.

2.8   You cannot solve this by just adding an exception handler: you have to add code to the rest of the block. If a null value of type Magtape_Type exists, initialize the magtape variables to it. In the exception part, release only those that do not have a null value; be sure to reset the values to null upon releasing the units in the code. Otherwise, declare a Boolean variable for each magtape unit and use these to record what you possess.

2.9   If it did that, it could be used in its own initialization expression.

2.10 The first makes the decision when pr sq is declared, depending on the value of debug at that time, the second makes the decision each time pr sq is called, using the value of debug at call time.

2.11 procedure Put(S: String) renames Text_IO.Put;

Chapter 3

3.1 Definitely not. A computer is not a disk or a power supply, it *contains* such components. In other words, the 'has' relation applies here, not the 'is-a' relation. You should thus not use inheritance here, but you should use the existing classes for defining the members of the new class.

3.2 See the Smalltalk-80 book by Goldberg and Robson (1983).

3.3 There are important commonalities, as shown by the fact that some languages treat classes as abstract data types. Both classes and ADT introduce a type whose internal representation is hidden from the user. A class is more general, however, as it also supports inheritance and dynamic binding.

3.4 A generic function is a static construct. A separate, compile-time instantiation is needed for every new use of the function. Each such instantiation has a unique name, so if an instantiated function is called, the types of its parameters are determined statically.

A polymorphic operation is one operation that can be called with different types of parameters. No compile-time instantiations are needed. If the actual parameter is a pointer to an object, the actual class of the object may not be determined until run time.

3.5 If A, B and C each have a copy of object R, they all get the same sequence of random numbers. If they share a copy, the random numbers generated by R are distributed among its users, so they get different numbers. Moreover, with three different copies, the objects do not depend on each other; a change in object A will not affect the random numbers seen by B or C. With one shared copy, the random numbers each object gets depends on how the other two objects consume random numbers. Which semantics is desired depends on the application.

3.6 The second and fourth invocation execute S.f, the others execute T.f. The fifth invocation also executes T.f, since C++ uses dynamic binding only for pointers.

3.7 Automatic garbage collection of objects is much easier for the programmer and it is more secure. As a disadvantage, it will have some execution overhead. In C++, objects created through a data declaration are deleted automatically, at little or no cost, but objects created dynamically must be freed explicitly by the programmer.

3.8   Eiffel has only one concept for program modularity: the class. C++ and Ada 9X have several different concepts (files and classes in C++; packages and tagged records in Ada 9X). Eiffel uses dynamic binding for invocations on objects; C++ and Ada 9X use a mixture of static and dynamic binding.

3.9   The C++ approach violates the principle of information hiding by allowing users of a class access to its internal data structures. Smalltalk-80 faithfully obeys the principle of information hiding. If the value of a variable is to be made available outside the class, an operation can be defined that returns this value. The advantage of the Eiffel approach is that such additional operations are not needed. Eiffel hides the difference between a variable and a parameterless value-returning procedure (this is called uniform access in Eiffel), and thus allows read-access to a variable from outside its class, if the programmer wants it.

Chapter 4

4.1   a. Most of the usefulness of the paradigm would break down. For one thing, it would no longer be true that the result of a function call depends only on the values of its parameters.

b. This would be much better and would restore the normal functioning of the program.

4.2   List data structures can be updated without doing a destructive update, as for arrays. Also, they are more suitable for the recursive programming style. Finally, functional languages are primarily intended for symbolic applications, while FORTRAN and Algol 60 are mainly used for numerical applications

4.3   A polymorphic function is a single function that can be called with different types of arguments. An overloaded function is actually a set of different functions with the same name.

4.4   Generics are a static (compile-time) mechanism. A separate generic instantiation is needed for each use of the generic function. So, if the function need be called with F1, F2 and F3 as arguments, three instantiations are needed, each having a different name.

Higher-order functions are dynamic. There is only one function, but it can be called with any function as an argument. This function argument need not be determined at compile time; it can, for example, be a variable containing a function value. So, higher-order functions are more flexible.

4.6 Miranda is strongly typed and it is not possible to define a type that is a list containing itself. Lisp does not have this restriction, since it is not typed.

4.7
```
runhanoi n = hanoi n "A" "B" "C"
hanoi 0 src dst aux = []
hanoi (n+1) src dst aux =
    hanoi n src aux dst
    ++ "from peg " ++ src ++ " to peg " ++ dst ++ "\n"
    ++ hanoi n aux dst src
```

4.8
```
runprimes = sieve[2..]
sieve (a:t) = a : sieve [x | x <- t; x mod a > 0]
```

4.9 Orca does not have referential transparency. For example, consider a function F that doubles its first (call-by-reference) parameter and returns the original value. An invocation such as 'F(x) + F(x)' cannot be optimized into '2 * F(x)'.

On the other hand, allowing call-by-reference parameters makes it much easier to modify parts of large data structures. As noted in the text, for example, changing one element of an array is inefficient in a functional language. With call-by-reference parameters and assignments, this is easy to do. Finally, by disallowing global variables, most programs will probably be easier to read, which is an advantage shared with functional languages.

4.10 The different parts of an expression can be executed in parallel on different processors. For example, to compute 34∗56 + 78∗21, one processor can do the first multiplication and another can do the second. In general, this can be done for all expressions in the program.

Chapter 5

5.2
```
count([], 0).
count([H|T], N) ← count(T, N2), N is N2 + 1.
```

5.3
```
hanoi(1,I,J)← !, out(['move','peg','from',I,'to',J]).
hanoi(N,I,J) ←
    K is 6-I-J,
```

```
M is N-1,
hanoi(M,I,K),
hanoi(1,I,J),
hanoi(M,K,J).
```

Here, out prints a given list of strings on the output, separated by spaces.

5.4

```
reverse([], []).
reverse([H|T], Rev) ←
   reverse(T, Trev),
   append(Trev, [H], Rev).
```

5.6

```
grandfather(X,Y) ← nonvar(X), father(X,Z), father(Z,Y).
grandfather(X,Y) ← father(Z,Y), father(X,Z).
```

5.7   First put a tile in the centre. Next try tiles on each of the four sides of the square, and finally try the four corners. Backtrack automatically whenever there is no suitable tile left over for the next position.

5.8   See Chapter 6.

Chapter 6

6.1   A process may be 'too late' in reading a shared variable, in that another process overwrites it before the value is read. If a print statement is added to the second process, its assignment to the shared variable will occur later.

6.2   It can be used for implementing higher-level synchronization primitives, such as locks and semaphores. For example, a lock can be implemented by a shared variable containing a zero (not locked) or one (locked). To set the lock, do a test-and-set; if the result is zero, the lock was not previously set, so the process now has the lock. If the result is one, the lock was already taken, so the process has to try again (probably after some delay). To release the lock, a zero value has to be assigned to the variable.

6.3   It is easy to miss a wakeup. If a wakeup is executed just before the sleep, the wakeup has no effect, so the sleep may block for ever. The **P** and **V** operations on semaphores, on the other hand, always have an effect. If a **V** operation is done before the **P** operation is executed, the semaphore will be incremented, so the **P** operation will succeed immediately.

6.4   If F2 blocks, other processes in M2 are allowed to continue. However, F1 will be blocked as well, but it is not suspended on a **wait** primitive. According to the monitor rules, no other process should therefore be allowed to enter M1. Unfortunately, this strategy may easily cause a deadlock. In particular, if M2's operations are always invoked through M1, no other process can enter M2 and do a **signal**. In this case, deadlock will certainly happen. A solution is to allow other processes to enter M1, although that makes the semantics of monitors less clear.

6.5   Add an operation no_more_data that sets a Boolean flag done within the monitor. Also, the get operation returns a Boolean indicating whether it succeeded or failed. In the get operation, test if 'count = 0 **and** done'. If so, let the operation fail. Also, do not forget to test the value of done after the **wait** operation on NotEmpty.

6.6   No, not really. If a select statement is started, it may not be possible yet to determine which selection will be made. All alternatives may initially block, so the choice must be deferred until one or more alternatives are enabled (by the arrival of messages). With a case statement, it is not possible to express such behaviour. One could put the **case** in a loop and retry it until one or more alternatives succeed. This solution uses polling (busy waiting), however, which is inefficient.

6.7   The solution is given in Figure B.1.

Chapter 7

7.1   1. B has the same number of elements as A; 2. for each value V which occurs N times (N >= 1) in A, there are exactly N elements of value V in B; 3. for each i and j in the index range of A, B[i] <= B[j] if i < j.

7.2   Similarities: most data flows through parameters and functions (= operators); Differences: no functional composition; no lazy evaluation; no single-assignment; no referential transparency; global variables.

7.3   For the same reason imperative languages allow iteration: it is much more efficient.

7.4   C: For the interrupt, issue a call to signal. For the byte, the expression *(char *)128 will cast 128 to a pointer to character, which is then dereferenced to obtain the contents of byte 128. Ada 83: For the interrupt, have an entry Interrupt in a task and use an address clause for Interrupt use at ...;. For the byte, declare a character Byte and

```
        protected type Buffer_Object is
          entry Put(Line: Line_Type);
          entry Get(Line: out Line_Type);
        private
          Max: constant := 10;
          Buffer: array(Integer range 0..Max-1) of Line_Type;
          Write_Pos: Integer := 0;
          Read_Pos: Integer := 0;
          Nr_Lines: Integer := 0;
        end Buffer_Object;

        protected body Buffer_Object is

          entry Put(Line: Line_Type) when Nr_Lines < Max is
          begin
            Nr_Lines := Nr_Lines + 1;
            Buffer(Write_Pos) := Line;
            Write_Pos := (Write_Pos + 1) mod Max;
          end Put;

          entry Get(Line: out Line_Type) when Nr_Lines > 0 is
          begin
            Nr_Lines := Nr_Lines - 1;
            Line := Buffer(Read_Pos);
            Read_Pos := (Read_Pos + 1) mod Max;
          end Get;
        end Buffer_Object;
```

Figure B.1 Type Buffer_Object.

use an address clause for Byte use at 128;. Ada 9X: For the interrupt, attach a parameterless procedure to the system-defined interrupt
identifier, using the procedure Attach_Handler. For the byte, declare
a character Byte and use an attribute definition clause for
Byte'Address use 128;. Modula-2: Interrupt handling is
implementation-dependent; Wirth (1985) gives an example using a
procedure IOTRANSFER which is supplied by the implementation.
The chapter 'Device handling, concurrency, and interrupts' in Wirth's
book shows that byte 128 in memory can be overlaid with a variable,
say x, by declaring VAR x [128]: CHAR; this feature is not described
in the accompanying grammar.

7.5 {x: x IN {2..n} | NOT EXISTS p IN {2..n}, q IN {2..n} | p*q = x}

7.6 In Ada, the programmer would have to compute the exact coordinates
of the start and end points of the lines (because they start and end on
the circles rather than in their centres). PIC does this automatically if

the programmer specifies 'chop'. (See Figure 7.11.)

7.7 We could try to write constraint(C, F) :– 9*C + 160 is 5*F. but then the is would evaluate its right-hand side.

References

Abelson H., Sussman G. J. and Sussman J. (1985). *Structure and Interpretation of Computer Programs*. Cambridge MA: MIT Press

Adobe System Inc. (1989). *PostScript Language Reference Manual*. Reading MA: Addison-Wesley

Agha G. (Oct. 1986). An overview of actor languages. *ACM SIGPLAN Notices*, **21**(10), 58-67

Aho A. V. and Kernighan B. W. (1988). *The AWK Programming Language*. Reading MA: Addison-Wesley

Ahuja S., Carriero N. and Gelernter D. (Aug. 1986). Linda and friends. *IEEE Computer*, **19**(8), 26-34

Almasi G. S. and Gottlieb A. (1989). *Highly Parallel Computing*. Redwood City CA: Benjamin/Cummings

Ambler A. L., Bunnett M. M. and Zimmerman B. (1992). Operational versus definitional: a perspective on programming paradigms. *IEEE Computer*, **25**(9), 28-43

Andersen Ch. (1964). *An Introduction to ALGOL 60*. Reading MA: Addison-Wesley

Andrews G. R. (1991). *Concurrent Programming – Principles and Practice*. Redwood City CA: Benjamin/Cummings

Andrews G. R. and Olsson R. A. (1993). *The SR Programming Language: Concurrency in Practice*. Redwood City CA: Benjamin/Cummings

Andrews G. R., Olsson R. A., Coffin M., Elshoff I., Nilsen K., Purdin T. and Townsend G. (1988). An overview of the SR language and implementation. *ACM Trans. Prog. Lang. Syst.*, **10**(1), 51-86

Andrews G. R. and Schneider F. B. (Mar. 1983). Concepts and notations for concurrent programming. *ACM Computing Surveys*, **15**(1), 3-43

Appleby D. (1991). *Programming Languages – Paradigm and Practice*. New York NY: McGraw-Hill

Arthur L. J. (1990). *UNIX Shell Programming*. 2nd edn. New York: John Wiley

Backus J. (1978). Can programming be liberated from the von Neumann style? A functional style and its algebra of programs. *Commun. ACM*, **21**(8), 613-641

Bailey R. (1990). *Functional Programming with HOPE*. New York: Ellis Horwood

Bal H. E. (1991). *Programming Distributed Systems*. Hemel Hempstead, England: Prentice Hall

Bal H. E. (1992). A comparative study of five parallel programming languages. *Future Generations Computer Systems*, **8**, 121-135

Bal H. E., Kaashoek M. F. and Tanenbaum A. S. (1992). Orca: a language for parallel programming of distributed systems. *IEEE Trans. Softw. Eng.*, **18**(3), 190-205

Bal H. E., Steiner J. G. and Tanenbaum A. S. (Sep. 1989). Programming languages for distributed computing systems. *ACM Computing Surveys*, **21**(3), 261-322

Bal H. E. and Tanenbaum A. S. (1991). Distributed programming with shared data. *Computer Languages*, **16**(2), 129-146

Barnes J. G. P. (1994). *Programming in Ada, Plus an Overview of Ada 9X*. 4th edn. Reading MA: Addison-Wesley

Bauer F. L. and Wössner H. (July 1972). The "Plankalkül" of Konrad Zuse: a forerunner of today's programming languages. *Commun. ACM*, **15**(7), 678-685

Bent R. J. and Sethares G. C. (1990). *Basic – An Introduction to Computer Programming*. 4th edn. Pacific Grove CA: Brooks/Cole

Bentley J. (Aug. 1986). Programming pearls – little languages. *Commun. ACM*, **29**(8), 711-721

Bentley J. L. and Kernighan B. W. (1986). GRAP – A language for typesetting graphs. *Commun. ACM*, **29**(8), 782-792

Bershad B. N., Lazowska E. D. and Levy H. M. (1988). PRESTO: a system for object-oriented parallel programming. *Software – Practice & Experience*, **18**(8), 713-732

Bird R. and Wadler P. (1988). *Introduction to Functional Programming*. Hemel Hempstead, England: Prentice-Hall

Birrell A. D. and Nelson B. J. (Feb. 1984). Implementing remote procedure calls. *ACM Trans. Computer Syst.*, **2**(1), 39-59

Black A., Hutchinson N., Jul E., Levy H. and Carter L. (Jan. 1987). Distribution and abstract types in Emerald. *IEEE Trans. Softw. Eng.*, **SE-13**(1), 65-76

Blair G., Gallagher J., Hutchison D. and Shepherd D. (1991). *Object-Oriented Languages, Systems and Applications*. London: Pitman

Boehm B. W. (1976). Software engineering. *IEEE Trans. Computers*, **25**(12), 1226-1241

Borning A. (Oct. 1981). The programming language aspects of ThingLab, a constraint-oriented simulation laboratory. *ACM Trans. Prog. Lang. Syst.*, **3**(4), 353-387

Brainerd W. S., Goldberg C. H. and Adams J. C. (1990). *Programmer's Guide to Fortran 90*. New York NY: McGraw-Hill

Bratko I. (1990). *Prolog Programming for Artificial Intelligence*. Wokingham, England: Addison-Wesley

Brinch Hansen P. (June 1975). The programming language Concurrent Pascal. *IEEE Trans. Softw. Eng.*, **SE-1**(2), 199-207

Brodie L. and Forth, Inc. (1987). *Starting Forth*. 2nd edn. Englewood Cliffs NJ: Prentice-Hall

Budd T. (1991). *An Introduction to Object-Oriented Programming*. Reading MA: Addison-Wesley

Burns A. (1988). *Programming in occam 2*. Wokingham, England: Addison-Wesley

Burns A. and Wellings A. J. (1990). *Real-Time Systems and their Programming Languages*. Wokingham, England: Addison-Wesley

Carriero N. and Gelernter D. (Sep. 1989). How to write parallel programs – a guide to the perplexed. *ACM Computing Surveys*, **21**(3), 323-357

Clark K. L. and Gregory S. (Jan. 1986). PARLOG: parallel programming in logic. *ACM Trans. Prog. Lang. Syst.*, **8**(1), 1-49

Cooper D. and Clancy M. (1982). *Oh! Pascal!*. New York NY: W.W. Norton & Co.

Cooper T. and Wogrin N. (1988). *Rule-based Programming with OPS5*. San Mateo CA: Morgan Kaufmann

Cox B. J. (1986). *Object Oriented Programming – an Evolutionary Approach*. Reading MA: Addison-Wesley

Date C. J. (1989). *A Guide to the SQL Standard.* 2nd edn. Reading MA: Addison-Wesley

Date C. J. and Darwen H. (1993). *A Guide to the SQL Standard.* 3rd edn. Reading MA: Addison-Wesley

Davie A. J. T. (1992). *An Introduction to Functional Programming Systems using Haskell.* Cambridge, England: Cambridge University Press

Dijkstra E. W. (1968a). Cooperating Sequential Processes. In *Programming Languages* (F. Genuys, ed.), pp. 43-112. New York NY: Academic Press

Dijkstra E. W. (1968b). Go To statement considered harmful. *Commun. ACM,* **11**(3), 147-148

Dybvig R. K. (1987). *The Scheme Programming Language.* Englewood Cliffs, N.J.: Prentice-Hall

Eliens A. (1992). *DLP – A language for Distributed Logic Programming.* Chichester, England: John Wiley

Ellis M. A. and Stroustrup B. (1991). *The annotated C++ reference manual.* Reading MA: Addison-Wesley

Emerson S. L. and Paulsell K. (1987). *troff Typesetting for UNIX Systems.* Englewood Cliffs NJ: Prentice-Hall

Field A. J. and Harrison P. G. (1988). *Functional Programming.* Wokingham, England: Addison-Wesley

Gaudiot J.-L. and Bic L. (1991). *Advanced Topics in Data-Flow Computing.* Englewood Cliffs NJ: Prentice Hall

Gehani N. and Roome W. D. (1989). *The Concurrent C Programming Language.* Summit NJ: Silicon Press

Genesereth M. R. and Ginsberg M. L. (Sep. 1985). Logic programming. *Commun. ACM,* **28**(9), 933-941

Geschke C. M., Morris Jr J. H. and Satterthwaite E. H. (Aug. 1977). Early experience with Mesa. *Commun. ACM,* **20**(8), 540-553

Geurts L., Meertens L. and Pemberton S. (1990). *The ABC Programmer's Handbook.* New York NY: Prentice-Hall

Ghezzi C. and Jazayeri M. (1987). *Programming Language Concepts.* 2nd edn. New York NY: John Wiley

Goldberg A. and Robson D. (1983). *Smalltalk-80: the Language and its Implementation.* Reading MA: Addison-Wesley

Grimshaw A. S. (1993). Easy-to-use object-oriented parallel processing with Mentat. *IEEE Computer,* **26**(5), 39-51

Griswold R. E. and Griswold M. T. (1983). *The Icon Programming Language.* Englewood Cliffs NJ: Prentice-Hall

Halstead Jr R. H. (Oct. 1985). Multilisp: a language for concurrent symbolic computation. *ACM Trans. Prog. Lang. Syst.,* **7**(4), 501-538

Hoare C. A. R. (Aug. 1978). Communicating sequential processes. *Commun. ACM,* **21**(8), 666-677

Holt R. C., Matthews P. A., Alan Rosselet J. and Cordy J. R. (1988). *The Turing Language, Design and Definition.* Englewood Cliffs NJ: Prentice-Hall

Hudak P. (Sep. 1989). Conception, evolution and application of functional programming languages. *ACM Computing Surveys,* **21**(3), 359-411

Hughes J. K. (1986). *PL/I Structured Programming.* 3rd edn. New York: John Wiley

Hughes J. (1989). Why functional programming matters. *Computer Journal,* **32**(2), 98-107

IEEE (Mar. 1985). Special Issue on Ada Environments and Tools. *IEEE Software,* **2**(2)

Ichbiah J. D., Barnes J. G. P., Heliard J. C., Krieg-Brueckner B., Roubine O. and Wichman B. A. (June 1979). Rationale for the design of the Ada programming language. *ACM SIGPLAN Notices,* **14**(6B)

Intermetrics, Inc. (Sep. 1993). Programming Language Ada – Language and Standard Libraries (Draft Version 4.0).

Iverson K. E. (1962). *A Programming Language*. New York NY: John Wiley

Kacsuk P. and Wise M. J. (1992). *Implementations of Distributed Prolog*. Chichester, England: John Wiley

Karp R. M. and Miller R. E. (Nov. 1966). Properties of a model for parallel computations: Determinacy, termination and queueing. *SIAM J. Appl. Math.*, **14**(6), 1390-1411

Katzan Jr H. (1971). *APL User's Guide*. New York NY: Van Nostrand Reinhold

Kernighan B. W. (1982). PIC – a language for typesetting graphics. *Software – Practice & Experience*, **12**(1), 1-21

Kernighan B. W. and Ritchie D. M. (1988). *The C Programming Language*. 2nd edn. Englewood Cliffs NJ: Prentice Hall

Kligerman E. and Stoyenko A. D. (1986). Real-time Euclid: a language for reliable real-time systems. *IEEE Trans. Softw. Eng.*, **SE-12**(9), 941-949

Korson T. and McGregor J. D. (1990). Understanding object-oriented: a unifying paradigm. *Commun. ACM*, **33**(9), 40-60

Kowalski R. (1979). *Logic for Problem Solving*. New York NY: North-Holland Publ. Co.

Kramer J. and Magee J. (Apr. 1985). Dynamic configuration for distributed systems. *IEEE Trans. Softw. Eng.*, **SE-11**(4), 424-436

Kuhn T. S. (1970). *The Structure of Scientific Revolutions*. Chicago IL: University of Chicago Press

Lampson B. W. and Redell D. D. (Feb. 1980). Experience with processes and monitors in Mesa. *Commun. ACM*, **23**(2), 105-117

Landin P. J. (1966). The next 700 programming languages. *Commun. ACM*, **9**(3), 157-166

Lee J. A. N. and Sammet J. E. (Mar. 1993). History of Programming Language Conference HOPL II. *ACM SIGPLAN Notices*, **28**(3)

Leler W. (1988). *Constraint Programming Languages – Their Specification and Generation*. Reading MA: Addison-Wesley

Levine J. R., Mason T. and Brown D. (1992). *lex & yacc*. 2nd edn. Sebastopol CA: O'Reilly & Associates

Li K. and Hudak P. (Nov. 1989). Memory coherence in shared virtual memory systems. *ACM Trans. Computer Syst.*, **7**(4), 321-359

Lindsey C. H. and van der Meulen S. G. (1980, c1977). *Informal Introduction to ALGOL 68*. 2nd edn. Amsterdam: North-Holland

Liskov B., Snyder A., Atkinson R. and Schaffert C. (Aug. 1977). Abstraction mechanisms in CLU. *Commun. ACM*, **20**(8), 564-576

Luker P. (Feb. 1989). Never mind the language, what about the paradigm?. *ACM SIGCSE Bull.*, **21**(1), 252-256

MacLennan B. J. (1990). *Functional Programming – Practice and Theory*. Reading MA: Addison-Wesley

McGraw J. R. (Jan. 1982). The VAL language: description and analysis. *ACM Trans. Prog. Lang. Syst.*, **4**(1), 44-82

Meyer B. (1988). *Object-oriented Software Construction*. New York NY: Prentice Hall

Meyer B. (1990). Lessons from the design of the Eiffel libraries. *Commun. ACM*, **33**(9), 68-88

Meyer B. (1992a). Applying "Design by Contract". *IEEE Computer*, **25**(10), 40-51

Meyer B. (1992b). *Eiffel: the Language*. New York NY: Prentice Hall

Milner R., Tofte M. and Harper R. (1990). *The Definition of Standard ML*. Cambridge MA: MIT Press

Oram A. and Talbott S. (1993). *Managing Projects with make*. Sebastopol CA: O'Reilly & Associates

Owens B. B. (1992). Comparative Review. *Computing Reviews*, **33**(1), 49-56

Peyton Jones S. L. (1987). *The implementation of functional programming*. Englewood Cliffs NJ: Prentice-Hall

Pohl I. (1989). *C++ for C Programmers*. Redwood City CA: Benjamin/Cummings

Pooley R. J. (1987). *An Introduction to Programming in SIMULA*. Oxford: Blackwell Scientific

Reiser M. and Wirth N. (1992). *Programming in Oberon: Steps Beyond Pascal and Modula*. Reading MA: Addison-Wesley

Robinson J. A. (1965). A machine-oriented logic based on the resolution principle. *J. ACM*, **12**(1), 23-41

Sammet J. E. (1969). *Programming Languages: History and Fundamentals*. Englewood Cliffs NJ: Prentice-Hall

Sammet J. E., Lee J. A. N. and Wexelblat R. L. (Aug. 1978). History of Programming Language Conference HOPL. *ACM SIGPLAN Notices*, **13**(8), 310

Schwartz J. T., Dewar R. B. K., Dubinsky E. and Schonberg E. (1986). *Programming with Sets – An Introduction to SETL*. New York NY: Springer-Verlag

Scott M. L. (May 1983). Messages vs. remote procedures is a false dichotomy. *ACM SIGPLAN Notices*, **18**(5), 57-62

Shapiro E. (1987). *Concurrent Prolog: Collected Papers*. Cambridge MA: MIT Press

Shapiro E. (Sep. 1989). The family of concurrent logic programming languages. *ACM Computing Surveys*, **21**(3), 413-510

Shaw (ed.) M. (1981). *Alphard: Form and Content*. New York: Springer-Verlag

Steele Jr G. L. (1984). *Common Lisp*. Burlington MA: Digital Press

Stefik M. J., Bobrow D. G. and Kahn K. M. (Jan. 1986). Integrating access-oriented programming into a multiparadigm environment. *IEEE Software*, **3**(1), 10-18

Sterling L. S. and Shapiro E. (1986). *The Art of Prolog*. Cambridge MA: MIT Press

Stern N. and Stern R. A. (1991). *Structured COBOL Programming*. 6th edn. New York: John Wiley

Strom R. E., Bacon D. F., Goldberg A. P., Lowry A., Yellin D. M. and Yemini S. A. (1991). *Hermes: A Language for Distributed Computing*. Englewood Cliffs NJ: Prentice-Hall

Stroustrup B. (1991). *The C++ programming language*. 2nd edn. Reading MA: Addison-Wesley

Sutherland I. E. (1980, c1963). *Sketchpad: a Man-machine Graphical Communication System*. New York NY: Garland Publications

Turner D. A. (Dec. 1986). An overview of Miranda. *ACM SIGPLAN Notices*, **21**(12), 158-166

US Department of Defense (Jan. 1983). Ada Programming Language. *Technical Report ANSI/MIL-STD-1815A*, American National Standards Institute, Washington DC

Ueda K. and Chikayama T. (1990). Design of the kernel language for the Parallel Inference Machine. *Computer Journal*, **33**(6), 494-500

Ungar D., Smith R. B., Chambers C. and Hölzle U. (1992). Object, message, and performance: How they coexist in Self. *IEEE Computer*, **25**(10), 53-64

Van Wyk C. J. (Apr. 1982). A high-level language for specifying pictures. *ACM Trans. Graphics*, **1**(2), 163-182

Veen A. H. (Dec. 1986). Dataflow machine architecture. *ACM Computing Surveys*, **18**(4), 365-396

Vossen G. (1991). *Data Models, Database Languages, and Database Management Systems*. Wokingham, England: Addison-Wesley

Wadge W. W. and Ashcroft E. A. (1985). *Lucid, the Dataflow Programming Language*. London, England: Academic Press

Watt D. A. (1990). *Programming Language Concepts and Paradigms*. New York NY: Prentice Hall

Watt D. A. (1991). *Programming Language Syntax and Semantics*. New York NY: Prentice Hall

Watt D. A. (1993). *Programming Language Processors*. New York NY: Prentice Hall

Werum W. and Windauer H. (1983). *Introduction to PEARL: Process and Experiment Automation Realtime Language*. 2nd edn. Braunschweig, Germany: Vieweg

Wiederholt G., Wegner P. and Ceri S. (Nov. 1992). Towards megaprogramming. *Commun. ACM*, **35**(11), 89-99

Willey E. L., d'Agapeyeff A., Tribe M., Gibbens B. J. and Clark M. (1961). *Some Commercial Autocodes – A Comparative Study*. London, England: Academic Press

Wilson L. B. and Clark R. G. (1993). *Comparative Programming Languages*. 2nd edn. Reading MA: Addison-Wesley

Winston P. H. and Horn B. K. P. (1989). *LISP*. 3rd edn. Reading MA: Addison-Wesley

Wirth N. (1985). *Programming in Modula-2*. 3rd corrected edn. Berlin, Germany: Springer-Verlag

Yokote Y. and Tokoro M. (Nov. 1986). The design and implementation of ConcurrentSmalltalk. *ACM SIGPLAN Notices*, **21**(11), 331-340

Yonezawa A., Briot J.-P. and Shibayama E. (Nov. 1986). Object-oriented concurrent programming in ABCL/1. *ACM SIGPLAN Notices*, **21**(11), 258-268

Zuse K. (1989). The Plankalkul. 2nd edn. *Technical Report Mathematische Berichte Nr. 175*, Gesellschaft für Mathematik und Datenverarbeitung, München, Germany

van Wijngaarden A., Mailloux B. J., Peck J. E. L., Koster C. H. A., Sintzoff M., Lindsey C. H., Meertens L. G. L. T. and Fisker R. G. (1975). Revised report on the algorithmic language Algol 68. *Acta Informatica*, **5**

Index

4GL **10**, 241

ABC 43, 90, 246
ABCL/1 216, 246
abstract data type 21, **99**, 115, 240
abstraction 19
accept statement **207**, 208
access-oriented programming 228
acknowledgement message 205
activation record 77
active object 215
actor language 215
actual parameter 85
Ada 206, 210, 217, 243
Ada 83 **33**, 246
Ada 9X **33**, 217, 246
adicity 60
ADT 99
aggregate 42
Algol 60 105, 246
Algol 68 36, 53, 89, 91, 216, 246
Algol-like language 105
algorithmic language 17
alias **37**, 86
aliased in Ada 47
allocator **46**, 72, 217
Alphard 246
AND/OR tree 169
AND-parallelism 215
anonymous data 34, 240
anonymous subroutine 91

anonymous type 39, 46, 53
APL 17, 230, 244, 246
apostrophe 13
append relation on lists 174
applicative language 144
applicative order reduction 153
applied occurrence 79
argument of a function 144
arity 60
array **41**, 67, 110, 230
array bound checking 52
array of procedures 49
assembly language 3
assert predicate 184
assignment operator 57
assignment statement **56**, 62
associative array 43
associativity of an operator **59**, 89, 230
asymmetric direct naming 204
asynchronous error 71
asynchronous message passing **205**, 216
Autocode 5, 246
automatic garbage collection **130**, 138,
        150, 161
Awk 240, 246

backtracking **169**, 170, 176, 180, 182
Backus Naur Form 14
bag 44
base class 120
base class argument 120